Getting a Social Media Job

FOR DUMMIES®

A Wiley Brand

by Brooks Briz and David Rose

FOR DUMMIES®
A Wiley Brand

Getting a Social Media Job For Dummies®

Published by: **John Wiley & Sons, Inc.,** 111 River Street, Hoboken, NJ 07030-5774, www.wiley.com

Copyright © 2015 by John Wiley & Sons, Inc., Hoboken, New Jersey

Published simultaneously in Canada

For general information on our other products and services, please contact our Customer Care Department within the U.S. at 877-762-2974, outside the U.S. at 317-572-3993, or fax 317-572-4002. For technical support, please visit www.wiley.com/techsupport.

Wiley publishes in a variety of print and electronic formats and by print-on-demand. Some material included with standard print versions of this book may not be included in e-books or in print-on-demand. If this book refers to media such as a CD or DVD that is not included in the version you purchased, you may download this material at http://booksupport.wiley.com. For more information about Wiley products, visit www.wiley.com.

Library of Congress Control Number: 2014957116

ISBN 978-1-119-00266-6 (pbk); ISBN 978-1-119-00271-0 (ebk); ISBN 978-1-119-00278-9 (ebk)

Manufactured in the United States of America

10 9 8 7 6 5 4 3 2 1

Table of Contents

Introduction

Social media. It sounds so captivating. It's loose and flowing, yet rigid at times. There are unwritten rules and advice from experts. Social media is evolving rapidly, and the line between social and traditional media is blurring.

Social media is the social interaction among people where they create, share, discuss, exchange information, and modify content in virtual communities. Social media relies on mobile and web-based technologies to create highly interactive platforms, and is evolving day to day.

Social media has changed the way information is received and disseminated. Because information is so accessible, companies have embraced tools to share and deliver their messages.

Companies are developing relationships directly with their consumers.

Professionals across all industries — virtual communication, marketing, public relations, branding, cultural and professional influence — are developing, enhancing, communicating, engaging, educating, and protecting the brands they represent via social media.

Social media has embedded itself in our everyday lives and is an intricate part of employment. Anyone who's interested in a social media job has to be ready to read about the proven methods for scoring one of these countless positions.

About This Book

Companies are looking for highly qualified social media professionals who are experienced users and can deliver quantifiable results.

Social media is a quick, efficient way to communicate a message to a big audience. It allows for engagement and brand building. Companies need people with these unique talents of engagement and brand building.

This book helps you brand and promote yourself in a highly competitive market.

We help you with your career strategy: how to create your ideal position, whether it's within an established or start-up company, as a consultant, or in a part-time role.

You'll see some text that stands out, too:

- ✔ Text that you're meant to type just as it appears in the book is **bold**. The exception is when you're working through a steps list.

- ✔ Words that we're defining are *italicized.* If you're unsure about a word, you can use the Glossary, too.

- ✔ Web addresses are in monofont, like this: `www.dummies.com`. If you're reading this book on a device connected to the Internet, you can tap the address to visit that site.

Foolish Assumptions

When we were writing this book, we imagined someone with a genuine interest and understanding of the scope of social media — its subtleties and complexities — who needs a guide to help navigate a career path. We offer a diverse mix of resources and tools.

You might be a social media novice who's intrigued, or you might be a marketing/communication/PR pro who wants to expand your reach. You might already be a social media pro but looking for more responsibility.

We have these assumptions about you:

- ✔ You want to work in the social media field.

- ✔ You have basic computer knowledge (word processing and Internet surfing).

- ✔ You're comfortable with social media and you're familiar with one or more platforms (including Facebook or Twitter).

- ✔ You want to add to your skills.

- ✔ You're curious about social media, and want to use your current experiences and skills.

Icons Used in This Book

You'll notice icons in the margins of this book:

Heed the paragraphs marked with the Warning icon to avoid potential disaster.

Remember icons mark paragraphs that have stuff you'll use regularly, or that you'll need to remind yourself as you look for — and work in — a social media job. This information is especially important to know. To get the most important information in each chapter, just skim through these icons.

Whenever we share a hint that might save you time, effort, or money, we mark it with the Tip icon.

The Technical Stuff icon marks information of a more technical nature, or a personal anecdote, that you can skip over.

Beyond the Book

In addition to the material in the book you're reading now, we compiled other helpful material on the web.

This book has an online Cheat Sheet at www.dummies.com/cheatsheet/gettingasocialmediajob. It's filled with information you'll need to reference, like interview prep and tips for better online job searching.

You'll find links to the articles on the parts pages and at helpful points in the chapters, too. Visit www.dummies.com/extras/gettingasocialmediajob.

Where to Go from Here

You can begin reading this book anywhere. We wrote it so you can pick areas of interest to you. Look for topics in the table of contents or check out the index. Everything is explained in the text, and important details are cross referenced.

This book has information that helps you before, during, and after your job search. We help you get started in your new role and provide a guide to your career path.

Leaf through and seek out what makes sense for you, but be sure to skim for new and specialized information too.

Part I
So You Want to Work in Social Media

In this part . . .

- ✔ Understand why companies might push back on the idea of social media and how you can educate them.

- ✔ Get exposed to the returns and the metrics that most companies are after from a social media professional.

- ✔ Discover in what kinds of companies, organizations, and departments you can find social media jobs.

- ✔ See more at `www.dummies.com`.

Chapter 1

The Big Picture of Social Media Jobs

In This Chapter

▶ Understanding social media's future

▶ Explaining what social media is — and what it isn't

▶ Realizing that every single person is a part of social media

▶ Defining what types of entities hire social media professionals

Social media isn't a fad or a temporary business practice. Social media has forever changed the Internet's identity and has shifted the way people around the world communicate with one another. It's where people can interact as seamlessly as on the telephone. Social media has connected thought leaders and fostered innovation, collaboration, and creativity.

For-profits and nonprofits no longer ask *whether* organizations should participate, but rather *how* to engage and participate in a meaningful way. Because social media is a constantly evolving industry, people who are willing to cultivate their knowledge and skills have plenty of opportunities.

The best part of the social media growth curve is how new the industry is and how quickly the job market is growing. This means that anyone with the desire can learn the information and refine the skills that define a top-notch social media professional. It's a good thing that you have this book!

In this chapter, you discover how social media has evolved, why social media is different than any other medium ever created before, and how to set yourself up as a highly regarded expert.

Defining Social Media

Defining what social media is can be tough. Various types of online entities such as web logs (blogs), video blogs *(vlogs)*, virtual game worlds (like World of Warcraft), *wikis* (websites that gather information from contributors all over the world), and Internet forums all can be classified as social media. For example, an Internet marketing forum such as warriorforum.com would be classified as a social network since the users share text, links, and pictures and can directly talk to one another.

Videos are typically the most engaging form of content. Vlogs are the most efficient way to accommodate different learning styles. Some people learn by seeing, hearing, reading, or doing. Video lets consumers see, hear, and read.

What social media is:

- ✔ A website or web-based app such as Facebook.
- ✔ A smartphone or tablet app to use the platform the same as they would on a desktop. Every big social networking site has a mobile app.
- ✔ A platform, such as Twitter, that lets users share different kinds of content whenever they please.
- ✔ An online community, such as deviantART, where users communicate directly with each another.
- ✔ A combination of technology and social interaction, such as Instagram comments.

Understanding how social media is completely different from every other communication channel is important.

What social media *isn't:*

- ✔ Traditional or industrial media that is defined by one-way communication; see Figure 1-1
- ✔ Offline
- ✔ A standalone resource that prohibits interaction
- ✔ Static content from one source
- ✔ Temporary content that isn't archived

The current top players in social media — the Big Five — are Facebook, Instagram, Twitter, LinkedIn, and YouTube. Those front runners will change, and not long from now.

Understanding each platform's identity — its culture — is vital. A platform's identity is made up of its content length, the multimedia content, the audience demographics, and the overall tone. Chapter 7 goes into these respective social media identities in more detail.

A bit of history

Many people argue about where the term *social media* started. Some social media analysts say that 1994, when Geocities enabled its one million users to create websites, was really the start of the social media phenomenon. Other people claim it started from blogging and America Online (AOL) Instant Messenger in 1997. Though these breakthroughs certainly had features that exist in modern social media, the real start began in 1999, when Friends United launched in Great Britain, allowing users to reconnect with former classmates.

Social media has aliases that can be a bit confusing. For example, you might be familiar with these terms, all of which refer to the same types of communication:

- ✔ Social networking
- ✔ Social media
- ✔ Social broadcasting
- ✔ Web 2.0
- ✔ Virtual online networks

What's the difference between web 2.0 and social media? The time periods, the constantly evolving networks, the allowed communication, and the content forms. Web 2.0, which mainly featured MySpace, Friendster, Flickr, and Second Life, had person-to-person communication or broadcast communication (from one person to their entire network).

Social media has expanded the communication types to allow people to segment their network and choose specifically who should receive their message and who shouldn't.

For more information on the particular networks and impending social media trends, be sure to check out Chapter 3.

Finally, you can create more dynamic content via social media. Web 2.0 used limited text, pictures, and emoticons. Social media has built upon this base and brought the ability to create multimedia content, higher quality photography, animated GIFs, stop-motion video, and much more. Not only are there more *types* of content available, but each network allows different content.

WARNING!

Social media professionals who use the same voice and content type across platforms are seen as novices. Always know the cultural best practices on a platform.

Separating social media from traditional media

The biggest confusion about the term *social media* is the idea that it's just a newer form of traditional media — magazines, television, billboards, and radio. See Table 1-1 for the very clear opposites.

Many social media professionals come directly from advertising and mass-communication fields. They use the knowledge and experiences that they got from traditional media.

Social media isn't the online form of traditional media.

Table 1-1   Comparing Traditional Media with Social Media

Traditional Media	Social Media
One-way communication. The company talks to the customer but never the other way around.	Two-way communication happens, leading to open conversation.
Temporary messaging. Once the messaging has been sent, it's almost never repeated.	Messaging's recorded for posterity.
Significant production costs for messaging.	Little to no production costs for messaging.
Little to no sales tracking.	The most sophisticated communication analytics ever created.

Traditional media has a difficult time establishing how their marketing efforts correlate to sales. It's hard to prove that a billboard on the side of the road or a television commercial brings money into the business.

Assimilating to the world of social media

How can you shoot yourself in the foot and wind up making the most common mistakes in the social media profession?

✔ **Expect instantaneous results.** A company (or person) can't set up a Twitter account, spout information about products, and expect immediate sales increases. Success on social media is never overnight; you must build a responsive network. Remember: The key is to be social rather than communicating one way to the masses.

✔ **Focus on you.** Social media emphasizes the need for community, interaction, and mutually beneficial relationships. Avoid thinking about what others can do for you. Look for ways you can benefit others first. Social media pros who contribute value up front always win.

✔ **Use automated and easy.** Social media requires — above all else — manpower and dedication. Some parts can be automated, but social media success mandates that users authentically connect with other users and build genuine relationships.

If you can't automate the process in real life, then it probably won't work on social media. Chapter 3 talks about how to use automation successfully.

All the top social media professionals know (and show) the following:

✔ **Slow and steady results.** Social media is the common marathon versus a sprint. You have to build significant relationships and find enough people who trust you and your brand to accomplish your goals. That takes time and effort.

✔ **Two-way dialogue.** It's more important to listen than to talk. Maybe you're charged with getting word out about a social media conference. You might be tempted to hit Twitter with "The ABC social media conference is going to be awesome and there's a super special sale going on!" Don't. Instead, first read tweets about the product and its competition. Then ask other influencers their thoughts and broadcast to the social media community an open-ended question for their feedback.

✔ **Laser focus on relationships.** Without significant thought leadership via content (such as writing a periodical to demonstrate your knowledge) and context, efforts fall flat. Fast. One reason social media works so well is because it helps create more relationships than you could dream of in person. But you have to continually improve these relationships. This process can be difficult and time consuming, but work at least 30 minutes per day to keep in touch with your key people.

✔ **Native storytelling.** Every social media site speaks its own language: different content, optimal content lengths, and cultural standards for participating. Not only do you need to know how to speak the language, but you must quickly tell your story. *Storytelling* is the essence of effective marketing. Chapter 3 explains this kind of communication. See Figure 1-1.

A social media pro knows how to tell the right story to the right people on the right platform at the right time.

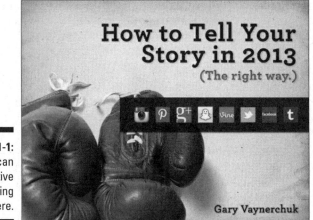

Figure 1-1:
You can
find native
storytelling
help here.

Demonstrating the Value of Social Media

All social media pros face this question: What's social media's *return on investment (ROI)?*

If someone asks what social media's ROI is, have a few thought-provoking statements prepared. Don't get defensive or attack traditional media. Explain its metrics, direct response measurables, and customer-retention abilities.

Soft benefits

Consider some of social media's ancillary benefits:

- The total amount a customer will spend over a lifetime
- Better direct response and metrics
- Extending consumer relationships with two-way communication
- Increased brand recognition
- Free opportunity to convert customers
- Enhanced brand loyalty
- Increased in-bound web traffic
- Search engine optimization (SEO)

Unfortunately, qualitative information and customer retention aren't as valued as customer acquisition and sales metrics. In business, definitive sales metrics still rule all.

Hard benefits

The simplest ways to prove social media's value from an ROI perspective follow:

- ✔ **Direct response.** The best way to measure social media's impact is to directly correlate the results with social media content.

  Establish marketing mechanisms that are tied only to specific platforms. Then, you know that platform is the only way a consumer could have made a specific purchase. Examples of direct response mechanisms are:
  - 1-800 or specialized phone numbers
  - Campaign websites or landing page websites
  - Specialized email addresses

- ✔ **Web traffic.** Free traffic tools (such as Google Analytics, found at www.google.com/analytics) can show you not only where the traffic came from but where they were referred from. For example, a brand fan might share a social media purchase link, which allows an analytics system to show the additional web traffic that resulted from sharing.

- ✔ **Social mentions.** Social media aggregators such as SocialMention.com let you search across all social media engines to see all consumer comments around any keyword: a brand name, product, service, or industry, for example. You can put together this information to tell a brand what the general public thinks.

- ✔ **Social media analytics.** Social media provides metrics that are unmatched by traditional media and can provide information such as actual impressions, actions taken, engagement ratios, and sharing metrics. Some of the more sophisticated social media tools, including raventools.com, provide exponentially more information than traditional marketing sources such as billboards and magazine ads. Not only that, social media analytics are more accurate since all the information is digital.

- ✔ **Social media ad sales.** Using a website *conversion pixel* (code placed on a website), you can measure how many sales come from platform advertisements.

Finding an In

Because social media is so popular, organizations and corporations are being pushed to use it for their outbound communication: companies that are publicly traded on the New York Stock Exchange, private companies, government, education, nonprofits, and religious institutions.

Companies are skeptical of self-proclaimed "social media gurus." Stay away from terms such as *guru;* they're typically used for shock value. Instead, emphasize that you're a professional or illustrate a specific skill set.

Internal and external jobs

Social media opportunities exist for internal and external communications. It's common for brands to have internal social networks (courtesy of vendors such as yammer.com).

They provide these internal networks for several reasons:

- To help facilitate creativity.
- To have different departments collaborate on projects.
- To streamline their brand's critical activities.

When choosing your career, you also must decide what type of work environment that you prefer. If potentially making it big and working extremely hard is up your alley, then start at Chapter 10. You might also be interested in starting your own business and consulting with brands, which is covered in Chapter 8. You might even want to start your own social media agency where you manage social media for clients, which is what Chapter 11 is all about.

Regardless of your route, make sure you know what you want out of a job. If you're not excited to get up in the morning and rush off to work, then you're probably in the wrong career!

Going where the jobs are

More companies are building context with their customer base rather than advertising. As such, companies are making larger financial commitments to people and systems that help grow and manage their social media presence.

Social media can lead to automated two-way communication systems. Don't let it!

However, the emphasis for these brands should be on hiring leaders and building relationships with their customer base. You have even more opportunity if you can help brands reach their target goals.

Some of the immediate opportunities for social media pros are in the following areas:

- **Strategy.** How to create the positioning, organizing, and execution of a social media plan. Chapter 12 gives you a basic plan.

- **Advertising.** Creating, promoting, and continually improving advertisements on social media platforms such as Facebook and Pinterest.

- **Analytics.** Metrics that show you how many impressions and sales happen as a result of social media. Chapter 16 talks about metrics in detail. Chapter 7 dishes on the tools you need to reveal those metrics.

- **Referral marketing.** These are programs where customers can refer their friends via social media and be given rewards such as money for telling others about a company.

- **Graphic design.** As more players rush into the social media space, top-notch graphic designers are needed to help brands establish a unique, professional style on social media.

Knowing Who Does the Hiring

You might specialize in social media, but you can wind up on task forces or committees within a business department such as information technology or human resources. Chief Social Media Officer positions are being created at Fortune 500 companies; social media internships are ready in nonprofit start-ups.

How can you get involved?

Being a consultant or an employee

You might be hired as one of two position types when you're applying for a job:

- Employee
- Consultant

Even if you're a full-time employee, you might wind up working with a consultant. Employers can ask consultants to become full-time employees at any stage. And on the other hand, a full-time employee may start his or her own consultancy as a side job (and consult for the company he or she worked for).

What's the difference between a consultant and an employee? Consultants generally have more billable hours but less security. If a company needs a specific skills set (such as social media advertising), it may choose to hire a contractor for three month's trial.

Also, a consultant typically has the following:

- ✔ Ownership of a consultancy or work for a business consulting entity
- ✔ An hourly pay rate or consulting pay rate via government tax form 1099
- ✔ Accountability for their own business taxes, insurance, and benefits
- ✔ A signed consulting agreement that encompasses specific deliverables and a working timeframe
- ✔ More freedom in terms of work hours and location

An employee typically has the following:

- ✔ Strict work hours, standards, and corporate expectations
- ✔ Guaranteed hourly rate or yearly salary
- ✔ Health, dental, vision, and other insurance benefits
- ✔ Retirement and other savings investment benefits

Brooks's business

Brooks has done both, but prefers a combination. Brooks is a full-time Chief Marketing Officer for FilterEasy, Inc., but also does social media consulting with other brands such as ENDcrowd.com. The rationale behind this decision comes as a result of Brooks establishing that he wanted the stability of a full-time position but still had the ability to build a longer-term career within social media by helping grow other brands within his portfolio.

Figure out your risk tolerance versus the reward that you can receive and make your decision accordingly:

- ✓ If you have a high tolerance for risk and want the greatest reward, then the full-time consultant route is the one for you.
- ✓ If you have a medium tolerance for risk and want options, then a full-time job and consulting on the side is your best option.
- ✓ If you have a low tolerance for risk and are comfortable with a smaller reward at first, a full-time position with a company is your best bet.

Public and private organizations

Both public and private organizations hire social media professionals.

- ✓ *Public organizations* have shareholders that invest money; public organizations are publicly traded on the NYSE, NASDAQ, or AMEX markets. Public sector organizations can include government and educational institutions such as state-run universities.
- ✓ *Private organizations* can be for-profit, nonprofit, governmental agencies, and educational institutions. Private, for-profit companies are not traded on the stock exchange and all *non-governmental organizations (NGO)* are private institutions. All governmental and educational entities will clearly state whether they're supported by the government or independently operated.

Both public and private entities typically have the same departments: marketing, information technology, human resources, and executive management.

Though social media positions often cross into different departments or functional teams, the following sections cover the most common.

Marketing

Social media marketing is currently one of the most desired skills.

A social media marketing job might take form as a community manager, social media strategist, or a social media manager. Marketing departments typically rely on social media professionals to perform the following tasks:

- ✓ **Social media management.** You create content, figure out communication strategies, and respond to any social media users contacting the brand and social media as a whole.
- ✓ **Community management.** The building, growth, and management of a brand and a cause's online community. For example, responding to anyone who directly talks to a brand or tags the brand in a social media post.

✔ **Social media metrics.** You show, with criteria, social media's reach and impact. The most important metrics are explained in Chapter 16.

- Impressions

- Cost per 1,000 impressions (CPM)

- Click-through rate (CTR)

- Website clicks

- Mentions

- Overall social reach

✔ **Social media advertising.** The marketing department creates and manages advertisements. These ads include graphics, sales copy, and targeting of consumer demographics and interests. Social media platforms including Facebook, Instagram, LinkedIn, Pinterest, Twitter, and YouTube offer ads.

Targeting is why social media ads are so effective. Platforms gather data based on what the users interact with and the demographic data that they provide.

Information technology (IT)

Social media integration requires top-notch IT professionals that specialize in different social media aspects. IT social media pros may also be in charge of internal social media websites and helping other departments from a technical standpoint.

Knowing how to program in computer languages such as HTML, CSS, and PHP is extremely useful for social media platforms.

Human resources (HR)

HR is another common department for social media professionals to be placed in.

Social media is becoming an intricate part of HR departments because social media communication represents organizations as a whole both internally with the company and their external communication.

A social media pro in HR might have the following responsibilities:

✔ Research potential candidates throughout the social web and report findings to HR in charge of hiring.

✔ Facilitate and strengthen relationships with potential candidates for open and upcoming positions with headhunters and potential candidates.

✔ Monitor and report findings regarding the personal social media accounts of shareholders such as employees, vendors, and investors. This is done to strengthen relationships and protect the brand from anything unsavory or controversial.

✔ Manage an internal social network and help moderate communication.

Executive management

The new need for accomplished social media professionals forced organizations to create social media manager positions. Sometimes a person in that position is a department head, and sometimes he's a social media executive that oversees all efforts.

Chief Social Officers (CSOs) or *Chief Social Media Officers (CSMOs)* are becoming more common. Any information that passes to, from, or within an organization would fall under a CSO. This includes social media strategy, planning, and all aspects of execution.

A CSO does the following:

✔ Drives awareness and *impressions* (the number of times that a brand is seen)

✔ Manages and builds sales

✔ Ensures consumer satisfaction and superior service

✔ Builds, refines, and synthesizes consumer feedback

These departments are where most social media professionals are hired, but it isn't a complete list. Departments such as accounting, finance, operations management, and procurement sometimes need specialized social media positions. Chapter 9 talks about in-house social media positions in more depth.

Chapter 2

Seeing Yourself in a Social Media Job

In This Chapter

▶ Transitioning to the social media field

▶ Uncovering the biggest job opportunities

▶ Knowing how social media influences an entire organization

▶ Understanding how to demonstrate value in your new career

*I*t might be difficult knowing what a new job in such a new industry will look like. Social media positions are being created so quickly, and some have never existed before.

If no one can tell you all the details of the job or what your typical workday will look like, that uncertainty might be intimidating. We encourage you to look at this challenge as exciting. In time, you'll be able to focus on the activities that you enjoy the most (if they provide optimal results for your employer).

In this chapter, you discover the best practices for getting acclimated in your new social media career, what to expect as you progress into your job and helpful hints for effectively conveying the value that you will inevitably provide.

Preparing to Prove Your Worth

Because the industry is so new, social media efforts are constantly under strict scrutiny because of the questionable *return on investment (ROI)*.

Can a brand possibly quantify the *actual* impressions and correlation to top-line sales of a billboard or a magazine ad? Yes — if there are direct-response mechanisms with this traditional advertising media — but the fact remains that traditional media doesn't have great metrics.

Social media can measure just about anything and everything with its digital reach from click-through rates, brand impressions, top-line sales, and much more. These important deliverables should be defined as follows:

- **Click-through rates (CTR)** is the percentage of people that click a link posted on social media to take them to another website.

- **Brand impressions** is the total number of people that can potentially, and actually, see the content that you post on social media.

- **Top-line objectives** are sales numbers that can come in the form of leads, a consumer contacting your employer, and the actual sale of products and services.

You'll be challenged to establish immediate value, but in social media you also have the distinct advantage of being in control of the future benefits. For instance, social media provides ongoing brand equity and the opportunity to build a relationship with your employer's customers.

Social media careers offer the most accurate snapshot of a brand. Social media provides more in-depth metrics than any other advertising and marketing medium and accurately shows key sales numbers, unlike many traditional marketing outlets. In essence, social media provides the most data, and it shows brands exactly where they stand against competitors and with consumers and communities. This is one of the many reasons social media careers have become so valuable to many employers.

Social media careers are clearly different from traditional marketing jobs. What are the top reasons?

- There's no precedent in terms of expectations, standards, performance, or value-driven results. Organizations commonly create jobs based on what other brands put together. They don't necessarily know what to expect.

- The person hiring often has limited (or no) practical experience with social media. As such, you can define your value more clearly.

- Social media provides the strongest metrics out of any advertising and marketing media. A social media pro can interpret and deliver results since social media can be integrated into web analytics and tracking programs. Chapter 16 covers these analytics in detail.

✔ Social media has reinvented how to attract new customers. Traditional marketing spends its time finding, converting and keeping its base in that order. However, social media marketing flips this process upside down and focuses its time on keeping, converting and finding customers.

Checking Your Daily To-Do List

What will a new career in social media include? You have to be prepared for having daily responsibilities that vary greatly. When showing how your efforts correlate to sales and brand impressions, more opportunities will come your way.

You'll encounter these common responsibilities and tasks when starting a new social media job:

✔ **Daily reporting:** Full quantitative reporting (available through software such as `www.simplymeasured.com`, shown in Figure 2-1) on the day's progress and how this correlates to ongoing goals is typically expected. The reporting will usually involve impressions, click-through rates (CTR), social reach, top-line sales, and other brand KPIs. Chapter 16 delves into these tools and reporting.

✔ **Daily progress:** You'll provide a list of tasks that you completed. They're often requested at the end of your work week. Include information that other departments need to drive sales.

✔ **General promotion:** Since brands put a heavy emphasis on sales and brand impression, your responsibility is geared toward anything that's newsworthy on behalf of your employer. This may involve advertising products, services, specials, company initiatives, company news, and limited-time promotions.

✔ **Community management:** Most brands simply want a pro to answer and help any social media users who are contacting the brand. More progressive brands focus on building and using a community around the company. A lot of great community management software programs provide more information. (Try `lithium.com`.) Upload your employer's information and social media handles; the software generates any type of report that your employer may need.

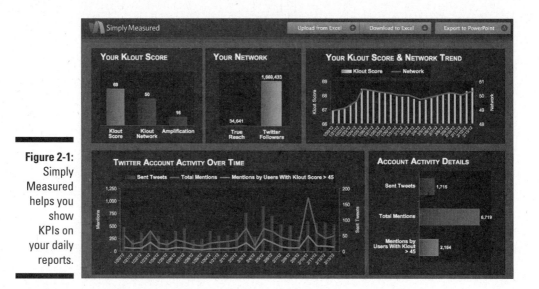

Figure 2-1:
Simply
Measured
helps you
show
KPIs on
your daily
reports.

Trading Off Between Bigger and Smaller Entities

You may take a small role with a big company or a big role with a small company. Each has advantages and disadvantages.

At a smaller company, you'll typically have:

- ✔ Much larger scope of responsibility
- ✔ Job flexibility and the ability to create your own roles and responsibilities
- ✔ Lower initial salary and limited benefits
- ✔ Opportunity to make a huge impact on a company's direction and its corporate culture
- ✔ Heightened opportunity for larger equity and ownership
- ✔ Ability for larger payout as a member of executive management, ownership, or an acquisition of the entity

Working for a smaller company is the right path if you're a risk taker who desires a bigger reward sooner. If you're more risk averse, then you'll certainly prefer the comfort and security of a larger company.

Typically, social media jobs at larger entities have the following:

- ✔ Focused role and scope of responsibilities
- ✔ Set schedule with the same daily work
- ✔ Higher salary and guaranteed benefits
- ✔ Difficulty working into executive management

Again, the opportunities for social media employment are everywhere, but you decide what level of risk, reward, impact, and versatility you want.

Jobs Coming from All Sides

Social media jobs are coming from everywhere:

- ✔ Public industry
- ✔ Private industry
- ✔ For-profit organizations
- ✔ Nonprofit organizations

Figure out the top three positions that you'd be excited about and narrow your company choices to a maximum of three as well.

Search these resources to find a job:

- ✔ careerbuilder.com/jobs/keyword/social-media
- ✔ jobsinsocialmedia.com (See Figure 2-2.)
- ✔ socialmediajobs.hootsuite.com
- ✔ socialmediajobs.com

Keep your eyes on the websites of the organizations that you want to work for. Connect with the decision makers of the companies on LinkedIn and Twitter and communicate with them.

Set up a Google Alert around the type of job that you want and the company that you're eyeing. For example, if your dream job is to be a social media strategist for the Dollar Shave Club, go to Google Alerts and set up your search query as *social media strategist* and *Dollar Shave Club*.

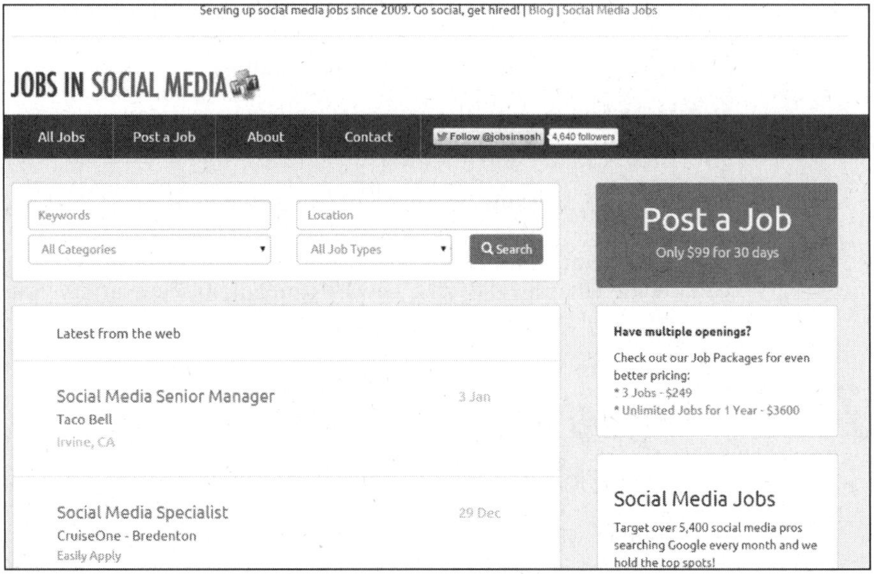

Figure 2-2:
Jobsin
Social
Media.
com is a
good place
to search.

Here's how to set up a Google Alert:

1. **Go to** `google.com/alerts`.

2. **Enter your query.**

   It might be *dollar shave club* and *social media.*

3. **Enter your email address.**

4. **Click the Create Alert button shown in Figure 2-3.**

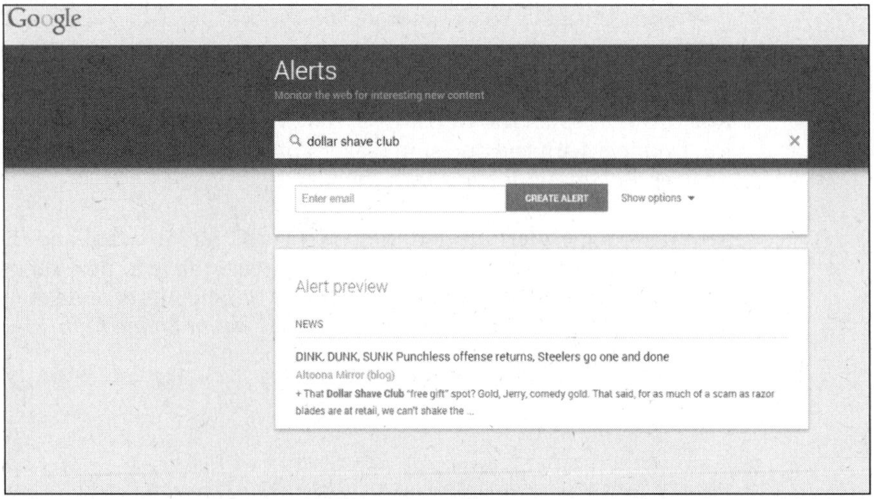

Figure 2-3:
Google
Alerts help
you stay
updated.

Eyeing the Trends

What are some of the biggest trends and opportunities for 2015?

- ✔ **Social media advertising:** The main revenue driver with engines such as Facebook, Twitter, and LinkedIn is advertising. The larger social media networks constantly get more effective. This job opportunity becomes larger when considering networks such as Pinterest, Instagram, Snapchat, and Google+ emerging with their advertising platforms. A social media advertising professional should be well versed in copywriting, graphic design, and social media analytics. If you're considering more education on this topic, check out Chapter 5.

- ✔ **Real-time marketing:** Real time is versus *reactive marketing,* which happens after the fact and doesn't involve two-way conversation. You can use Facebook, Twitter, or Instagram for real-time marketing, which includes brands monitoring and participating in trends. You can target large and small current events to specific audiences. For example, the Grammy's produced huge net results for Arby's and Quaker Oats, which jumped into a Twitter conversation with witty banter; multiple media sources were talking about the brands.

- ✔ **Content marketing:** Social media pros create and distribute valuable, relevant content to attract and acquire a clearly defined audience for this marketing technique. Content marketing's ultimate objective is to drive profitable customer action. An opportunity exists in the storytelling process around the user rather than the product. Brands have jumped onto platforms like medium.com, where stories can be told with beautiful imagery and create a more enjoyable reading experience for the end user. For great examples of content marketing and how to optimize this methodology, visit `contentmarketinginstitute.org`.

- ✔ **Data aggregation and analysis:** Can you synthesize social media information and turn it into actionable data for brands? A professional who knows how to use social media data and turn it into sales is valuable to organizations. For more information about the specific social media metrics that are the most relevant, please see Chapter 7.

Be aware of your own strengths and talents when considering opportunities. Don't take a big data job if the monotony bores you to tears. The money and benefits will never outweigh the happiness that you get from work. (Chapter 15 talks more about job satisfaction.)

To be prepared for the impending changes, continually do the following:

- ✔ Know what's happening in the social media trenches. Be part of the work that is going on, even if you are in a management capacity.

✔ Learn. Block out at least one hour per day to brush up on articles or tutorials and engage with other social media professionals about best practices, tips, strategy and so forth. Create Google Calendar reminders to stay on schedule. When you let a day or two of study go by, the sooner you're likely to give up this tactic. Chapter 12 talks more about education.

Be *transparent* (share) about your responsibilities at work to give back to the social media pro community — as long as your employer allows it and it doesn't violate your employment agreement — and try to provide as much value as you can to other social media professionals.

Understanding the Social Media Department

The social media department typically lives in the confines of the advertising or marketing departments.

Ultimately, social media deals with two things:

✔ Information

✔ Communication

Information and communication can come from current customers, prospective customers, competitors, stakeholders, vendors, the community that you serve, the community that you don't serve, and virtually everyone else in between.

The value of social media comes from the synthesis and analysis of the information and communication that happens on the social media networks themselves. The social media department's job is to figure out how the components that they see can make all departments more efficient.

Winning friends and influencing departments

Because social media revolves around information and communication, it touches most business segments, including

✔ Marketing and advertising

✔ Sales

- ✔ Customer service

- ✔ Executive management

- ✔ Operations management

- ✔ Accounting

- ✔ Finance

- ✔ Information technology

For example, customer service is impacted because you can use information gathered from social media to improve internal customer support systems. Information such as customer feedback and comments offer insight about buying habits and tendencies. Sales can use social media information to hone in on better customer acquisition and retention.

You can use customers' email addresses to strengthen the marketing, advertising, IT, sales, and customer service departments:

- ✔ Plug email addresses into Facebook and find out what types of Facebook pages your customers like. Put the information into a spreadsheet so you can see different attributes and interests to target on Facebook's advertising software (at facebook.com/advertising) when creating advertisements.

- ✔ Plug the customer email addresses into Facebook's advertising to create a lookalike audience that automatically targets users with similar demographics and user habits.

- ✔ Plug email addresses into Twitter so you can follow and engage with current customers; this interaction helps you add more information to your customer profile database (if applicable) such as `nimble.com` or `exacttarget.com`. For more information on social media customer relationship management (CRM) databases, see Chapter 7.

Social media can impact an organization in so many ways. Figure out how you can benefit other departments and give them the information that they care the most about.

Using social media in unexpected ways

Don't hesitate to offer social media know-how beyond your expected responsibilities. Your social media skills come in handy other times:

- ✔ **Short-term or ongoing projects:** Brands often create projects that fulfill a business need, conduct research, or develop future products and services. The projects need input from multiple parts of a business. As a social media pro, you can provide the information and communication for pulling off internal initiatives. For example, you can bring real comments and feedback from social media customers when you're developing new products or evaluating how effective consumers find a new service.

✔ **Task forces:** In crisis mode, or when an urgent need has to be met, temporary task forces are put into place to handle the issue. For example, if a company puts out a product that negatively impacts consumers, the company may need multiple professionals (public relations, advertising, legal, accounting, and social media, for example) to help handle the repercussions.

✔ **Committees:** A company's continuous improvement might be handled by committee. For example, a committee may be evaluating the way they ship their products. You can fill in the rest of the company on surveys that customers have taken via social media. You can share feedback and relay suggestions made by consumers.

✔ **Community initiatives:** A company's main goal is to make money and improve stakeholder returns, but great companies contribute value to their communities. As a social media pro, you might become a part of a community group because you have your finger on the pulse of how online communities think and feel about a brand. In fact, you might become instrumental in this role, because you can bridge online and offline relationships by meeting your customers and local social media influencers through local gatherings. Chapter 3 details these local networking opportunities.

Measuring Your Results

A restaurant owner asked why the new chain couldn't get 10,000 followers and fans on social media and "just sell them stuff." Brooks was under pressure to deliver his value through a combination of proper expectation setting, education on the subject matter, and focusing on what the owner thought the key performance indicators (KPIs) to be.

It falls squarely on your shoulders to prove your merit. Be prepared to measure and quantify your results.

Setting up expectations

Ask your employer questions about their expectations, document the answers, and saving the document in a shared space such as Dropbox or Google Drive. Here are a few examples of what you absolutely need to ask:

✔ What are the most important *key performance indicators (KPIs)* to you?

✔ What would you consider an absolute home run success as a result of my work?

✔ How and when do you expect me to quantify my work and overall results?

✔ Who will I report to and who will I collaborate with on projects?

 Make sure that expectations on both sides are realistic. Just because your employer asks for a deliverable doesn't mean that it's right. If you have any doubt that you can't meet an expectation, say so up front and come to a resolution before you begin work. Chapter 16 talks more about setting expectations.

Meeting expectations

After you clearly understand what work you should deliver, you can ensure that you're continuously improving at your job. Do this is by constantly sharing your results with your employer, asking for objective feedback, and being proactive.

These tasks will help you meet expectations:

✔ Keep a daily log of your accomplishments. This can be an hour-by-hour breakdown or a snapshot of your weekly progress. The more information you have, and the more easily understood you make your results, the better.

✔ Create simple charts and diagrams that show the progress that you're making in the KPIs that your employer identified. For example, if you can show impressions, sales, and follower counts for respective networks, then display this information. This doesn't have to be visually stunning. A simple Excel chart will get the job done.

✔ Use a project-management system such as `Wrike.com` or `Basecamp.com`. Your use becomes more impressive if your employer doesn't use project-management software. Showing a clear breakdown of your work means that you can organize projects. For example, Wrike has built-in Gantt charts (see Figure 2-4) that show when projects are supposed to begin and end and the manpower you need to complete the project. By doing this, you're setting yourself up for managerial roles.

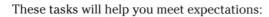 Be aware of the skepticism that surrounds social media. Prove that you're useful. Establish the quantitative and qualitative value that you bring to the table.

Get out and vote

Poll your social media user base to confirm your social media efforts. You can use a free service such as `EasyPolls.net`, or a paid system such as `PollDaddy.com`. Ask your audience simple questions about what they value, what they like most about your social media presence, additional wants that they have, and so forth. Many of these polling systems automatically create simple charts that easily quantify your results.

Brooks used PollDaddy when he was a restaurant general manager. With the information he got from users, he was able to say how many people were coming into the restaurant and were returning as a result of the restaurant's social media presence. He even put together direct-response coupons for specific platforms.

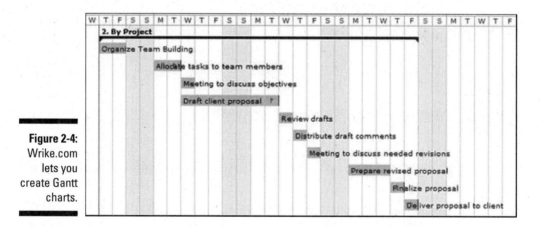

Figure 2-4:
Wrike.com
lets you
create Gantt
charts.

Chapter 3

Key Social Media Concepts You Should Know

*T*he amount of information about social media is one of the most daunting factors that social media professionals face. You can't read a magazine, watch a television show, or glance through a newspaper without seeing information about social media.

You can read and study and still not get anywhere. We call this "paralysis by analysis." In other words, you run the risk of spending all your time absorbing information but not taking action.

Using your knowledge in the trenches, failing on occasion, and dedicating yourself to continuous improvement is where you'll see the most significant results.

In this chapter you discover the key networks that you need to master. You also read about where to put your time and efforts. This chapter focuses on the basics that you need to know. Make it your mission to take the knowledge from this chapter and apply it.

Knowing Your Value

When you're looking for opportunities within social media, ask yourself two questions:

- ✔ **Is it fun?** Why not focus on finding or creating positions that make you feel good? For example, if you've read that social media big data or social media ad management provide great jobs, but neither of these topics interest you, focus on what you enjoy.

- ✔ **Can I make money?** How are you going to sustain yourself? If you can't tell how your value can earn money, you run the risk of doing a lot of work with no immediate rewards. For example, Brooks advises smaller companies and *non-governmental organizations (NGOs)* but doesn't work with them full time because they typically can't afford his full-time expertise. This isn't a knock on entities with smaller budgets but rather being self-aware and knowing your value.

The more value you provide one on one, the better you'll build long-lasting relationships. This value and approach put you in the good graces of the thought leader or business and gives you an entire network for your business page.

Looking for opportunities

We recommend finding opportunities wherever you can. There's a distinct possibility that you'll have to volunteer or intern for little or no money and prove your worth to get the position that you want.

For example, Brooks volunteered for three months to manage and grow the social media presence of a developing restaurant chain. He worked long hours, got no pay, and moved 500 miles away from his friends and family.

We aren't proposing that you quit your job and risk everything for opportunity (especially if you have a family to help provide for). You might have to hedge the risks; knowledge and experience might trump the short-term sacrifices. The advantage of doing pro bono work is that you'll know exactly what knowledge you need and focus on the *key performance indicators (KPIs)* that social media provides.

Ensuring Success with Social Media

Think of social media as an upscale networking and cocktail party. Who gets the most attention? The interesting party guest who listens to others and knows how to work the room. This person has high credentials but they don't flaunt their accomplishments or ask everyone to join them in business. This person doesn't need to be aggressive because everyone wants to be around him or her. They're already beating down the door in hopes of building a relationship.

Many traditional businesspeople stereotype social media pros as "professional networkers" that want to "save the world" with engagement and *vanity metrics* (such as Likes and comments). Nothing could be further from the truth. Smart, savvy social media pros understand the value of genuinely connecting with other human beings, as well as finding new ways to grow their brand and direct response measurables via social media.

The following sections explain the top rules to follow when establishing yourself as a top-notch social media pro:

- ✔ Respect each social media platform. (Read about the Big Five in Chapter 7.)
- ✔ Always look to help others without looking for anything in return.
- ✔ Define your value and look to be a friend and helpful professional rather than wonder what everyone else can do for you.
- ✔ Create helpful content worth talking about. The more people get the help they want from you, the closer you'll be to getting what you want.

Respecting the platforms that you play on

For example, if you try to share an Instagram photo on Facebook and Twitter, the users may be annoyed with an Instagram best practice of using lots of hashtags. Conversely, if you share a Facebook photo on Instagram, then the quality may be greatly diminished and the website URL in the description won't work. Making these mistakes makes you look like a novice.

To get to know a platform's culture, study each one to

- ✔ See how users interact.
- ✔ See what type of content that they produce.

✔ Understand top thought leaders.

✔ Learn what type of content seems to work really well based on engagement and when optimal times to post are.

Chapter 7 talks about the top platforms in depth.

Speaking natively to your audience

Speaking natively means that you understand each site's culture and post relevant content. For example, you wouldn't post pictures of the pretty flowers in your backyard as a LinkedIn update; this content isn't relevant to LinkedIn's business-oriented discussions and content standards. You would, however, post flower pictures within a Facebook group related to botany, or within your Instagram account if this is one of your interests that you position yourself with.

Probably the most important aspect of speaking natively is to avoid coming across as a blatant advertisement in people's feeds. For example, if your target audience is NFL fans who are streaming through their Instagram feeds to look at pictures of players, practice, games, and NFL gear, and you put up a PowerPoint image advertising your "super social media management special," then you'll quickly be ignored — or worse, unfollowed and reported for not being relevant.

Thanking people for saying something nice or telling someone else about you is important. Being grateful is a part of effectively listening.

Domo arigato: Automating authentically

Often, social media pros are looking for new ways to automate their social media posts and engagement. The problem is that human interaction can't be completely automated. We're not suggesting that you sit on your computer or smartphone and monitor social media sites all day, every day. Find a balance between scheduling posts for optimal times and the genuine interaction that needs to transpire.

✔ Schedule your content posts via Facebook, Twitter, and LinkedIn using tools such as Hootsuite or Sprout. Check the number of impressions, shares, and overall engagement that your posts get to find the best times and days to post.

✔ Interact with people who show any sort of interest in the content that you're producing. Thank everyone and continue the dialogue by asking open-ended questions about their thoughts.

One of the best types of content is what is known as a *picture quote,* a vibrant image that has a quote, saying, or advice on top. Figure 3-1 shows a picture quote. If you're not comfortable with graphic design, make these sorts of images on `quotescover.com` or `pagemodo.com`.

Figure 3-1: A picture quote tends to be upbeat.

Reaching Beyond Social Media

Arguably the most important thing that you can do via social media is bridge your online and offline relationships.

Though the social media community is full of wonderful people, be cautious when meeting new people. Always meet in public, let at least one other person know where you'll be, and don't give out your personal contact information.

Here are some of our favorite ways to start meeting more people offline:

- ✔ **Tweetups:** A *tweetup* is when local Twitter users meet locally to network. Sometimes the tweetup is just for fun. Other times it's for business or to help raise funds for a nonprofit. Read more about them and how to use them to your best advantage in Chapter 5.

- ✔ `Meetup.com`: Local people get together in person because of mutual interest in a cause or hobby. *Meetups* can be virtually anything, from bicycling to business networking. The more of these connections you can make, the better it is for business in the long haul. See Figure 3-2.

✔ **Nextdoor.com:** This site helps you discover your neighborhood. Knowing what's going on in your community could help your job search.

✔ **LinkedIn:** Local groups meet for more business. Search for these groups on LinkedIn (with a search query such as **social media pros**) and use your general geographic area. Sometimes the group administrator must approve your admittance into the group but from there, finding out when and where the meetings are is a breeze.

Almost all social networks organize events locally for users to meet face to face. If you're not sure where and when they meet, ask some of the people who you communicate with. Look for local influencers; they always know the answer to this question.

Another option is to start organizing your own events. We've helped organize local basketball games, *mastermind meetings*, and local speaking groups through Facebook, Twitter, and LinkedIn. Brooks found that building restaurants in new communities was difficult, but that inviting the social media users that he communicated with *to* his restaurant gave him a leg up. Even better, he let frequent guests know where to find the restaurant on social media by using in-store signage (and even sewing his social media handle onto his chef jacket).

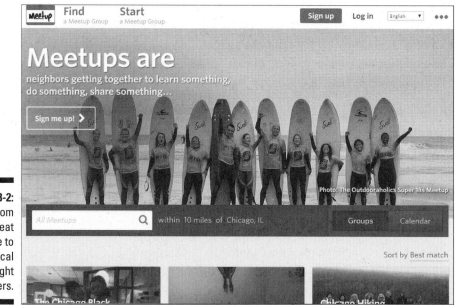

Figure 3-2:
Meetup.com
is a great
place to
meet local
thought
leaders.

Mastermind meetings are where local business leaders come together to share ideas and facilitate business partnerships.

Defining Your Social Media Talents

Find the subset of social media that you're the most passionate about and focus your efforts as an expert in that area. When establishing your talents, ask yourself the following questions:

- ✔ What industries am I most passionate about?
- ✔ What groups of people do I like to help and serve?
- ✔ What types of people do I love working alongside?
- ✔ What problems do I enjoy solving?

You might be especially interested in graphic design, managing people, or strategizing.

- ✔ Find positions by keywords and phrases on LinkedIn. Jobs that interest you will require common knowledge and skills.
- ✔ Conduct searches that are related to interesting business verticals so you can get the big picture of your ideal jobs.

Keep trying different skill sets and in different segments. Over time, you'll find the work that you're most passionate about. That will help you clearly identify your talents and skills.

For more information on the types of positions available for the talents and skills that you identify, check out Chapter 4 and Chapter 5.

Establishing your voice

Think of your *voice* as your content and tone. It's important to define how these two aspects are different from everyone else's in your marketplace — and the trick is doing so without telling anyone why you're different.

- ✔ **Content:** Think about what you share, create, and say, and the reasons why. For example, your content can be seen as succinct, transparent, based on real-world experiences, or offering practical implementation.

Whatever form of content is the most enjoyable to you is what you should share with the world. Don't try to create content that other "pros" say that you should, or you'll merely churn out the same old, run of the mill information. Be unique, be yourself and have fun with it.

✔ **Tone:** You can choose to be wise, snarky, witty, kind, or bubbly. Again, it's about picking a tone that's in tune with who you are as a person and as a professional. For example, many people view Michael Hyatt as a very honest, thoughtful leader. Seth Godin positions himself as a very perceptive thinker who establishes profound points but makes them simple to understand. Your voice will evolve as you create content. See Figure 3-3.

Make sure that your tone is authentic, consistently professional, and in tune with the potential entities that you're approaching. Tone is always about your subject matter, word choice, and overall writing style. If you try to write in a funny manner, make sure it doesn't come across as arrogant or demeaning. Above all else, communicate in a way that's becoming of the companies that you're applying with.

Refining your unique selling proposition (USP)

Your *unique selling proposition (USP)* should clearly and succinctly answer why your target audience should listen to you above anyone else.

Figure 3-3: Michael Hyatt is a social media thought leader whose voice is considered honest and thoughtful.

Refine your USP so your audience — current and target — clearly understands your offerings:

✔ Who you are as a person and how you communicate

✔ What type of expert information you offer

✔ The audience's benefit

Have a clear idea of how a colleague or superior would briefly explain them to someone else. If you're not sure how someone would explain what kind of expert you are, or why they should listen to you, figure it out.

Your audience must be able to clearly explain what your USP is to others within their networks. The best way to do this is to continually brand yourself around a very short phrase that lets people know what you do.

Some notable experts within the social media field include Derek Halpern from socialtriggers.com and Scott Stratten of UnMarketing.com; see Figure 3-4. Halpern chooses to position himself as an online sales psychology expert and Stratten has made his offering synonymous with effective storytelling. Both have very narrow focuses but their USP is extremely clear and their names immediately come to mind when it comes to these niches.

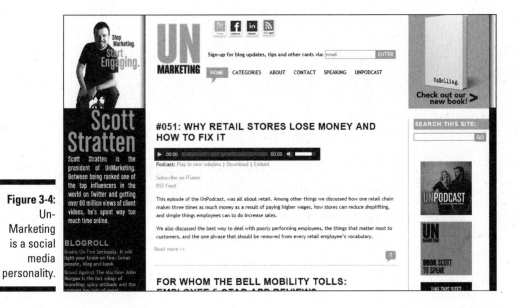

Figure 3-4: UnMarketing is a social media personality.

Creating Remarkable Content

The content that you create must aim to educate (and hopefully entertain) and have a heavy dose of your personality. You can choose different content types. Create a video or compile research that helps a potential employer achieve an objective. Look for influencers asking questions on their personal blog or on LinkedIn comments; respond with the answer via a YouTube video.

The best types of content let the audience take immediate action to see results. Your content should provide specific instructions and guidance so the audience can see an ideal outcome. If your audience has questions, you'll be the first one they contact. Provide your direct contact information!

The top forms of social media content have specific benefits:

✔ **Audio:** This can be in the form of an audio recording or podcasting. A *podcast* is audio, digital radio, or other documents that are subscribed to and downloaded through web syndication or streamed online to a device such as a laptop, tablet, or smartphone. Podcasting has huge markets, such as iTunes; see Figure 3-5. If you've been told that you have excellent inflection or cadence, then this is for you.

Figure 3-5: Apple iTunes is the premiere podcasting platform.

Discovering Podcasts

With hundreds of thousands of free podcasts at your fingertips, it's easy to find and enjoy your next favorite podcast on your iPhone, iPad, iPod touch, computer, or Apple TV.
Learn more ›

Making a Podcast

Join thousands of public and commercial broadcasters, renowned celebrities, and independent podcasters on iTunes. Easily create, maintain, and submit your podcast to the iTunes Store.
Learn more ›

✔ **Written word:** Blogs on networks such as WordPress sync well with search engines, which make up about a third of the world's website traffic. If you can organize information, create excellent actionable advice, or inspire others, then this is an excellent medium to choose.

✔ **Video:** YouTube is consistently the third-highest trafficked site in the world and is also integrated into search results. If you're extroverted and perform well on camera, then this highly visual medium is a great place to build your personal brand.

✔ **Imagery:** If you have photography or graphic design skills, then this is a fantastic way to set your personal brand apart. Creating distinct content that influencers want to use is a quick way to get noticed. This content can come in the form of graphics, stock photography, infographics, and much more.

✔ **Original research:** Creating original studies, gathering statistics, and putting together numbers pertaining to the social media industry from an academic standpoint is a great way to build your personal brand. Thought leaders are constantly looking for scientific information to support their claims, and you can brand your research with logos or a specific style that you create.

Promoting your work

One of the biggest mistakes social media pros make is failing to effectively tell others about the content that they've created. Most social media pros also fail to understand that your content and promotion may fail repeatedly, and that's completely okay.

Tenacity — sticking to it and getting better — is really what matters. Those mistakes typically boil down to a fear of failure (or a fear of success). The only way to get a social media job is by effectively promoting your work. Your audience decides whether your work is great.

Content promotion has an ever-changing nature, but your goal is to continually challenge yourself to produce the right message at the right time to the right audience on the right platform. If you get all four of these components right, then you'll be a household name. However, continually challenging yourself to refine all four is where you'll see results that steadily improve over time.

Follow these best practices when it comes to promoting your work:

✔ **LinkedIn:** Unless they unsubscribe, people you're connected to are automatically notified when you publish a post.

You can pay for targeting toward specific groups, companies, and people, but set a strict budget and evaluate whether paying for exposure is netting a return for you.

✔ **Google+:** You can directly email anyone within your circles and share it on the Google+ network. These are by far the best ways to distribute highly targeted content in different media.

✔ **Email:** One of the most valuable assets that you can possibly build is an email list full of loyal readers. Many social media pros say that email is useless because no one reads it anymore, but it's not necessarily the medium that's ineffective. Email success depends on whether the recipient is familiar with the sender. One way to set yourself apart is by using engaging video newsletters or beautiful email templates through vendors such as `iContact.com` and `benchmarkemail.com`.

✔ **Syndication:** Facebook emphasizes advertising, which forces you to pay for your content to be seen. Larger platforms are your best options. It takes time, but applying to be a contributor for huge social media publications such as Mashable and Social Media Examiner, and for business publications such as AMEX Open Forum (see Figure 3-6) and `Inc.com`, is a terrific way to get tons of traffic.

Syndication can get a bit sticky when it comes to search engine results. Your original content on your blog can be penalized from a *search engine optimization (SEO)* point of view. Google pushes a website down in the search engine rankings if Google has seen the content before. To combat this, use the Fetch as Google feature in the Google webmaster tools. The tool ensures that Google gives you credit for your content. Just put your URL in Fetch as Google and submit it to Google's index. See Figure 3-7.

Figure 3-6:
The AMEX
Open Forum
is a thought
leader
platform.

Figure 3-7:
The Fetch as Google tool comes in handy.

Volunteering with influencers

You certainly have a talent or skill that you can offer influencers. This can be something as basic as researching or compiling data, or as advanced as graphic designing or programming.

Examine

- ✔ Their blog
- ✔ The comments on their blog
- ✔ What they post on social media

For example, if she talks about the five hours of research she did to write a blog post, then you have the opportunity to step in and help. This approach is especially effective if you offer to help them without them having to ask. The worst that can possibly happen is that she won't take you up on your offer — but you'll at least have practice offering value to others.

To contact thought leaders, find their contact information. Most publicly list their email addresses or have contact forms on their websites. Keep these guidelines in mind:

- ✔ Use the person's supplied email address or contact form unless she explicitly states some other way to make contact. (Social media influencers often do.)
- ✔ Be very specific about what you can do for them. Define your value, whether it's in the form of copywriting or graphic design or connecting them with someone of interest.

✔ Provide evidence from social media or their thought leadership blog comments. For example, you might say, "I noticed that many of your readers have requested information about the top time-saving apps. I've attached a list of the 34 best time-saving apps, along with the website and price for each."

After you've helped someone, you can propose a working relationship. Be brief and clear about the benefits you bring. Then establish what you're looking for. It's completely acceptable to say what the person can do for you; leaders are interested in mutually beneficial relationships.

Don't get discouraged if someone you contact doesn't answer you immediately (or at all). To get the attention of an influential person, you must remain value driven, succinct, and persistent. You'll most likely "fail" repeatedly, but your determination to keep in contact will win over time.

Part II
Getting Your Social Media Education

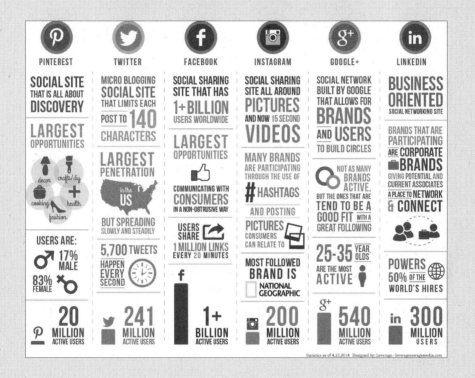

PINTEREST

SOCIAL SITE THAT IS ALL ABOUT **DISCOVERY**

LARGEST OPPORTUNITIES

decor · crafts/diy · cooking · health · fashion

USERS ARE:
17% MALE
83% FEMALE

20 MILLION ACTIVE USERS

TWITTER

MICRO BLOGGING **SOCIAL SITE** THAT LIMITS EACH POST TO **140** CHARACTERS

LARGEST PENETRATION in the US BUT SPREADING SLOWLY AND STEADILY

5,700 TWEETS HAPPEN EVERY SECOND

241 MILLION ACTIVE USERS

FACEBOOK

SOCIAL SHARING SITE THAT HAS **1+ BILLION** USERS WORLDWIDE

LARGEST OPPORTUNITIES

COMMUNICATING WITH **CONSUMERS** IN A NON-OBTRUSIVE WAY

USERS SHARE 1 MILLION LINKS EVERY 20 MINUTES

1+ BILLION ACTIVE USERS

INSTAGRAM

SOCIAL SHARING SITE ALL AROUND **PICTURES** AND NOW 15 SECOND **VIDEOS**

MANY BRANDS ARE PARTICIPATING THROUGH THE USE OF **#HASHTAGS** AND POSTING **PICTURES** CONSUMERS CAN RELATE TO

MOST FOLLOWED **BRAND IS** NATIONAL GEOGRAPHIC

200 MILLION ACTIVE USERS

GOOGLE+

SOCIAL NETWORK BUILT BY GOOGLE THAT ALLOWS FOR **BRANDS** AND **USERS** TO BUILD CIRCLES

NOT AS MANY BRANDS ACTIVE, BUT THE ONES THAT ARE **TEND TO BE A GOOD FIT** WITH A GREAT FOLLOWING

25-35 YEAR OLDS ARE THE MOST **ACTIVE**

540 MILLION ACTIVE USERS

LINKEDIN

BUSINESS ORIENTED SOCIAL NETWORKING SITE

BRANDS THAT ARE PARTICIPATING ARE **CORPORATE BRANDS** GIVING POTENTIAL AND CURRENT ASSOCIATES **A PLACE TO NETWORK & CONNECT**

POWERS 50% OF THE **WORLD'S HIRES**

300 MILLION USERS

Statistics as of 4.25.2014 Designed by: Leverage - leveragenewagemedia.com

web extras

Get the scoop from social media experts about four things every job candidate should know, at www.dummies.com/extras/gettingasocialmediajob.

In this part . . .

✔ Get a look at what kinds of roles social media offers, as well as their skills and responsibilities.

✔ Compare certification courses to college degrees to self-taught education.

✔ Determine your strengths and weaknesses and what to do with both.

✔ Investigate the essential tools you need to get and keep a social media job, including aggregation and automation.

✔ Nail down the culture and best approaches to the Big Five social media platforms: LinkedIn, Facebook, Instagram, Twitter, and YouTube.

✔ See more at www.dummies.com.

Chapter 4

Roles in Social Media Revealed

*I*f you want a job in social media, then you need to understand the job landscape. Maybe you have a few skills that are relevant but don't know how to apply these skills to the available positions. Or maybe you see opportunities but don't know what skills these jobs require.

This chapter discusses the opportunities that are currently available, what types of skills you need for success, and how to find the jobs that are best matched to your skills.

Honing Your Skills

First you have to figure out what your strongest skills are. Then focus on them. If you're not sure where you stand, read the descriptions for your ideal positions. By focusing on specific job descriptions, you'll know what type of experience you need and how skilled you have to be to get that job.

✔ **Write out your "perfect work day."** This is the best activity for establishing what you enjoy and defining how you could spend your work days. Go into as much detail as you can.

- Who do you spend time with?

- What is the corporate culture like?

  • What sort of functional work team are you on?

  • What type of results do you get?

  • Where will you be one year after you're hired.

The more detail you describe, the more beneficial it will be for your development.

✔ **Take online social media skills tests.** Lots of tests are out there, but the best place to get started is `smarterer.com`. Get signed up and take a few social media-related tests to find out what your top skills are and get recommendations for what jobs you should consider. To get a jump start, see Figure 4-1 for an example.

✔ **Ask people what you're good at.** Ask former and current colleagues, a close friend, and family members where your talents lie. Record the answers and look for trends. Ask people the following questions:

  • What do I talk most about?

  • Where does most of my passion lie?

  • What do I spend most of my free time reading about?

  • What type of position do you think I'm best suited for?

  • What skills and abilities am I truly gifted with?

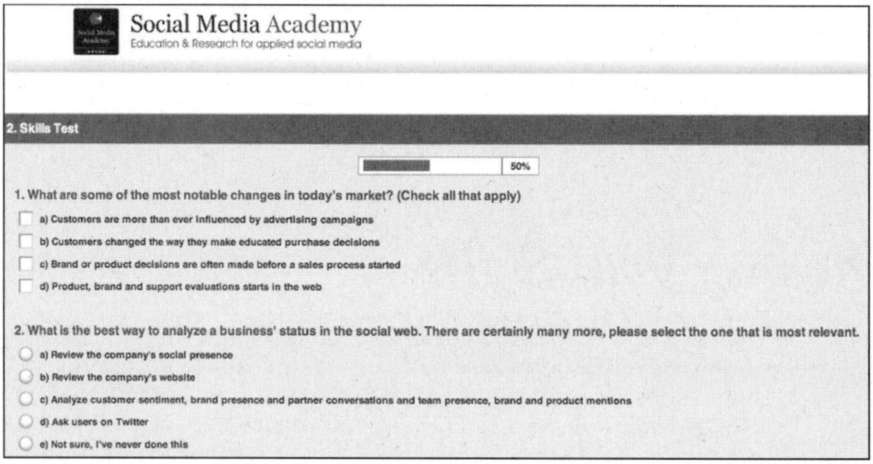

Figure 4-1:
A social media skills test can help you focus your search.

Copywriting

Maybe you're thinking about Peggy Olsen from the TV show *Mad Men* when you hear the term "copywriting." Copywriting typically persuades someone to buy something, or it influences their overall beliefs.

Copywriting is used in online periodicals, social media updates, content descriptions — and virtually anything that a company releases via social media. For more information on effective social media copywriting, consider a leading resource such as `copyblogger.com,` which you can see in Figure 4-2.

The most effective copywriters do the following tasks to create their writing pieces:

1. **Identify a problem.** Clearly stating the issue that a potential customer is experiencing is key here. For example, a potential customer's need for more time and more money would be the problem that your employer can help solve.

2. **Stir up the problem.** Effectively explain why that problem exists and drive home the negative consequences that the issue causes consumers. From the previous example, a copywriter would emphasize that the lack of time is causing the consumer to miss important events and diminish their quality of life.

3. **Define the solution.** Offer a definitive solution that's guaranteed to solve the pain or problem. And finally, your employer will emphasize that the product or service that they offer will solve the problem and is the best possible solution for the consumer.

Figure 4-2: Copy blogger. com is a social media copywriting resource.

Graphic design

Another crucial social media skill is that of graphic design which can be summed up as the graphical representation of the brand. Graphic design typically sets the tone for the brand in terms of its typography, color scheme, logos, promotional campaigns and overall personality.

Elements

Though it's important to understand at least one (and the more you understand, the better) graphic design software, it's also important to know what results are important to companies.

No one can be fluent in all graphic design software. But they do build on one another. If you understand GIMP, then you'll have a basic understanding of Photoshop and can build your way up within the Adobe Suite.

Graphic designers typically create these deliverables:

- ✔ **Pictures.** A graphic designer typically takes a picture and manipulates it to represent the brand's voice. These pictures may be created for specific social media platforms and may involve the company's logo or slogan, or a quote, or other factors to enhance the content piece.

- ✔ **Website development.** You might design an aspect of a website, or even the entire site, to help promote the brand. With website-development resources such as www.tumblr.com, www.strikingly.com, and www.wordpress.com, graphic designers can be web developers even though they don't know how to code.

- ✔ **Infographics.** Social media has helped make infographics popular because they present information and have attractive graphics. Infographics list important statistics, quotes, and facts and are presented in an attractive, linear fashion to drive home important points. See Figure 4-3 for an example infographic.

- ✔ **White papers and books.** *White papers* are reports that help educate readers, or help solve a problem or make a business decision. White papers are typically shorter than books. Books are usually electronic (so the company can save money) and are usually longer-form content to serve the same purpose as white papers. Both white papers and books must be branded for companies to give out to prospective clients, partners, and other audiences.

Tools

Graphic designers typically rely on a suite of tools and most commonly use the following programs:

- ✔ **Adobe Suite.** This graphic design industry standard includes Photoshop, Illustrator, and InDesign. Adobe offers free trials but is the most expensive tool.

- ✔ **Microsoft Suite.** The Microsoft equivalent of Adobe includes Publisher and Expression Design. Microsoft also offers free versions of these software packages.

✔ **Free tools.** The *open-source* (free) equivalents of Adobe and Microsoft include gimp.org, gimptools.com, and inkscape.com. These tools come under a lot of scrutiny because they're free. The trade-off is typically a longer learning curve, limited support, and a little less reliability.

Udemy.com offers a wide range of courses and graphic designers prefer it as a quick, inexpensive knowledge source.

Information technology

Information technology (IT) can take many forms within social media. An IT professional typically serves as the intermediary between copywriters, graphic designers, and the strategists. The other roles can create the ideas and content, but they usually need IT to help carry out the ideas from a technical standpoint.

Sites like SocialMediaToday.com offer the latest and greatest strategies for social media IT.

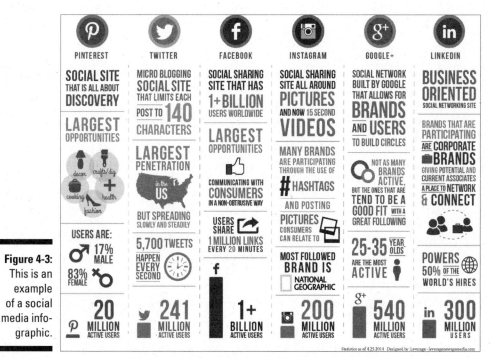

Figure 4-3: This is an example of a social media infographic.

An IT professional typically specializes in either *search engine optimization (SEO)*, web development, or data, though some positions combine these skills.

Search engine optimization (SEO)

Search engine optimization (SEO) increases the odds that a website will show up higher in a search engine's results. In general, the higher the result and the more often a website appears in the search results, the more web traffic that website gets.

Often, people think SEO is at odds with social media because it focuses on creating content and an overall process that's conducive for search marketing. However, search is becoming heavily influenced by social media and the need for IT professionals to merge the two marketing areas is more important than ever.

For example, social media platforms are often very trusted with search engines. Google uses a quality score known as Page Rank, scored from 0–9, that heavily influences where websites are listed in search engine ranking pages. Sites such as Facebook, Twitter, Pinterest, Google+, and YouTube are almost always listed on the first page and the content on these social media platforms is vital to a company's SEO strategy.

Web development

Though most social media platforms don't require much technical knowledge to use, the web visitors who visit a company's website should be targeted and presented with information that applies to them.

Some platforms, such as `strikingly.com`, allow you to develop landing pages that require minimal coding; see Figure 4-4. A *landing page* is a simple website with limited user actions that visitors start on when clicking an online advertisement or specific web result. The landing page usually shows specific sales copy that works with the initial ad or search engine result.

Web development may also include systems (such as social media aggregators or *customer relationship* integration) necessary for streamlining social media efforts and organizing information efficiently.

Data

The data component in IT can vary from getting *(procurement)* to synthesizing to interpreting social media efforts and results. There's a big call for IT professionals who can create systems that can correlate social media efforts to a *return on investment (ROI)* and *brand impressions.*

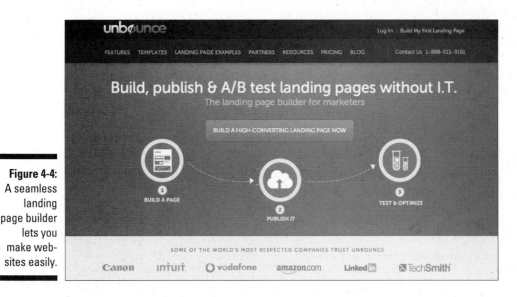

Figure 4-4:
A seamless
landing
page builder
lets you
make web-
sites easily.

Marketing and sales strategy

Without a thorough plan that includes great copywriting, graphics, and IT, you can't carry out a successful social media strategy. Typically these plans are constructed in phases and include each department's specific responsibilities.

A person who's good at creating effective marketing and sales strategy has a firm grasp on how to accomplish the following:

- ✔ **Positioning.** A strategy should have a clearly defined *unique selling proposition (USP)* and communicate to consumers, in a consistent voice, what the company does and why it's worth paying attention to.

- ✔ **SMART goals.** These goals should be *specific, measurable, accurate, realistic,* and *time related.* The more objective these goals are, the more likely they are to achieve a company's desired results. Chapter 17 goes into more detail about SMART goals.

- ✔ **Clear communication.** Other departments should be crystal clear how products, services, and goals are explained within the company and presented to the general public. This strategy has to be consistent across the organization so that everyone's accountable for their progress. It keeps things efficient

- ✔ **Focused on the Four Rights.** The strategy should promote the *right product* to the *right audience* on the *right platform* at the *right time.* If it focuses on those, the odds of effective social media marketing are increased.

Knowing Your Type (or Someone Else's)

You might have multiple skill sets and want to avoid being pigeonholed. The good news is that the following roles are often merged together and they're evolving.

Stay up-to-date with the latest types of social media jobs available at `indeed.com` and `jobsearch.about.com`, which is shown in Figure 4-5. Set up job alerts that are related to you!

These are the most common types of positions.

Figure 4-5: About.com is a social media job-searching portal.

Community manager

A *community manager's* primary focus is to educate, engage, and entertain the fans or followers of the social media account that he's managing. The community manager's reign can range from blogs, Facebook fan pages, Twitter, YouTube, Tumblr, LinkedIn, and much more.

The networks and responsibilities vary drastically between companies, but the community manager's often focused on the company's brand and how much money and time are dedicated the company's social media efforts.

A community manager's responsibilities are best summed up with the following collection of duties:

✔ Post company-approved content on a variety of social media platforms.

This content may include text, pictures, videos, or animated GIFs. Sometimes the community manager creates the content; sometimes she works on a team to create the content, or she posts the content and continually improves the content for promotional purposes.

✔ Quickly and efficiently respond to all consumer requests, complaints, and problems.

Most of the time, the community manager creates best practices that dictate decisions, and will know exactly what to do in the event of a crisis or if any other type of roadblock emerges.

✔ Present customer issues found on social networks to all applicable departments.

The departments that would be interested in the information may vary from accounting to advertising to marketing and sales.

✔ Monitor blogs, websites, and forums — virtually the entire Internet — for opportunities to

• Strengthen customer relationships

• Create strategic partnerships

• Establish local outreach activities

Entry-level or intermediate employees typically do the social media monitoring. The social media community manager may progress into a strategist or manager, or explore graphical or copywriting roles within the social media department.

 Social media community managers don't sit and play on Twitter and Facebook all day. Community managers are actively involved in the branding of the company and are crucial to enhancing the company's overall image.

Graphical social media jobs

Graphics are in social media's DNA. If a company doesn't have consistent, attractive graphical presentation, it's going to lose. This branding becomes even more important on platforms such as Facebook, Instagram, and Pinterest, where most content is visual.

This sequence of jobs, from entry level to expert, is available for graphic designers within social media:

- Graphic design internship
- Marketing assistant graphic designer
- Graphic designer
- Creative director

These positions don't have to happen in order. For instance, as an intern you might be promoted to full-time graphic design rather than to a junior role.

Graphic designers in social media typically have the following skill sets:

- **Mastery of a graphics suite.** Some companies are slanted toward Adobe, and others prefer Microsoft or open-source programs. A graphic designer knows how to use at least one, if not all three, of the suites.

- **A firm understanding of effective social media content.** A polished social media graphic designer knows exactly what type of content performs on each platform. For example, animated GIFs are native to Tumblr and work well on Google+, whereas a picture quote is more likely to be shared on Facebook.

- **Continuously providing ideas and solutions** about how the company can grow brand equity, leads, sales and overall social media ROI from a graphical standpoint.

- **Knowledge about the latest trends in graphic design.** The designer will know that the design itself must embody the tone, values, and voice of the brand as well.

Graphic design jobs in social media typically include the following tasks:

- Create attractive landing page websites that go with specific social media platforms.

- Develop animated GIFs for sites such as Google+ or Tumblr. An *animated GIF* is a sequence of images that are combined to look like a video.

✔ Design periodicals such as white papers, ebooks, press releases, and other short promotional pieces for release on websites and professional social media sites.

✔ Create informative, attractive infographics for sources such as LinkedIn and Twitter.

✔ Ensure consistently branded profile pictures, icons, *favicons* (16-x-16 images in a website tab), *header images* (large images within a social media profile), and status updates across multiple social media accounts.

✔ Form platform-specific images for social media campaigns.

Be willing to bring more important deliverables to the table when exploring a social media job related to graphic design.

Technical social media jobs

Companies value targeted web traffic, analytics, and data, so there's never a shortage of technical jobs. Technical, or IT, social media jobs are typically the easiest to find because

✔ The skills are specialized.

✔ IT can measure the most important quantitative factors that social media provides, such as sales and impressions.

✔ Social media sites often are listed very high in search engine results.

A social media IT role typically has the highest pay.

Companies are looking for people with these skills for social media IT roles:

✔ Web developer

✔ Search engine optimization (SEO) specialist

✔ Data and analytics professional

Web developer

The *web developer* typically is fluent in computer languages such as HTML, CSS, and PHP. A web developer within the social media framework can also make simple WordPress *Content Management System (CMS)* websites or landing page websites without needing significant time or resources.

If you need to brush up on the basic computer languages, or you're interested in learning about them, consider a resource such as codecademy.com, which is in Figure 4-6.

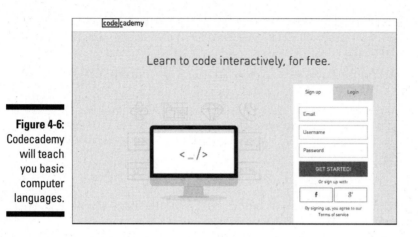

Figure 4-6:
Codecademy
will teach
you basic
computer
languages.

The web developer may work with the graphic designer, and he's typically responsible for launching, measuring, and making the most of *(optimizing)* the websites geared toward specific social networks.

SEO specialist

An SEO specialist often blends the line between optimizing websites and social media. *Website optimization* is typically how fast a website loads, but this term also refers to relevant keyword and phrases on the website. Ultimately, a website has to follow specific rules to be accessible to a search engine and improve the overall probability that the website appear in search engine results.

An SEO specialist has the tall order of ensuring that all web content from social media platforms has the proper *backlinks* (one website linking to another), website structure, and other base SEO principles.

The SEO specialist typically works with content producers and a strategist to ensure that results are being driven back to landing pages and websites. For more SEO knowledge, `SearchEngineLand.com` is a great resource; see Figure 4-7.

Data and analytics professional

A *data and analytics professional* collects, synthesizes, and optimizes data harvested from social media. The data professional is responsible for translating the numbers — engagement, shares, likes, and other performance metrics — into quantifiable sales.

Figure 4-7:
A sample
SEO and
social media
resource.

The essential tools for collecting social media analytics follow:

- ✔ **Brandwatch.com** monitors social media conversations. Brandwatch is widely known as the most powerful social media monitoring and analytics tool and is used by huge brands and agencies all over the world.

- ✔ **LocalResponse.com** helps you determine the intent of social media posts and focuses on delivering and optimizing targeted social ads. LocalResponse.com specializes in social media advertising.

- ✔ **SalesforceMarketingCloud.com** pulls together social media content by keywords and phrases, and the company's social media updates, and ties them into smarter social advertising solutions. Salesforce Marketing Cloud specializes in using traditional and social media solutions to create one-on-one relationships with customers.

Social media strategist

A *social media strategist,* typically an executive or mid-management position, is in very high demand. A strategist has a firm grasp of social media platforms and can translate social media execution into measurable results. Strategists may come from different backgrounds and have an advertising, graphic design, IT, or writing slant. However, all strategists are proven leaders that have been tested in multiple functional areas within social media.

A social media strategist can deliver the following:

- ✔ **Develop and maintain an in-depth social media strategy.** The strategy defines how a company's social media marketing techniques will be applied for increasing brand equity, impressions, and web traffic.
- ✔ **Mentor and provide training** throughout the organization on best practices for creating, managing, monitoring, and developing content for a variety of social media platforms.
- ✔ **Establish standards** for companywide social media-management policies and the best practices for using, monitoring and optimizing social media.
- ✔ **Apply marketing research** for understanding emerging trends and technologies; clearly communicating this knowledge to the whole company.
- ✔ **Define** *key performance indicators (KPIs)* and implementing executive-level measurement, analytics, and reporting methods to gauge success.

Additionally, companies are typically looking for these key requirements when hiring a social media strategist:

- ✔ BS or BA degree from an accredited university, and a minimum of four years' experience in advertising, communications, or marketing.
- ✔ Exceptional leadership capabilities and strong interpersonal skills.
- ✔ Effective communication and presentation skills.
- ✔ Two to four years of experience in social media project and web campaign management.
- ✔ Demonstrated experience and an unprecedented passion for social media and social technology.
- ✔ Knowledge of graphic design management and best practices for web projects and campaigns.
- ✔ Orientation toward data, analytics, and metric performance.

Chapter 5

Foundations of Social Media Education

*T*he amount of information available about social media marketing is astounding: websites, conferences, webinars, blogs, Google hangouts, magazines, and — what do you know? — even whole books about the subject matter. Knowing which sources to trust can be tough.

This chapter helps you identify the best sources for social media information. We give you our recommendations for interacting with top social media pros, as well.

Surfing the Learning Curve

We each dedicate at least five hours per week to reading social media articles, writing about topics within the social media space, and networking with other social media professionals.

Schedule continued learning time with reminder tools such as Evernote.com and Google Calendar.

Researching nonstop

It can always be more fruitful to apply your knowledge to the real world rather than just consuming information and never using it. We call this process of researching and never taking action "Paralysis by analysis." You can certainly spend time learning and synthesizing information but without the practical part, you'll never become a social media professional.

A true social media pro absorbs the right material, surrounds him or herself with the right people, learns from mistakes, and strives to continually improve.

The other pitfall to avoid is never paying attention to how social media is behaving in current day and where social media is headed. If it's 2015 but you're marketing like it's 2011, then you're going to lose. Social media is a living and ever changing entity and must be treated as such.

Consider this tactic:

1. **Go to** www.stickK.com.

   See Figure 5-1.

2. **Register and accept the terms of service.**

   You can customize your profile with your picture and interests.

3. **Click Create a Commitment.**

4. **Type your goal.**

   For example, it could be *completing a graphic design course* or *attending a social media conference.* Make sure the goal is attainable and challenging yet realistic.

5. **Click Go.**

6. **Choose Commitment Type, such as ongoing.**

7. **Enter your commitment, a starting date, and a duration.**

8. **Choose Career from the list on the right, then click Next Step.**

9. **Choose Anti-Charity. Choose a group you loathe from the drop-down menu.**

   You could choose Charity, Friend or Foe, or No Money at Stake, but you're here to put your money where your mouth is!

10. **Enter the amount of money you're willing to risk, enter your credit card information, and accept the terms of service.**

If you don't reach your goal, the money you put up goes to a charity you don't want supported. Make sure that you put a dollar amount that would make you uncomfortable.

11. **Click Next Step.**

You get instructions via email that tell you how to organize your goal into steps. If you accomplish your goal, your money's returned to you.

The following sections go over the types of online social media education programs and emphasize those that give you the best bang for your buck.

Custom Goal

Your privacy is important to us. You can adjust your privacy settings once you're done creating your Commitment

Create your own goal: Complete a graphic design course

Example: Drive car to work less often.
Example: My history paper.

Commitment Type: ◉ Ongoing ◯ One-shot   what's this?

I commit to: Enroll in a graphic design course at
*optional (500 characters max)   lynda.com and commit five hours per
week to learn

This Commitment Starts: Today ▾

Figure 5-1:   **My Reporting Days will be:**   **Fridays**
stickK.com
has you put   **Length of my Commitment:**   16   week(s)
your money
where your
mouth is.

Goal Category: (Check all that apply)
☐ Career
☐ Diet & Healthy Eating
☐ Education & Knowledge
☐ Exercise & Fitness
☐ Family & Relationships
☐ Green Initiatives
☐ Health & Lifestyle
☐ Home Improvement & DIY
☐ Money & Finance
☐ Personal Relationships
☐ Quit Smoking
☐ Religion & Spirituality
☐ Sports, Hobbies & Recreation
☐ Weight Loss

Choose a new goal   Next Step

Investigating Certification Programs

Your social media education is a direct trade-off between your time and money. You can spend money to attend a class or you can spend time researching.

Degree and certificate programs get attention, but they aren't required in the current job market. You may consider other educational opportunities if the costs associated with a formal degree program are too high.

Self-guided learning is a realistic option if you have the discipline and commitment required to further your knowledge.

Practicing your skills on social media and learning from your mistakes and successes is the best way to improve.

Potential employers care much more about proven results and applied knowledge than degrees. However, if you can bring results *and* education to the table, and a candidate you're competing with brings one or the other, then you'll have a significant advantage.

Always focus on certifications and education that are mentioned in the descriptions of the jobs that you'll be applying for.

Ask employers if an accreditation would benefit you. See if the company is willing to pay for a degree or if it reimburses you for tuition.

If you're considering a social media certification program, consider the following factors:

- ✔ What's the return on investment with this accreditation or education? For example, if you spend $10,000 on an online course, are you guaranteed being worth that much more?

- ✔ What's the time commitment for each social media educational system? If you can't set aside the time necessary to complete the requirements, don't pursue this avenue.

- ✔ Does the social media educational service have connections within the social media job space? Many networks have strong relationships with employers of social media professionals and offer exclusive or preferential opportunities for their members.

  A great question to ask before you enroll in a program is whether the service has a job board full of opportunities that appeal to you. The best way to find out is by investigating the jobs yourself and judging whether they appeal to you.

- ✔ Which do you have more of to spare: time or money? Are you willing to use your time scouring the web, and or would you rather make a capital expenditure now for the convenience of a well-organized education?

- ✔ What types of relationships can you create with the program organizers, teachers, alumni, and other students? Typically, social media professionals are helpful and generous; plus, the more people you know, the better it is for your long-term success.

Hootsuite University

Hootsuite is the premiere software that allows professionals to view, manage, and automate social media participation. See Figure 5-2. Hootsuite created two learning platforms:

- ✔ **Social media education.** The course is geared toward entrepreneurs, employers, and business managers. You get comprehensive training on how to use the Hootsuite software, various courses, and a lecture series that offers over 40 webinars. It's a little over $20 monthly to access this course.

- ✔ **Hootsuite certification.** This program is geared toward marketing agencies, social media consultants, and full-time social media professionals. The program offers a variety of social media exams and a certification badge for your website and social profiles. You can try for certification anytime, but Hootsuite recommends that you go learn from all of their social media education materials before attempting to get certified.

You pay a monthly subscription to learn how to use Hootsuite's software (see Figure 5-3), so keep that in mind if you're also attending Hootsuite University. You can cancel your Hootsuite University subscription at any time but then you won't have access to the Hootsuite University network, job boards, and internal networking possibilities.

Ultimately, Hootsuite provides an affordable, recognizable option for social media beginners or novices.

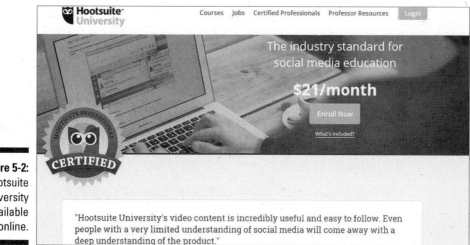

Figure 5-2: Hootsuite University is available online.

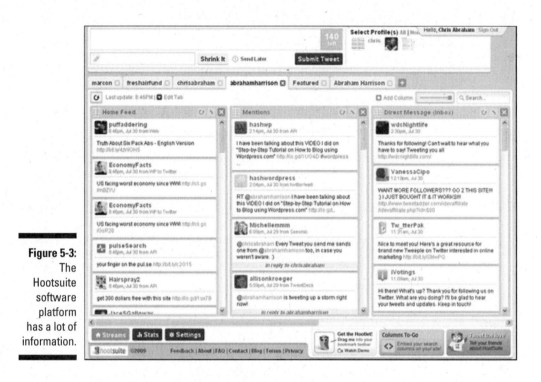

Figure 5-3:
The Hootsuite software platform has a lot of information.

National Institute for Social Media (NISM)

The National Institute for Social Media (NISM) is a strong way to show off your social media knowledge. See Figure 5-4. It's important to clearly communicate your goals to NISM about whether their return on investment will parallel the type of career you're after.

The website, at `nismonline.org`, has partnered with the Assessment Systems Corporation (ASC) and has developed an internal committee of social media subject matters called the NISM Industry Advisory Committee (IAC).

NISM offers a social media strategist exam that costs $295, plus a $65-to-$85 proctoring fee. The exam covers the following topics:

✔ Social media strategic planning (see Chapter 4)

✔ Social media compliance and governance

✔ Social media project and campaign management

- ✔ Social media marketing
- ✔ Community management
- ✔ Research and analysis

To take (some people say *sit for* instead) the NISM exam, you must apply and be accepted to the program. To apply, you need one of the following:

- ✔ An Associate Degree (64 credit hours) in business, marketing, computer science, communications, or other type of educational discipline
- ✔ Two years of practical business experience related to social media

After you get approved, use the self-study bundles, the NISM online course, or the in-person course (which is offered at colleges across the United States). All the options include a voucher for the NISM exam, except for the standard self-study bundle.

Overall, the NISM social media certification is an extremely strong program. Consider these factors before pulling the trigger on this program:

- ✔ NISM is the most expensive social media training product on the market. Its price tag starts at over $1,000.
- ✔ You have to renew your NISM certification every three years.
- ✔ The NISM certification price pales in comparison to the price of most social media conferences. They range anywhere from hundreds of dollars to $10,000 just for admission to some of the big shows.

Getting a Degree

Several universities now offer advanced degree programs in social media.

These institutions have reputations for embracing innovation and technology. As such, each program provides a structured learning framework for participants. Most of these programs are offered as online programs rather than classroom curriculum.

There's a distinction between a certification program and a degree program. *Certification programs* offer specialized training and education in a given area. They require less time to complete than a degree program. A *degree program* offers specialized training and education in addition to a foundation of general education including mathematics, science, English, history, and humanities.

The graduate programs in Table 5-1, online except for Rutgers and NYU, are in social media.

Table 5-1	Social Media Graduate Programs		
School	*Degree(s) Offered*	*Anticipated Cost*	*URL*
West Virginia University (Morgantown, WV)	Master of Science in integrated marketing communication, certificates in integrated marketing communication and digital marketing communication	$33,000 for M.S.; $13,000 for certificate program	imc.wvu.edu
University of Florida (Gainesville, FL)	Master of Arts in mass communication, Master of Arts in social media, certificate in social media	$13,000 (in state)	socialmediadegree.jou.ufl.edu/

School	Degree(s) Offered	Anticipated Cost	URL
Rutgers University (New Brunswick, NJ)	Mini-MBA in marketing	$5,000	business.rutgers.edu
New York University (New York, NY)	Master of Science in integrated marketing, certificate in digital media marketing	$17,000	scps.nyu.edu
Southern New Hampshire University (Manchester, NH)	MBA with a concentration in social media	$21,000	snhu.edu
University of Washington (Seattle, WA)	Master of Communication in digital media, Master of Communication in communities and networks, certificate in social media technologies and implementation	$2,200/course (resident), $4,000/course (non-resident), $925/course for certificate	commlead.uw.edu/ and pce.uw.edu

Going Online for Education

Here are our top recommendations for online learning platforms:

- ✔ Udemy.com lets you search a subject and choose a course based on its rankings, features, and feedback. Some courses are free but some can cost thousands. The average price is around $40 per course.

  People who teach Udemy courses aren't necessarily professors or experts, so the quality can range significantly.

✔ **Skillshare.com** has many classes available at about $25 per course. Or, you can join Skillshare for $10 per month and get 20 percent off all their classes. Joining has lots of other benefits too, but you should anticipate spending at least $50 per month.

✔ **Alison.com** has over 600 courses that are completely free. The selection is diverse but its focus on finance, digital literacy, and information technology are top notch for social media pros.

We also like these options:

✔ Comply Socially at `http://complysocially.com`; see Figure 5-5

✔ Boot Camp Digital at `http://bootcampdigital.com`; see Figure 5-6

✔ Social Media Online Classes at `http://socialmediaonlineclasses.com`

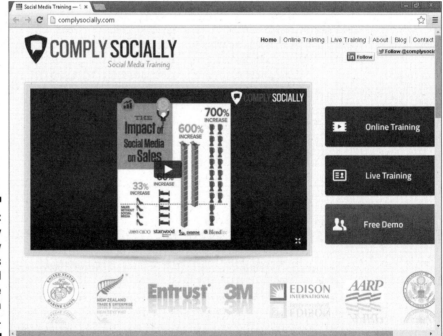

Figure 5-5: Comply Socially provides web based and live social media training.

Figure 5-6:
Boot Camp
Digital offers
customized
social media
training.

Attending and Participating in Conferences

Virtually every principle, platform, and strategic area of social media is covered in conferences. Social media conferences offer

- ✔ *Speakers,* where speakers have sessions to talk about a particular subject matter.
- ✔ *Roundtable sessions,* which feature a host of subject matter experts who all share their views on a topic. Roundtables are handled by a moderator.
- ✔ *Breakout sessions* tend to be more like a workshop seminar, with a lot of Q&A. Enhancing skills and abilities is the focus.

It seems crazy, because people travel from far and wide to attend conferences, but it's very common for conference speakers to have virtual meetings via sponsored webinars, Google Hangouts, and even Skype sessions.

You get these main benefits from going to a social media conference:

- ✔ **Thought leadership:** Know what content you'll be exposed to. The content should overview the tools, processes, and technology that you currently use or want to use. You can get an idea of what each informational session is about ahead of time through the conference's website and in the conference program.

- ✔ **Future planning:** Conferences expose you to current and coming trends, technologies, services, and buying habits. This information keeps you ahead of the curve instead of playing catch-up.

- ✔ **Networking:** You can contact speakers, thought leaders, potential partners, vendors, and other attendees. This contact is by far the most valuable aspect of conferences because you can strengthen existing relationships, merge an online relationship with a face-to-face one, and facilitate new connections.

Keep your eye on conference hashtags and meet with people for coffee, a meal, a round of drinks, or to attend a party. It doesn't always have to be about work, either!

Saving up to go

Conferences offer benefits, but they're not cheap. Admission and expenses can run into tens of thousands of dollars.

In addition to conference admission, keep these costs in mind:

- ✔ Material fees such as a program, books, or courses that you buy from vendors
- ✔ Lodging
- ✔ Transportation mileage or flights to and from
- ✔ Parking
- ✔ Food and beverage

Even though you'll carefully research before attending a conference, it's tough to quantify the value. If you offer social media services, then it's easier to figure out whether you break even. For example, if a conference costs $10,000 total and your employer's average client is worth $2,000, then you'll need to successfully lock down five clients to break even. Of course if you're on the job hunt, then getting a job will be your break-even point.

You can try to cut costs a few ways:

✔ Volunteer at the conference. You can get an attendance discount or maybe even go free. Find the conference's website and check the Volunteer section. If not, the website ought to have contact information for the organizers. Asking about volunteering is another way to get this done.

✔ Go to social media and ask if anyone has an extra attendee ticket they're willing to give you. If you're uncomfortable asking for a ticket, offer your services in exchange.

✔ Work to be selected as a workshop leader or speaker. You have to compete with professional speakers, but if you have an expertise and can show that you provide a lot of value, try it. Contact the conference organizers far in advance and offer your services pro bono.

Prominent conferences

Conferences are nearly a corporate rite of passage. Give them a try. The following sections talk about the biggest or best, but we also like these:

✔ **Social Media Strategies Summit** at
http://socialmediastrategiessummit.com

✔ **The Corporate Social Media Summit** at
http://events.usefulsocialmedia.com/newyork/index.php

✔ **Social Media Week** at http://socialmediaweek.org

✔ **Summer Brand Camp** at summerbrandcamp.com

South by Southwest (SXSW)

South by Southwest is by far the most prominent conference. Its subject matters cover a lot of area, but SXSW is widely regarded as the primary place for social media and electronic communication innovation. The conference has been around since 1987 and takes place annually in Austin, Texas. The interactive conference (meaning you can watch a lot of the conference from home and interact with attendees via social media) has included the unveiling of technologies such as Twitter, Foursquare, and Digg 2.0.

SXSW has expanded the innovation aspect of the conference to Las Vegas, launching SXSW Vision to Venture (V2V). V2V focuses on entrepreneurship in terms of finding, financing, and developing new businesses, with a heavy slant toward social media sites and electronic communication.

Some SXSW attendees don't get a lot of value because they're overwhelmed and unprepared. Don't let that happen to you! Check out sxsw.com/first-timers-guide.

Social Media Marketing World (SMMW)

Social Media Marketing World (SMMW) is put on by SocialMediaExaminer.com, which helps social media pros increase sales and improve branding using social media. The SMMW conference is held in San Diego, California, in March and hosts over 100 of the top social media experts. Though it's significantly smaller than SXSW, SMMW has a laser focus and packs a punch.

SMMW features over 100 expert led workshops, round table discussions, question and answer sessions, and keynote sessions. With its intimate setting, you are able to directly interact with many of the best social media pros in the world and absorb targeted information about effective social media strategy, content creation, and general social media tactics.

SMMW provides two big advantages:

- ✔ **A sales pitch-free environment:** SMMW markets itself as the only conference that features high-quality information minus pitches from presenters. You can attend this conference with peace of mind that the presenters are trying to give you the best information rather than trying to sell you their goods and services.

- ✔ **Full access to every session:** If your chief motivation for conference attendance is to network, then this particular conference is unique; you can watch the videos at a later date and focus solely on meeting people.

MozCon

MozCon was developed by Moz.com (originally SEOmoz.com) and is held in July in Seattle, Washington. Moz focuses on *in-bound marketing* (online content that pulls people toward your products and services. Moz also focuses on search engine optimization (SEO), but MozCon has grown into social media, brand, and content marketing. This conference has versatile subject matter and does an excellent job of quantifying social media's impact on facilitating sales.

MozCon chooses speakers who share revolutionary advice about how to build loyal brand customers and how to make better marketing decisions based on data from online sources. For example, a brand's messaging or marketing spending may change based on the sales and consumer feedback that they get from social media. In addition, MozCon promises actionable information in the following areas:

- ✔ Search engine optimization
- ✔ Social media
- ✔ Community building
- ✔ Brand development
- ✔ Social media analytics
- ✔ Mobile technology

Social Fresh

The Social Fresh Conference is put on by SocialFresh.com. The event is widely known as the "original" social media conference and typically attracts social media managers, community managers, content marketers, and social media consultants.

Social Fresh only allows single presenters to present for 25 minutes within one room rather than hosting additional breakout sessions, roundtable discussions, or panel question-and-answer sessions that are short and to the point.

Getting properly prepared

Plan out your conference attendance. You must know what value you hope to take away.

Consider these tips before going to any social media conference:

- ✔ **Come with a schedule, but be prepared for anything.** Let go of the feeling that you'll miss something great if you don't stick to your schedule. Instead, prioritize the speakers and breakout sessions and be willing to go with the flow or make other plans with other social media pros. Of course you want to absorb significant content, but you also need to have profound context (also known as *relationships*) with the other conference attendees.

- ✔ **Know definitively how you can help others.** If you meet a potential business partner, or a speaker, or an author you want to connect with, focus on how *you* can make *their* lives better. Have a plan for hooking the person with your value proposition and set a date for when you can connect further. You might say something like, "I create social media graphics that make people's heads turn. How about I make you one sometime soon?" No one in their right mind would say no to this.

✔ **Be prepared with extras.** Take more snacks, water, energy supplements, and technology accessories than you need. You'll be amazed how many friends you'll make by bringing an extra water, iPhone charger, or wireless hotspot that can help others.

✔ **Exchange business cards with everyone you meet.** Whether you believe you can help one another is irrelevant. Use an app such as Abbyy or CamCard to instantly capture information of the other conference attendees. Also scribble down notes about your conversation, ideas of how you can work together, and personal characteristics so that you generally remember the conversation that you have.

Asking great questions to stand out

Before the conference, carefully research so you can ask educated questions at the conference. Asking great questions helps market you and puts you on the radar of top social media professionals. Be sure to avoid painfully obvious questions and try to focus.

To properly prepare for the questions that you'll ask, do the following:

✔ **Research.** Who is speaking? What do they do? What have they accomplished? What are they interested in personally and professionally from social media?

✔ **Plan.** Craft questions that get to the point and inspire critical thought. Try to ask a question that will help you solve your own business problem but also contribute value to other attendees's. What question shows that you're aware of the speaker's work?

✔ **Ask.** Rehearse your delivery and execute flawlessly. Try to inspire a one-on-one follow-up conversation with the presenter. In a follow-up question, see if she'd be willing to talk to you afterward.

Hashtagging and live chats

Hashtags represent topics on social media; you can use hashtags at virtually any point. On Twitter you can search and find every single tweet that uses a specific hashtag and immediately jump into the conversation; the same for photos and videos on Instagram. Hashtags are a daily opportunity for social media professionals, but they also help promote and facilitate conferences.

Most conferences designate a hashtag to facilitate conversation and to give the attendees real-time information about what's happening. Hashtagging can also feed into planned chats both at a conference and at virtually any other time.

A *hashtag chat* is where a larger group plans to discuss a particular subject; you can see all the tweets based on a particular hashtag. See Figure 5-7. For example, some of the top hashtag chats on Twitter include the following:

- SMOchat (Social Media Organizer Chat)
- Socialchat
- SMManners (Social Media Manners)
- Mmchat (Marketer Monday Chat)

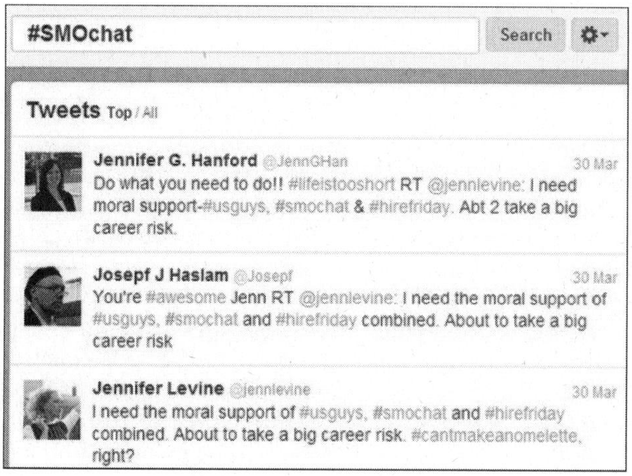

Figure 5-7:
You can
have a
hashtag
chat on
Twitter.

> **#SMOchat**   Search ⚙▾
>
> **Tweets** Top / All
>
> **Jennifer G. Hanford** @JennGHan   30 Mar
> Do what you need to do!! #lifeistooshort RT @jennlevine: I need
> moral support–#usguys, #smochat & #hirefriday. Abt 2 take a big
> career risk.
>
> **Josepf J Haslam** @Josepf   30 Mar
> You're #awesome Jenn RT @jennlevine: I need the moral support of
> #usguys, #smochat and #hirefriday combined. About to take a big
> career risk
>
> **Jennifer Levine** @jennlevine   30 Mar
> I need the moral support of #usguys, #smochat and #hirefriday
> combined. About to take a big career risk. #cantmakeanomelette,
> right?

Bushwhacking Your Own Path

No matter how prepared you are when starting a job, you're going to run into problems. Most of these problems won't have easy solutions. That's okay. Because social media is so new, you can create your own solutions, job requirements, and systems.

For example, Brooks had been running a successful ad campaign on Facebook when he noticed, abruptly, that none of his company's ads were being shown. The company had never faced this obstacle before. Brooks had to hound Facebook for weeks to get an ad sales rep to identify the problem.

Educating yourself

There will come times where you simply need to improve your skills or will not be able to figure out the answer to a social media problem yourself. The good news is that you have the Internet and a world chock full of social media experts that can help you improve your skills. Some of the top informational sources include:

- ✔ Social media conferences
- ✔ Formal social media education
- ✔ Webinars and Google Hangouts
- ✔ Online educational sources
- ✔ Asking experts on social media platforms

You can typically get your organization to pay for training or courses.

 Whether you can get ongoing education reimbursed depends on clearly communicating your organization's need for the education. You have to explain how it will help your employer. Present the options to solve a problem or bring a skill in house, and clearly identify why investing in your education is the best decision.

For example, you may need some basic HTML knowledge to style a content-management system or update a landing page. If your company hired a contractor, she could finish it for $10,000 over a month. What if you took a month-long course at khanacademy.org? This would benefit your employer and you, and it sets you up for additional advancement opportunities.

Though thousands of educational opportunities exist, these are our favorites:

- ✔ **Lynda.com:** This site features arguably the most comprehensive database of business courses in the world: web design, web services, photography, coding, and much more. Unlimited access per month is inexpensive.

- ✔ **Codecademy.com:** This free resource can teach you the basics of web languages such as HTML, PHP, CSS, and Javascript. Even if you don't have a web development background, Codecademy makes the information interactive and fun.

✔ **OnlineMarketingInstitute.org:** This website covers a comprehensive list of social and online marketing objectives that you may not have even realized that you needed. The scope is wide and the site offers accreditation and interaction with instructors. This website, per month, is inexpensive and has different features by subscription level. See Figure 5-8.

Innovation within social media comes from different ideas that are either combined or applied to a different set of circumstances.

Figure 5-8:
Online
Marketing
Institute.
org offers a
monthly sub-
scription.

Asking your friends

Try this exercise to jump start new learning:

1. **Choose three friends you've known for a long time.**

2. **Ask each person these questions about his or her profession:**

   • How did you get the job you have now?

   • What advice would you give someone who wanted to do what you do?

   • Aside from compensation, why do you go to work every day?

3. **Tell each friend what you think a typical work day looks like, based upon your existing knowledge and the new information.**

4. Ask your friend to fill in the gaps.

Talking through the details of a position, even in a different field, will help you to get to the most important bits. When you know the key parts of a job you want, you can identify the resources that will help you get those attributes.

Think of key attributes as *high-peforming behaviors* — the things successful people do to ensure their own success. If a job requires effective communication, for example, then highlight your ability to be clear.

Remain open to new options.

Chapter 6

Making Your Own Way

Challenging times force people to act in interesting ways. Some folks cower in the face of adversity, and others manage to rise to the occasion.

If you're employed, you are undoubtedly frustrated by the increase in responsibilities, and remorseful for the colleagues who were downsized.

If you were downsized, you're likely frustrated by the lack of human contact throughout the application and interview process, as well as the lack of real opportunities. You're probably disenchanted and concerned with maintaining your (and your family's) well-being.

Motivation is yours to channel. Whatever your circumstance, you have ample fuel to help you focus on your career utopia. In this chapter, we help you discover what makes you *you,* and we help you break down your career's past, present, and future. By doing so, you'll be able to assess where you've been, where you are, and where you'd like to take your career.

Reflecting and Adjusting Your Sails

When you find yourself in the candidate pool, you need a clear employment strategy. Blasting a résumé all over the Internet and hoping the content appeals to someone (or some system) isn't strategic — it's ineffective. You don't know who sees your information, or what decisions are being made about you, or with whom to follow up.

The number-one most important step in job hunting is taking time for yourself. Too often, candidates react frantically. Instead, reflect. Spend time thinking about what makes you happiest and where you were most successful, so you can discover (or rediscover) your passions and learn what sacrifices you're willing to make.

With reflection comes clarity. As you force yourself to focus on what matters, you can narrow your attention to companies, industries, and occupations that are in line with your ideals. Your personal and professional life will become more balanced, and more meaningful.

Once the personal and professional sides of life are aligned, you can develop impactful and thought-provoking questions (and answers) to dynamic interview questions. Interviewes become more conversational, and your connection with the interviewer becomes engaging.

Career utopia is a destination. To get there, you need a goal, a strategy, plans, support, and resources.

Taking stock

Taking stock in your experience can help you in the future.

✔ **Consciously think about your past successes and how to best explain them to a potential employer.**

Try this exercise:

1. Pull out your last résumé. It may be covered in dust.

2. Review each job on your résumé.

3. Try to recall three experiences, from each job, that resonated with you.

4. Write down the experiences as you remember them.

5. Read the stories, and re-read them until you know them so well it's like you're telling a joke to your closest friend.

This challenge helps you deliver the best, smoothest interview responses. To make your point perfectly clear. The ease, tone, and comfort of your delivery develops an underlying connection with your interviewer. He'll feel like you're having a conversation. In Chapter 14, you explore how to best prepare for interviews.

✔ **Delve into business books, blogs, networking groups, and organizations.**

Chapter 12 talks about networking and groups.

✔ **Get information from multiple sources on a regular basis.**

- Stay current on local and global news.

- Stay current on industry-specific news.

That knowledge helps you navigate an interview process well. Interjecting real-life experiences and framing them within much larger issues lends not only perspective, but emphasizes depth of understanding of your occupation and the industry for which you work. Chapter 22 lists the top ten social media resources.

Contemplating your successes

When you're in the middle of trying to find a job (or working in one), it's hard to pull back and fairly assess what's going on. Over time, however, you can gain valuable perspective. Also, people often forget the importance of contemplation. The act can add logic to a particular decision or thought process, and provide great clarity. By taking time, your emotions fade and logic prevails.

You're in a good position when you can look back at a situation or process, having knowledge of each stage, start to finish.

✔ How did you approach a particular situation?

✔ How did you manage through it?

✔ How did you complete it?

Success starts with knowledge

The importance of success may have been drilled into you at an early age. You had no clue what that meant, mind you, but you heard that with hard work, determination, and perseverance, you could get there. Talk about an abstract idea.

People define success differently, and it's hard to measure. It's a challenge to duplicate.

It's really more about priority. Success hasn't been the priority; survival has. But the tides are turning. Savvy job hunters are seeing more companies announce their need for talent in completely new venues, and through newly adopted platforms (texting, direct messaging, live chats, hashtagging, and so on). More information is accessible if you know where to find it.

There's an old saying: "Successful people know when to make the right move at the right time." It's not because successful people predict the future. Successful people identify how things are trending early on, and make decisions based on knowledge and confidence.

When you have the knowledge, you can use it as you see fit.

One decision might take you in an entirely new direction. Perhaps, upon reflection, you realize a missed opportunity. Gaining perspective and using your experience, helps you make better decisions when you're confronted with similar circumstances. The good news is that in the future, should you be in the same situation, you'll have experience to rely on.

Absorbing failures

There are many great stories about overcoming obstacles.

Albert Einstein wasn't able to speak until he was almost 4 years old. His teacher said he would never contribute to society. Walt Disney was fired from a newspaper job for a lack of creative ideas, originality, and imagination. Steve Jobs was removed from the company he started before returning to save Apple. The Beatles were rejected by Decca Recording Studios.

It's shocking — and almost comical — to read about the initial impressions of such successful people, knowing that they ultimately found success (by any respectable measure). Perhaps those critics offering their opinions were ill informed. Perhaps these judges of talent weren't so talented. But maybe, just maybe, these successful people used the failure and rejection as motivators.

The incredibly funny comedian Louis C.K. has a great quote about failure: "I think you have to try and fail, because failure gets you closer to what you're good at." He was on to something. Failure is simply an investment in future success.

Through failure, you

✔ Learn to anticipate.

✔ Develop a better understanding of how to identify outside factors more quickly.

✔ Discover resilience, determination, drive, and motivation, all attributes employers seek.

✔ Develop humility and sympathy for others.

Failure will make you a better future leader, too.

Knowing your strengths, weaknesses, and happiness

What *is* your greatest weakness? (No, really.) At some stage, an interviewer will ask you this question. You should also be ready to discuss a time you used skills and knowledge to overcome an obstacle and a time you were challenged and failed.

Questions about your strengths and weaknesses help the interviewer know

- ✔ How you deal with failure, how you fix it, and how you learn from it.
- ✔ How you'll handle constructive criticism in the future.
- ✔ How resilient and resourceful you are.

Start thinking about your own strengths and weaknesses. Reply to the preceding bullets. What are areas where you need improvement? This assessment forces you to be humble and helps you figure out how to best explain your point of view about these topics in an interview.

Be honest with yourself about your weaknesses and strengths, but don't let weaknesses kill your confidence.

The act of identifying weaknesses, and making a step-by-step plan to overcome them, is practical. When an interviewer asks about your weaknesses, you can talk about how you overcame them. You can be very specific about the skill, the actions that you took to elevate your skill level, and the ultimate outcome from your investment of time.

Keep it professional. This is about professional weaknesses, so don't drift down a personal path.

If you're still looking for reassurance, you may want to explore personality quizzes. Companies like Personality Max (www.mypersonality.info) offer free and low-cost testing to help you understand the different aspects of your personality. You can see the site in Figure 6-1. The more you know, the better chance you have of leaving weaknesses in the dust.

Exercising your weaknesses

Break down your social media strengths and weaknesses by comparing and contrasting your skills and experience with those required of all social media professionals.

The following general skill areas are necessary for all social media professionals:

- ✔ Community management: Coordinating common resources

- ✔ Search engine optimization (SEO): Increasing a website's visibility

- ✔ Creative design: Balancing art and function

- ✔ Writing skills: Proper grammar with clear messaging

- ✔ Comfort with emerging trends and technology: Knowing current systems and tools while keeping on top of new offerings

- ✔ Understanding (and valuing) analytics: Measuring a campaign's performance

- ✔ Strategic view: Big-picture understanding

- ✔ Knowledge of tactics: Time-sensitive actions used to accomplish goals

- ✔ Effective presentation delivery: Commanding a presence while disseminating information

- ✔ Leadership: Inspiring and motivating others

Here's a quick exercise to help determine how much preparation you'll need to ready yourself for the rigors of an interview process. (Further prepping for your interview is explained in Chapter 14.)

1. **Make a list containing each of the ten general skill areas.**

2. **Use a 1–10 scale to indicate your comfort level in each area.**

   1 is a novice and 10 is an expert.

3. **Do the math.**

   Your total score will range between 50 and 100. The closer you are to 100, the greater your overall confidence in social media skills.

4. **Rank your skills.**

   List the skill areas from strongest to weakest based upon your scores.

5. **Analyze your findings.**

   Areas where you scored 8+ don't require as much time or effort to maintain. Focus on the areas where you scored 7 or less.

6. **Prioritize and build.**

   Start making a plan to build skills. There are many formal and informal learning opportunities available to you. (See Chapter 5.)

Matching passions and values

Try this exercise: Think about what you value beyond work. Where would you most likely be able to make this type of contribution?

You may be active in your community. For you, a company that supports its surrounding community may align with your values.

Matching your values to an employer's is a key indicator of success. When it happens, individual performance aligns and connects, and both parties benefit.

Establishing your own social media systems

You've taken stock. You know your strengths, and you've explored your weaknesses. You're focused on your future, and ready to renew your commitment to your career.

Now is the time to initiate.

✔ Create, find, or share content.

✔ Comment on posts, forums, and group discussions.

✔ Participate in polls.

✔ Make your social media profiles robust.

Listen to your gut. Your experience provides a great frame of reference. Define and prioritize your short-term goals. Develop a step-by-step plan of action. Engage others. Track and measure your activities. As you find what works — what gets the greatest attention, response, or action — you can refine your approach.

You can further explore how to maximize your social media systems in Chapter 7.

Chapter 7

Knowing Your Social Media Tools

In This Chapter

▶ Realizing which social media tools to use for expediting your career

▶ Applying the tools in the trenches

▶ Practicing for further positioning

*M*astering tools will make you head and shoulders better than your competition. The good news is that social media has lots of tools that can help you reveal your knowledge, prospect a hiring company, and carry out your daily duties. The not-so-good news is that new tools come out constantly and the amount of information can be daunting.

This chapter tells you what tools make your job easier, and the basics of how to use them. Though the names or features might change, what they do will stay essentially the same. We also give an overview of the Big Five platforms that you'll need to use.

Strapping On Your Tool Belt

Tools are for

- ✔ Organizing information *(aggregation)*
- ✔ Automation
- ✔ Results-driven data (sales and customer information)

Social media tools come in the form of apps, software, platforms, and programs. Consider a few base functionalities when choosing your tools.

Aggregating information

Collecting all the appropriate information that helps run a business from a relationship standpoint is what we consider aggregating. When you're gathering and organizing information with software, you'll also have the ability to schedule your social media posts. Finally, you'll manage all of the relationships that you build in social media through a software program known as a customer relationship management (CRM) database and continually improve your progress by analyzing the numbers (also known as analytics) that these software programs develop.

The best tools for collecting and organizing information in one central place follow:

- ✔ **Buffer** lets you manage multiple social media accounts at once. Buffer lets you schedule social media content virtually anywhere on the web and collaborate with team members. You also get statistics about how your social media posts perform. See Figure 7-1.

- ✔ `Nimble.com` combines the power of a *customer relationship management (CRM)* database with your social media connections. Nimble is a contact-management system that organizes your past, present, and future interactions across multiple social media platforms. If you need a reminder to get in touch with certain people on particular dates, use Nimble. See Figure 7-2.

- ✔ **Tweetdeck** is a web-based software app that applies strictly to Twitter. Tweetdeck allows you to create columns where you can see various feeds including @ mentions, new followers, direct messages, and your general feed.

- ✔ `Hootsuite.com` has a dashboard that organizes all your social media profiles. With it you can automate your posts and measure the results with a sophisticated suite of analytics.

You can find a less expensive software program with more features than Hootsuite. Ask other social media professionals in your network, or broadcast a request via your social media accounts.

Figure 7-1:
Buffer
allows you
to manage
multiple
social media
accounts at
once.

Figure 7-2:
Nimble.
com is a
social media
CRM used
to organize
your
contacts.

Automating natively

Automating means creating content and scheduling its release in the future without having to release it manually. The unfortunate part about this strategy is that many people try to take the "social" out of social media and automate all their interaction. It's almost as though you're trying to get a software program or app to talk for you and build relationships.

To *automate natively* means creating content that's relevant and helpful to your audience.

Automating in an obtrusive manner such as generating automatic direct messages to someone that follows you on Twitter is deemed to be disingenuous and gives off the wrong impression.

Ultimately, automating pre-planned content across platforms will save you a lot of time and effort.

Use these:

- ✔ www.IFTTT.com, pronounced like *gift* without the *g,* is software you can program. Set up triggers to cause a particular action; IFTTT calls that a *recipe.* For example, you can set up a recipe where a photo that you upload to Instagram is automatically uploaded to a specific file folder within Dropbox almost simultaneously. This simple example saves time and increases team efficiency. Set up an account on IFTT.com and look at some of the collections to establish some helpful recipes. See Figure 7-3.

- ✔ Twuffer.com is probably the easiest way to schedule tweets. Compose a list of tweets that you want to release in the future and decide when you want them posted.

- ✔ Pagemodo.com is for automating Facebook and LinkedIn posts as well as for scheduling tweets. Pagemodo lets you create visually stunning imagery, and it tells you how to improve the images you're posting. See Figure 7-4.

- ✔ Zapier.com is by far the best tool on the market for connecting apps and automating tasks. Not only does Zapier feature hundreds of apps, it has open *applied programming interface (API)* so you can use other services with the platform (with the help of your in-house programmer).

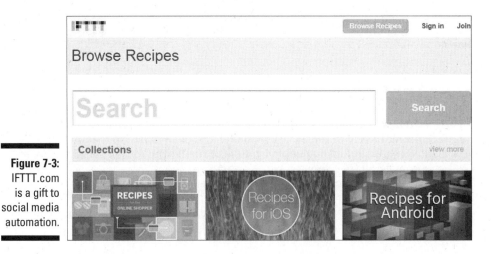

Figure 7-3:
IFTTT.com
is a gift to
social media
automation.

Many of the tools we mention earlier, in the "Aggregating information" section, allow you to schedule your social media content, but we list these tools specifically because of their simplicity, uniqueness, or breadth of capabilities.

Monitoring the social media landscape

Gathering information isn't the same as sorting through it. Monitoring tools allow you to look across multiple platforms for specific keywords and phrases.

These are the best monitoring tools out there:

- ✔ **Sproutsocial.com** is very similar to Buffer in that it schedules posts and offers in-depth analytics on your posts. Sprout also splits work among team members based on the projects you're working on and your team's responsibilities.

✔ **Keyhole.com** tracks keywords, hashtags, and website URLs across Facebook, Twitter, and Instagram. Keyhole also tracks news stories and trends across all social media. Its *influencer tracking* lets you see when key influencers mention terms related to your interests. Track terms that are related to a company's name, products, and overall image. See Figure 7-5.

✔ **Trackur.com** conducts monitoring of all social media and general news from Twitter, Facebook, Google+, and other sources. Its key advantage is that it allows you to understand your influence; its in-depth social analytics reveal trends and uncover target keywords. See Figure 7-6.

✔ **Topsy.com** searches virtually the entire social web for keywords. It also segments your searches across social media by links, tweets, photos, videos, and influencers. This feature lets you hone in on platforms and types of media that are most important to your company.

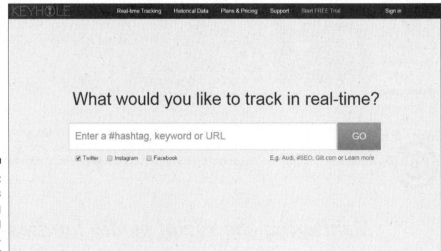

Figure 7-5: Keyhole is a hashtag tracking system.

Measuring results

How are your social media posts being perceived? How influential are you? How far are your messages traveling? It's important to measure your influence and overall results whether you're looking for a job or you're demonstrating your value for your employer. Results in social media are all that matter at the end of the day.

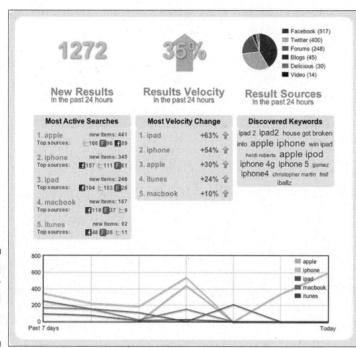

Figure 7-6:
Trackur allows full social media monitoring.

It's hard to quantify how much a relationship is worth. In fact, it might seem downright scandalous to put a value on a relationship or to figure out whether you can turn a profit or meet *key performance indicators (KPIs)* with them.

Bosses are looking to see how social media can show a positive. These sites can help you do just that:

✔ **SAS Social Media Analytics (SMA)** is an extremely sophisticated social media analytics system developed by the Statistical Analysis System (SAS) Institute. With the numbers accrued through social media, a company can integrate social conversations into business operations. For example, based on customer feedback, a company may decide that customer service is giving ambiguous information over the phone and can immediately focus on retraining their staff. SMA uses all customer touch points, including brand marketing, public relations, and customer service.

SAS is the closest to science supporting the effectiveness of social media. See Figure 7-7.

- ✔ **Socialbakers.com** features analytics software that focuses on social media measurement. You can compare your direct competitors and your industries.

- ✔ **TweetReach.com** offers in-depth analytics for Twitter, Instagram, and Tumblr. Enter a URL, hashtag, phrase, or username. TweetReach uncovers all the applicable information related to your search.

Figure 7-7:
SAS is a social media analytics platform supported by real science.

Digging In to Your Tools

How can you use this chapter's tools to build your personal brand and position your career? Think critically about how you'll position yourself, how you'll measure your results, and how you'll challenge yourself to continually improve.

Choosing an angle

You have to monitor and refine your personal social media use.

You'll get valuable experience using tools during your job search, which is useful down the line.

Above all else, choose whether you'll be using the tools as yourself, as a company, or as a "personality." It's okay if you change your mind, but commit yourself to an angle that leverages your skills and personality.

- ✔ **Personal brand:** You create and use platforms with your real name and information. A personal brand can include both personal and professional content that reveals who you are as a person and what you can do as a professional. Chapter 12 talks more about personal brand.

- ✔ **Social brand:** Your social brand isn't necessarily your actual name; a social brand is a bit more professional. We recommend injecting some personality into your content — people (in this case, the decision makers at your target companies) like to work with *people*.

- ✔ **Social media personality:** You have a fun option for branding yourself. Invent a character to entertain and educate the public with your social media knowledge. For example social media consultant, Andrea Vahl, decided to create a slightly grumpy character, Grandma Mary, who breaks down social media best practices. To see this social media personality on display, check out `andreavahl.com/grandmas-corner` or see Figure 7-8. This is a unique approach that can help reach more people but it may confuse the public if they can't distinguish between your character and who you are as a person.

Figure 7-8: Grandma Mary is a social media personality.

Improving your content quality

Avoid talking about whatever you want without considering whether there's a need in the marketplace. Focus on offering solutions to commonly asked questions and problems.

This approach works best if you do this daily on a one-on-one basis with influencers and people who you can help. As you create more content, you'll inherently improve your overall effectiveness.

These sources can help you get to the next level:

- ✔ **Copyblogger** is based around the concept of how to create content online that effectively increases exposure, leads and sales. This is also commonly known as sales copy, or writing to sell. The top social media and online marketing professionals go to `copyblogger.com/blog` to share their insight and best practices.

- ✔ **Soshable** is a social media marketing blog aimed toward best practices and emerging trends. JD Rucker is the main author and he shares his knowledge and tips from the trenches. See Figure 7-9.

- ✔ **Social Media Today** is an online periodical that covers social media topics as they pertain to technology, marketing, and the networks themselves.

As your content begins to improve, you might be invited to post it on other people's platforms. In fact, you may be invited to be interviewed, to serve as a panelist for online discussion, or to create content on other platforms. Always try to say "Yes." Every single connection matters.

Figure 7-9: Soshable is a social media marketing blog.

Why Social Media Won't Die Any Time Soon

October 5, 2014 by JD Rucker — 7 Comments

I remember the first "social media is dying" post that I read. It was early 2008 and MySpace was already showing signs of starting to implode upon itself. The article I read (wish I would have saved it) gave a very compelling argument about how social media was a fad and that privacy would eventually prevail once the glow of the "look at me" mentality that drives social media wears off.

It never did. It never will.

There's no going back. Social media is the ultimate legal voyeurism into the lives of those

Tapping into the Big Five and Further

Social medium platforms themselves are the most valuable set of tools. Mastering the Big Five (most powerful platforms), plus Quora, YouTube, and blogging in general, means you'll be able to practice the tools discussed in this chapter

The tools that you use to supplement your career can give you a lot of insight about how valuable your expertise is.

Communicating the right message with the right people at the right time on the right platform (also known as the Four Rights) starts with research and is refined with trial and error. Your success comes down to whether you're providing value for others. You can have all the knowledge and skill in the world, but people must trust or respect you.

Use the following networks. Chapter 12 has more information about the Big Five.

Maximizing: LinkedIn

LinkedIn is the most professional-oriented platform of the Big Five.

- ✔ **For five minutes every day, give endorsements to people within your network.** Endorsements list the knowledge and skills that other people in your direct network vouch for you having. The more you endorse other people, the more willing they are to endorse you. Endorsements help you see how credible you are in the eyes of your network. You might find that you have skills that you didn't recognize.

- ✔ **Write as many descriptive, honest recommendations as you can for ten minutes per day.** Or, ask for them via email. Recommendations are written by your network about your work experience; they show other LinkedIn users that other people are willing to put their names, faces, and reputations behind you. There is no higher compliment in the LinkedIn world.

  If just ten percent of people return the favor, then you have at least 36 referrals on your LinkedIn profile. That multiplies the average number of referrals for a job applicant by more than ten. If that's not a strong testament to your ability, we don't know what is!

Maximizing: Twitter

Hashtag chats are another great way to position your knowledge and expertise. For example, a group of social media power users may decide that they will meet every Tuesday at 8:00 PM EST around the hashtag #SocialMediaChat.

Try answering questions that you see thought leaders and influencers asking via their tweets. If you provide results faster, or offer better insight, you're contributing significant value to powerful people!

Maximizing: YouTube

YouTube is the third most trafficked site in the world behind only Google and Facebook. The even better news is that YouTube plays nicely with Google (since Google owns YouTube) and also integrates very well with Facebook for the time being. Ultimately, YouTube performs extremely well with search engines and video is arguably the most engaging form of content out there.

The challenge with YouTube is that videos are consumed in seconds. It's hard to capture someone's attention, much less get them to share what you offer.

Keep this in mind:

- ✔ **Focus on solving problems.** Resist the urge to create videos where you talk about what *you* want to talk about. Solve problems. Focus on one specific influencer and sufficiently answer his question.

- ✔ **Showcase decent quality.** If you're recording screen captures, use gamer headphones or another decent microphone. This shouldn't cost more than $100. If you go down the more expensive route with live video, then use a digital SLR camera, wireless lavalier microphone, and softbox light fixtures. All told, you'll spend about $750 — but you'll produce top-notch video that stands out from the competition.

- ✔ **Know what makes you different.** It's important to understand why people watch your videos. Consider creating a *unique selling proposition (USP)* and succinctly answering why your target audience should watch your video. After you answer that question, stick to it.

- ✔ **Create titles and descriptions for people.** Your tendency might be to create videos that perform well with search engines. Create titles that are an exact match for what people are looking for as your video has a much higher propensity for being found.

- ✔ **Collaborate with other YouTubers.** Create opportunities to leverage both audiences by appearing in each other's videos. Do this as often as possible!

Video and audio gear

Two great headphones options are Turtle Beach X12 and PX22, which you can find in any local electronics retailer or on Amazon. Upload your video to YouTube and Vimeo and distribute the content through a free service such as oneload.com.

Use video production software such as Final Cut Pro or Sony Vegas to isolate audio. You can also upload a YouTube link to a site such as youtube-mp3.org and upload the audio to a WordPress site using a plug-in such as Compact WP Audio Player.

Include a link in your YouTube description that takes people to your blog or website! Put the link in the very first line of text. Tell people what they can gain by watching your video, and give a call to action to click the URL.

Find what works best for your presentation style, and more importantly, your audience. For example, when Brooks was applying for a job with Google, he posted videos on YouTube to demonstrate his knowledge of Google Drive. The videos showed off his expertise with Google's product; it also gave him a chance to show off his personality and be much more engaging than you can with the written word.

The Internet never forgets so content that you put up once will receive residual traffic and can offer you benefits for years to come. The more video content that you have, the more potential opportunities that you'll create for yourself in the long run!

Maximizing: Google+

Google+ is a tough nut to crack. But there's hope:

- ✔ **Use strategic hashtags:** Google+ uses hashtags in search results, so you can position content that you post there so it shows up readily in organic search results and on Google+.

- ✔ **Message your connections:** Email people you're connected to (known as *circles*) any time that you post valuable content. Use the built-in Google+ email utility.

Maximizing: Quora

Quora.com is a website where people ask or answer questions. Quora will best serve you if you do two things:

- ✔ Ask thought-provoking questions and engage with other thought leaders and professionals within your field. This is similar to what you should be doing on social media all of the time, but Quora *only* focuses on building community around asking questions and the answers to them.

- ✔ Answer questions as completely and succinctly as you can.

You can share your answers on other networks. A valuable answer that you give on Quora might be shared on Google+, Twitter, Facebook, and LinkedIn.

Blogging

Think of your website or blog as the focal point of your thought leadership and positioning. If your online presence is a dinner party, then your blog is your house. Here's where you keep the most valuable information; social media sites are invitations to come over for supper.

- ✔ **Look for guest opportunities.** This goes both ways in terms of allowing other people to post on your blog or website and looking for opportunities to blog on other people's platforms. By allowing others to blog on your website, you'll be able to take the day off from writing and will strengthen your relationship with other thought leaders. The advantage to guest blogging on another platform is that you'll have the chance to get in front of a new audience and attract them to your offering. For more information on this topic, be sure to check out guestblogging.com.

- ✔ **Accommodate multiple learning styles.** Whenever possible, start with long-form written content and turn that information into video and audio.

- ✔ **Build an email list.** Use it to notify your audience when new content is out, when you want to advertise your services, or when you're looking for a job. You've provided value already, so don't be bashful when it comes to call in a favor.

- ✔ **Write for people.** We said it before and we're saying it again: Create long form content that answers people's questions and alleviates pain.

You have lots of blogging platforms to choose from, but we recommend starting with Tumblr and WordPress. These sites perform extremely well in search engine results and don't require any programming or web design experience.

Part III

Finding Your Fit with the Right Organization

In this part . . .

- ✔ Decide whether you're cut out for a full-time job or a potentially less secure job.

- ✔ Weigh the pros and cons of being a consultant with being a full-time employee.

- ✔ Look closely at what it takes to succeed in a start-up company.

- ✔ Figure out if you'd like to start your own social media agency and how to do it.

- ✔ See more at www.dummies.com.

Chapter 8

Life as a Social Media Consultant

In This Chapter

▶ Building your own social media consultancy

▶ Offering your services to partners

▶ Knowing the advantages and disadvantages of being a consultant

*T*o a full-time employee, being a consultant may seem like a dream. You get to tell companies exactly what they need to do and tell them what they need to pay you per hour or per project. Companies gladly pay you the asking price because you're the expert. You can outsource the work and charge a premium for managing the labor. Overall, the consultant's life sounds rather glamorous.

Of course, some people tell you that consultants are constantly struggling for business and that the consulting industry is as cutthroat as they come. That companies are loathe to spend money on this newfound cost. That companies will choose the cheaper option every single time.

A successful social media consultant will tell you success boils down to a few key factors:

✔ Listening effectively and offering solutions rather than pushing products and services that you want to sell

✔ Strictly defining your value and striving to under-promise and over-deliver

✔ Delivering value to relationships without looking for anything in return; staying in constant communication

✔ Carefully measuring results and effectively communicating your impact on the businesses you're serving

If you follow these four tips, you could build a social media consulting empire without reading the rest of this chapter. Luckily, the rest of this chapter teaches you how to position yourself for an executive career and details the pros and cons of being a full-time consultant.

Seeking Out Social Media Consulting Opportunities

The chance to serve businesses as a social media consultant is certainly there. You have to find them.

You're going to hear "No" a lot. There are many reasons not to take this "rejection" personally.

Figure out the real reason they're declining your services. They may be rejecting your offering because they don't have the budget, they aren't able to allocate the time to tackle the project or it just might not be the right timing for them in general.

Always interpret a "No" as a "Not right now." Keep in constant communication. Go out of your way to be kind and to provide value. An opportunity might not come through a prospect, but rather, from their network or someone else.

Offer only consulting services that you love; couple your services with companies, industries, and people that you love. If you chase after money and are willing to work with anyone, you'll burn out very quickly and get frustrated with consulting.

Knowing what you offer

You only have to figure out three things to start a successful social media consultancy:

- ✔ Where is there a need?
- ✔ How can I fill that need?
- ✔ Are they willing to pay a fair price for my services?

Don't	**Do**
Don't offer everything under the sun.	Offer services that you enjoy.
Don't dictate what you offer.	Determine your target market to find opportunities where there is pain, a problem or a need.

Figure out

- ✔ Who you're serving
- ✔ What work, if any, you'll be subcontracting out

For example, Brooks figured out that he was a much better strategist, copywriter, and planner when it came to social media advertising, but didn't enjoy graphics or ad monitoring. He found other professionals who could create images and ensure optimal ad performance; then he marked up their hourly rates to the client. In the end, Brooks got to focus on the parts that he loved and still make a decent profit.

Defining your ideal clients

This advice will contribute to your long-term happiness: Only work with clients that you enjoy.

You should enjoy working with them professionally and enjoy them as people. If you wouldn't ask them out to dinner as a friend, then they're probably not going to be very enjoyable business partners. Of course, you need experience and have to pay the bills, so you won't always be able to work with exactly who you want.

Critically think about the type of people that you enjoy being around personally and professionally. You might begin by asking these questions:

- ✔ What types of professionals do I enjoy working with? Why do I enjoy working with these people so much?
- ✔ What industries and companies do I prefer to serve?
- ✔ Would I have a vested interest in the client's success?
- ✔ What do my ideal clients do outside of work? Do we share common interests?

Answering these questions is worth the effort. In our experience, working with people and industries that you don't love is the fastest way to burn out in the consulting world.

Offering Your Services to Local Consultants

Many consultants have trouble finding new business; generating clients is always at the top of the list for social media consultants — especially if you're just starting out.

The good news is that you don't have to do all this on your own. Find established entities where you might be able to work as a subcontractor. Not only will you build your portfolio, but you'll build mutually beneficial relationships. Network effectively and establish relationships with other consultants and agencies that have client bases that you would like to work with or contribute to.

Consider non-compete clauses and never try to take business from entities that you work with or subcontract for.

Searching for established professionals

Search online for local consultancies and agencies that have similar offerings. For example, if you were a social media consultant in Raleigh, North Carolina, start your search with terms related to your industry, strategic focus, and your location. Search queries that you create might look like **ad agency Raleigh, NC** or **marketing consultant 27609**. See Figure 8-1 for search results.

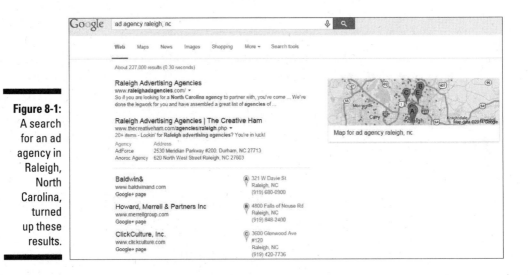

Figure 8-1: A search for an ad agency in Raleigh, North Carolina, turned up these results.

For example, if you're a social media manager, search for ad or marketing agencies that don't offer your services. Even if an agency's website states that it offers the service, often it is still looking for other professionals that can offer top-notch work.

Create a spreadsheet that includes the following:

- ✔ Company name
- ✔ Contact information
- ✔ Service offering
- ✔ Notes on the entity

Order the companies by how much you'd like to work with them. Consider the firm's reputation and values, billing rate, and clients.

Pitching what you bring to the table

To prepare for pitching companies, take these steps:

1. **Think about what your services include and how you compete in the marketplace.**

2. **List all the potential products and services that you feel comfortable offering.**

   Include as many as you can; you can then shrink this list to focus.

3. **Think about how you compete and what makes you different.**

   You should have your initial pitch down to a fluid, succinct presentation and then spend the rest of the time answering your client's questions and asking for their business.

For example, here's a weak service offering:

I'm a social media consultant and I specialize in anything social media related. If you're not satisfied for any reason then we no longer have to work together.

This value offering isn't specific, the consultant doesn't clearly define why he should be chosen, and the guarantee is weak. Consider this strong example:

I'm an established social media advertising professional that specializes in Facebook conversions. I guarantee a 250% ROI on all Facebook advertising campaigns or your money back.

This statement tells the audience exactly what you do. It makes a strong promise and backs it up with a guarantee.

Try to minimize your customer's risk. An example of minimizing risk is offering a money-back guarantee or a 30-day trial. This puts your prospect's mind at ease.

Deciding how to get in touch

You can approach a consultancy or agency the following ways, from least to more personable:

- ✔ **Email.** This is the least personal, but it also lets you reach the most people. You could send a BCC email to 50 different agencies and consultancies, but you wouldn't have any context or trust behind your message. If you use this method, get straight to the point. Tell the prospective partner how you can help them and what you're offering. They don't have the time to get into any further detail.

- ✔ **Social media.** Of course, using the medium that you're hoping to help a potential partner with is certainly wise. Social media is more personal than email. The only drawback is that social media should be used to build a relationship *first*. Trying to immediately sell your services to a potential partner is the opposite of how social media is supposed to work.

   Develop a daily action plan to contact a potential partner at least three times before asking for the sale.

- ✔ **Phone.** Make sure you're speaking to the proper decision maker, present a question that piques her interest, and set a meeting where you can get a "Yes." Your question might sound something like this: "I currently work with Competitor A and delivered [*your good result*]. Would you like me to do the same for you?" When she confirms her interest, present two time ranges and days that work for you. (You want to make it clear you're busy.) It might sound a bit crazy, but this works like a charm.

- ✔ **In person.** This is by far the most effective means to present your offering if you feel confident that you can dress and act the part of a top-notch social media consultant. This approach is also the least scalable. You'll have to consider whether the quality of the connection outweighs the quantity that you can achieve by prospecting online or on the phone. The advantage is that you can potentially get an answer that day but the trade-off is that in-person prospecting takes more time.

No matter how you approach a potential partner, your objective is to get a "Yes." We prefer to use the phone and social media, but your approach depends on what's most comfortable and most effective for you.

Presenting your offer with confidence

We can't understate the importance of confidence when it comes to pitching potential partners. Prospective partners have to fully trust you to buy into your service offering; that's why confidence in your offering and your delivery is so important.

Practice your prospective partner pitch with three friends. Encourage them to ask questions and be candid about evaluating your offer. Keep this pitch short; emphasize how you're benefitting the potential partner. Your wants and needs aren't relevant at this point. The more that you practice your pitch, the more confident you will be.

To practice, try Duarte's eCourse, which offers an entertaining, nontraditional approach to online learning that covers everything you need to develop and deliver a presentation. The price tag is steep at around $500, but you'll also become extremely effective with sales presentations and close a lot more sales. See Figure 8-2.

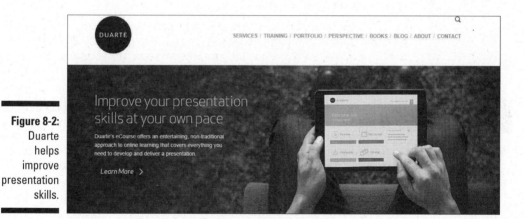

Figure 8-2:
Duarte
helps
improve
presentation
skills.

Improve your presentation skills at your own pace

Duarte's eCourse offers an entertaining, non-traditional approach to online learning that covers everything you need to develop and deliver a presentation.

Learn More ›

Negotiating your contract

The agreement that you put together for your clients should be fairly standard.

The contract should outline exactly

- What you'll deliver
- Timelines associated with your work
- Total costs
- All applicable rules and procedures

Have your attorney review this contract; your client's legal counsel should review it also. Legal review is important because the extra revision ensures that the expectations are rock solid and the likelihood for a legal dispute is greatly minimized.

Use these tips and tricks when you're negotiating your consulting agreement:

- ✓ **Always ask for more hours and money than you think you need.** For instance, if you think that a project will take 10 hours to complete and your hourly rate from your last consulting gig was $50 per hour, ask for 15 billable hours at $65 per hour. In this circumstance, you've almost doubled your fee from $500 up to $975 with a few basic tweaks. A client is never going to increase the number of hours or billable rate that you're asking so always start a bit higher.

- ✓ **Know your market rate.** How is your competition priced? Don't try to beat them on price. Having a comparable price is a great start but being able to outperform your competition in terms of value is way better. If you can offer more services or work a few pro bono hours, say so during negotiation. Chapter 14 offers websites that will tell you what the competition is getting paid.

- ✓ **Clearly understand your client's tendencies and payment rate.** For example, bigger companies won't even consider your services if they aren't priced what they're willing to pay. As such, do yourself a favor and understand what they typically pay for their service providers, the scope of expected work, and their overall expectations.

- ✓ **Have the read-only document signed and dated by decision makers from both sides.** Make multiple copies of the contract and scan it into a cloud-based storage system so both parties can access it. For more ideas on how to close the deal, check out The Negotiation Blog. This site has the best information in the negotiation industry. See Figure 8-3.

With practice, you can accomplish these goals with ease and begin beating your competitors.

Closing the consulting sale

Make your intentions clear and ask for the sale. Use the following formula:

1. **Reiterate the opportunities that the client has and how your solutions solve these problems.**

2. **Tell the client that you have a vested interest in their results and want to earn their business.**

3. **Ask for the sale and then remain silent.**

   For more information on how to effectively close sales, check out Jill Konrath's blog. See Figure 8-4.

   Remain silent after asking for the sale. Many consultants ask for a sale and then talk themselves right out of it.

Don't ramble on about additional services, explain why you're the best, or create barriers that weren't there in the first place. Your prospect is going to say Yes or No and present their objections. If they say No, then address the objections, offer more value (pro bono services or a trial period), and ask for the business again.

If you're not especially strong with closing sales, or you'd like more information on developing a better sales process, head over to `thesalesblog.com`. Anthony Iannarino is a world-class sales expert that freely gives away his knowledge about sales prospecting, the general sales process, and closing. See his blog in Figure 8-5.

Figure 8-3:
The Negotiation Blog discusses top negotiation tactics.

Figure 8-4:
Jill Konrath
knows how
to close a
sale.

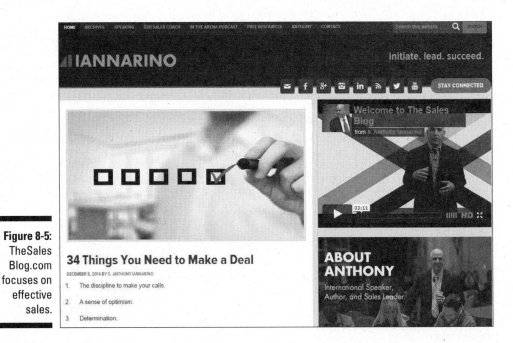

Figure 8-5:
TheSales
Blog.com
focuses on
effective
sales.

Looking at a Typical Day

Your day as a social media consultant varies because the number of clients, responsibilities, and scope of work varies. You're almost in complete control when it comes to when and how you do your work.

For example, some consultants understand how all the work is supposed to be done and subcontract out entire jobs. The only actual work that they do is project management and articulating to clients how the work was done. In essence, a consultant can theoretically do whatever he or she wants — avoid heavy lifting and still get paid the same as a full-time social media employee.

This is an extreme example but the point is that social media consultants have more freedom. Companies that you consult with don't normally care when and how you do the work, as long as you deliver the results they're looking for.

Typical workload

Aside from your primary deliverables, a majority of your work will be based around data reporting, results analysis, and managing subcontractors. Table 8-1 gives an example of a social media manager's average day.

Table 8-1	Social Media Manager's Average Day
Time	*Task*
9:00 AM–9:30 AM	Overview daily plan and check in with team and client to reiterate standards, expectations, and deliverables.
9:30 AM–11:00 AM	Answer all consumer questions on the Big Five and any other social media platforms.
11:00 AM–1:00 PM	Post and automate daily content on respective social networks. Connect with and try to help strategic influencers. For more information, see Chapter 12 for networking help.
1:00 PM–1:30 PM	Lunch or afternoon meeting with subcontracted team (if applicable).
1:30 PM–3:00 PM	Answer all consumer questions on Big Five and any other social media platforms. Network with strategic influencers.
3:00 PM–4:00 PM	Prospect potential clients via email, social media, phone and/or in person. Use available time for content planning and creation.
4:00 PM–5:00 PM	Compile data and submit daily report to client.

Even if you have no experience subcontracting, start subcontracting work as soon as you can. You'll burn out if you try to do the work all by yourself.

As a social media consultant, you can expect to put in between 15 and 50 billable hours per week.

When the work is done will also depend on the nature of the critical activities as well. For example, a social media manager has to provide real-time responses to consumers; a social media data aggregator or strategic planner won't have responsibilities that require that kind of timeliness. Chapter 4 talks more about social media roles and their responsibilities.

Delivering daily critical activities

The more you communicate with your client, the longer your contract and the better your referrals. Break down your hours and deliverables in as much detail as possible.

Though your clients may not care to know every nuance of your day, give them the option of having this information.

Don't send your clients an invoice billing for a large, subjective amount — especially when they're not seeing top-notch results.

You can format your daily critical activities two ways:

- ✔ Summarize each deliverable and what you did, along with a time increment (by 15 minutes).
- ✔ A complete hour-by-hour breakdown.

Ask your clients which method they prefer. They might tell you that this breakdown isn't necessary. Document your daily progress regardless. It helps you stay on track.

Documenting your results

In addition to logging your critical activities, document your overall results.

Clients care most about that part of your work, and it's your chance to showcase the benefits your client is getting.

Send a daily report that highlights what you accomplished that day and lay out the next day's objectives. Your daily results log should hone in on the deliverables and key performance indicators (KPIs) that the client has emphasized. Chapter 16 talks more about KPIs.

Include your daily results log with your invoice. Send an invoice bi-weekly or monthly. This way, a client can see an expense line item and have the information they need to account for the critical action item. Consultants rarely provide this level of detail; your clients will appreciate it and it sets you apart from competition.

Outline how your billing and deliverables will be provided in your contracting agreement. Or, you can pleasantly surprise your clients with these methods.

Clearing a Career Path: Consultant to Executive

You may enjoy working with a client full time and you may even be offered a job throughout the course of your gig. Clients like this route because a consultant's hourly rate is typically much higher than that of a salaried employee; becoming an employee shows that you have a vested interest in the company's success. Your benefit is more security in the form of an employment guarantee, benefits, and stock options for performance.

Another reason why this route is advantageous for you is because you will have delivered value from a high level standpoint and the entity views you as a true expert in your field. As such, you will have a significant advantage over the lower level employees and can assume a higher position rather than going through the organic route and being forced to climb the proverbial corporate ladder.

Establishing a clear-cut plan

Whether you have proposed an employment agreement or your current client has, create a definitive plan about to how your employment will look. If you're a consultant and looking for a full-time job, then the next section, "Asking for what you want," will give you clear direction for how to score a full-timer.

You can establish exactly what your roles and responsibilities will look like, and the client will be impressed by your foresight. The opportunity to create your own job is quite rare, so take advantage of the possibilities.

Outline the following:

✔ Compensation, perks, and benefits

✔ Roles and responsibilities

✔ Plan for the future in terms of growth, labor, deliverables, and timelines

✔ Expectations and standards for both sides

For more information about how to develop timelines, create explicit deliverables, and set realistic expectations, please see Chapters 16 and 17.

Asking for what you want

If you become a full-time employee, clearly establish what you want from your employment. If you guess what the company's going to offer and hope that they'll deliver, you're likely to be disappointed.

Always do the following when you're negotiating your employment package:

✔ **Define the future.** Clearly explain where you want to be with this company. Explain the positions you would need filled, the financial backing, the outcomes, and a clear plan of how you would build this all out.

✔ **Ask for more.** Use a resource such as salary.com (see Figure 8-6) to understand your market rate and ask for 5 to 20 percent more than what you believe you deserve. Also ask for more when it comes to benefits, stock options, perks, and bonuses. A potential employer will never give you an outright "No" when you ask for more; they might negotiate your agreement to a higher level than you expected in the first place.

✔ **Minimize your risk.** If your offer isn't enticing enough for the potential employer, then offer a trial rate.

✔ **Earn it.** After you've asked for what you want and created a game plan with your employer, it's time for you to work hard and earn your position. Go all in and prove your merit.

Defining your value

To finalize your agreement, show the documentation that clearly reveals your results, progress, and overall impact on the potential hiring company.

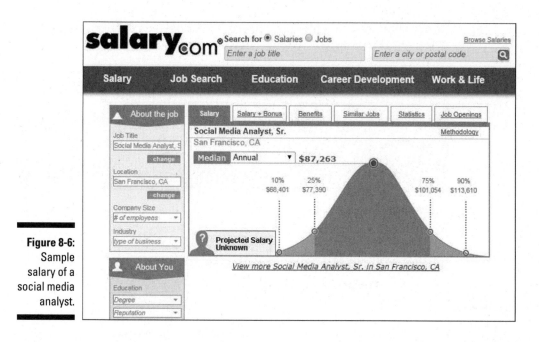

Figure 8-6:
Sample
salary of a
social media
analyst.

Do a cost benefit analysis. You'll justify your value by defining what knowledge, skills, and abilities you have and putting that into perspective regarding market-driven rates. Quantify roles that they'd have to hire if you weren't a full-time employee.

Say you could serve as a junior web developer, intermediate graphic designer, and social media strategic planner. In this example, between salary and benefits, a junior web developer costs $55,000, a mid-level graphic designer costs $60,000, and a social media strategist costs $85,000. That's a combined value of $200,000. Your initial asking price of $150,000 might sound steep, but it's a lot more affordable than taking on three separate employees.

Pros and Cons of Being a Consultant

Social media consultants are entrepreneurial people who are willing to take risks so they can get much bigger rewards. Consulting is a quicker route to substantial wealth, but you sacrifice the guarantees and luxuries of a full-time job.

It's foolish to give up the guaranteed income of a full-time job without a substantial book of business or contracts that can supplement your income. But you don't have to be a full-time consultant. A lot of pros have full-time jobs and consult in their free time. Building a portfolio that way can hedge your risk.

To get some great new ideas and improve your overall effectiveness as a consultant, read The Consultants Mind blog. See Figure 8-7.

Figure 8-7:
Consultants
Mind is a
top-notch
blog.

Pros

Consulting is a desired career for many reasons. Some people glamorize the pay or like the idea of being perceived as experts in their fields.

Consultants are often paid to be speakers or authors, and are asked to join business opportunities because of their perceived expertise.

The following top reasons are why consulting might be the right career choice for you.

Time freedom

Consultants don't check into an office or have superiors per se. This big responsibility takes a professional attitude and discipline. Though it's always wise to document your hours and show clients how your time is spent, you still get to spend your time as you see fit to get the job done.

Authority

As a consultant, you can structure agreements that outline expectations, standards, and decision making. If you plan around the results that the company wants, they'll almost always be willing to grant you full control over operations.

Some decisions still have to be run up the flagpole, but your autonomy is much greater than that of an employee.

Flexibility

You have two primary advantages: You choose how to get the work done. You can handle personal life obstacles when and how you please. And it doesn't particularly matter where you do your work. Go to the mountains; go to the beach. If you have internet access and don't need to meet with clients face to face, then you're free to work where you wish.

Ensure that you are on the same page with your client regarding when you need to meet directly. Make a plan. If your client wants a weekly in-person meeting and you prefer a bi-weekly Skype session, then you'll need to negotiate.

Referrals

If you do an excellent job, ask your client for referrals. This is by far the best way to build your business.

Another approach is a conversation at a results meeting. It might go like this:

> *You:* You all are completely satisfied with my work and would gladly tell others about my consulting services, correct?

> *Client:* Absolutely. You always under-promise and over-deliver with your results.

> *You:* Thank you for your kind words. Who else do you know would benefit from my offering?

> *Client:* I have a lot of other executive friends who would love what you do. Specifically, Sally from ABC Company would really be interested in your social media services.

> *You:* I'm happy to hear that. Do you have a moment to give Sally a quick call?

> *Client:* Absolutely. That would be my pleasure.

Because you're doing such a great job, a client is happy to do something nice for you. To get clients to refer clients *to* you, set up a referral program that rewards them. One of our favorite referral software programs is called ReferralCandy and it only takes minutes to set up. See Figure 8-8.

Figure 8-8: ReferralCandy focuses on referral marketing.

Increase your consulting rate 5 to 20 percent during each new agreement. That lets you adjust for inflation and ensure compensation for your growing expertise.

Other approaches might include

- Offering an incentive to any referring party. You can give rewards for each referral manually or you automate the process through customer referral software.

- Putting up an ad for a bird dog salesperson. A bird dog is someone who goes out and finds a prospective deal or even closes it for you. For every successful meeting, lead or sale that a bird dog brings, you offer a commission.

- Join a local networking group where you pay a membership fee in exchange for leads and introductions. Chapter 12 talks about more networking opportunities.

Results are all that matter

As long as you're delivering the results that you promised, then you can do virtually anything else that you want professionally and personally.

For example, if you've met your quota of 15 conversions for the day at 9:00 AM, then you're free to turn off your campaigns, schedule an end-of-day email to report your results, and take off the rest of the day. (But this only applies if you're working on a project basis. As an hourly rate for this type of work would be extremely unethical.)

For more information around social media consulting and to connect with the industry's top thought leaders, check out `socialmediaexplorer.com`. You can see the site in Figure 8-9.

Figure 8-9:
SocialMedia
Explorer.
com
comments.

Cons

There are obstacles that you need to be aware of. The following sections address some of the potential cons of working as a consultant but also provide perspective about these perceived disadvantages.

Stability

Consultants typically work on short-term contracts that may (or may not) have longer term provisions. Consultants are typically one of the first expenses cut to lower expenses.

Consultants have to continually look for new opportunities and bid for business. Their work can change at a moment's notice.

Many states have *at-will employment*, where either the employer or the employee can end their agreement at any time and for any reason. Both sides also have recourse for such instances and there are many federal and state exemptions which range from public policy, implied contract, and covenant of faith.

Employer perks, retirement, and benefits

Consultants sometimes get company perks, such as discounts with partners or a percentage off products. Retirement programs, stock and equity options, and medical benefits are even rarer.

Many consultants set up independent benefits programs through their consultancy. An example is setting up retirement through a more affordable system such as a *professional employer organization (PEO)*. TriNet, for example, helps small businesses establish payroll and health benefits, and advises clients about employment law compliance and overall risk reduction. See Figure 8-10.

You can establish your own medical, dental, vision, and 401(k) benefits. Start with PEOs and talk to as many companies as possible to find the options that fit best.

Figure 8-10:
TriNet is a professional employer organization (PEO).

Input rather than control

You can advise a client, but there are no guarantees that the client will accept your recommendations.

The quickest way a consultant-client relationship sours is when expectations aren't met. Set clear expectations for how decisions are to be made and where authority lies.

The more control and power you can get over decision making, the better your results will be. Your client might know their company and industry better than you, but you are the social media expert.

Chapter 9

Working as an In-House Social Media Specialist

In This Chapter

▶ Understanding the different team members

▶ Grasping social media projects and expectations

▶ Being a part of a team

*A*ffordable labor and authenticity from internal sources are leading many companies to manage their social media presence in-house. Authenticity gives you an inherent advantage over the competition. If you can truly embody the essence of the brand and provide quick answers to the public about the company's products, services, and culture, then you're in a position to win.

This chapter explains standalone social media departments: how they're structured, how they work, and the typical assignments they cover. Please note that this chapter assumes that you're a full-time employee of a company rather than a contractor.

Brands are creating entire social media departments, sometimes making them part of marketing or advertising.

Chief marketing officers (CMOs) have become branded as the more traditional, or *push*, marketing advocates; social media professionals are the new-age, or *pull*, marketing pioneers.

Chapter 4 talks about these roles in even more depth.

Typical Social Media Team Roles

Social media teams vary depending on the brand needs, the team's talents, and the budget. At a minimum there's a social media manager; sometimes contractors or the marketing department help.

Social media manager

The manager, typically the executive, is familiar with all functional areas of social media. The manager holds accountable all other departments — graphic design, strategy, customer service, public relations — and the social media department members report to her. She usually reports to the chief marketing officer or the executive board, or she may be on the executive team.

The social media manager typically is in charge of overseeing strategy, implementation, planning, budgeting, and reporting. Her main responsibility is to provide quantitative and qualitative reporting to the executive board. The quantitative data shows the brand's sales performance on social media, and the qualitative data reveals how the brand is performing in the consumer's mind.

Social media strategist

A strategist is usually second in command and reports directly to the social media manager. A social media strategist is mainly in charge of developing, executing, and measuring the results of the social media department.

The strategist typically defines the brand's social media voice, positioning, graphical presentation, unique selling proposition (USP), and overall strategic implementation.

Community manager

Behind a well-trained social media manager, a brand may also hire a community manager to speak and respond on various platforms. The community manager can speak in the brand's voice, is familiar with several social media platforms, and specializes in sales or customer service. The community manager not only monitors and talks with current and potential customers, but may provide additional customer service or look for opportunities to directly sell or start strategic partnerships. In larger organizations, this person may focus on only one platform (such as Facebook). See Figure 9-1 at https://www.marketo.com/_assets/uploads/Your-Sample-Social-Editorial-Calendar.pdf.

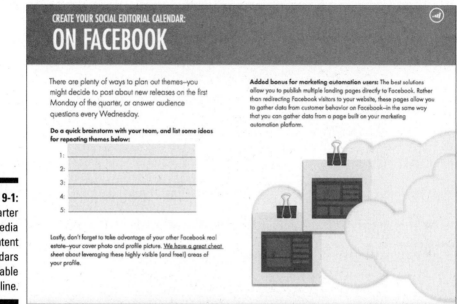

CREATE YOUR SOCIAL EDITORIAL CALENDAR:
ON FACEBOOK

There are plenty of ways to plan out themes—you might decide to post about new releases on the first Monday of the quarter, or answer audience questions every Wednesday.

Do a quick brainstorm with your team, and list some ideas for repeating themes below:

1:
2:
3:
4:
5:

Lastly, don't forget to take advantage of your other Facebook real estate—your cover photo and profile picture. We have a great cheat sheet about leveraging these highly visible (and free!) areas of your profile.

Added bonus for marketing automation users: The best solutions allow you to publish multiple landing pages directly to Facebook. Rather than redirecting Facebook visitors to your website, these pages allow you to gather data from customer behavior on Facebook—in the same way that you can gather data from a page built on your marketing automation platform.

Figure 9-1: Starter social media content calendars are available online.

Brands that only hire community managers to control their social media presence aren't allocating a significant budget to social media and are participating on social media because they "have to."

Copywriter

A copywriter writes the messaging for the overall brand on social media. The copywriter may also create the words for pieces such as infographics, social advertisements, and picture quotes. This person works with the strategist to create the content calendar; he works with community manager to refine broadcasts or advertisements. The copywriter position is often outsourced.

Graphic designer

The graphic designer is typically already a part of the advertising or marketing department, but may become part of the social media team if the volume of content and graphical needs are high enough. The graphic designer typically designs the brand's social media profiles and work with the copywriter or social media management to develop creative pieces; see Figure 9-2. For instance, a graphic designer may be responsible for designing an infographic, but the community manager is responsible for effectively promoting it.

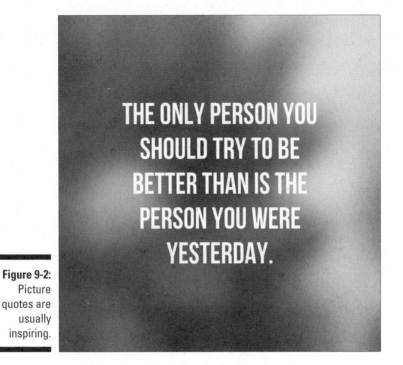

THE ONLY PERSON YOU SHOULD TRY TO BE BETTER THAN IS THE PERSON YOU WERE YESTERDAY.

Figure 9-2:
Picture
quotes are
usually
inspiring.

Programmer/web developer

Much like the graphic designer, the programmer/web developer is typically already contracted or a part of the brand's information technology department. The programmer may be responsible for developing smaller applications to make social media consumption easier for consumers and create smaller websites to drive social media traffic to take particular actions. The programmer may specialize in data and reporting. He is responsible for showing the quantitative performance of the social media department. Overall, the programmer works within the social media team to facilitate the team's needs from a technical perspective.

Knowing Your Role's Expectations

Though each team member has different deliverables and daily critical activities, the expectations of each member are similar.

Most brands require the social media team to meet these expectations:

- ✔ **Follow all rules and procedures.** This includes not compromising proprietary information, brand secrets, or other insider information. All the rules and procedures are established in a brand's employee paperwork, employee agreement, and *nondisclosure agreement (NDA)*.

  If you have to wonder if you're allowed to post particular content on social media, make sure your superiors give their blessing *before* you post it.

- ✔ **Report.** Reporting and analytic aspects are crucial. Most social media team members are responsible for a set of analytics. Typically the social media manager compiles and disseminates the information for the brand's executive team, while a graphic designer or programmer probably won't have the same deliverables. See Chapter 7 for more about analytics. Read Chapter 18 for more about reports.

- ✔ **Gather consumer feedback.** Find and compile what consumers are saying on social media using social media management software such as Hootsuite. Though a team member such as a graphic designer might not be in the trenches and participating on social media on behalf of the brand, they have insight about how the engines work and are expected to relay what they see in social media. The company uses compiled consumer feedback to create reports, case studies, and white papers.

- ✔ **Use platforms natively.** This seems obvious, but every team member must be able to speak in the native voice on each platform, including how and when to speak and listen. Most team members have already demonstrated their platform knowledge, but may have to go through an accreditation or course. The best option is just to read this entire book!

- ✔ **Keep consistent branding.** All team members keep the brand's image, voice, tone, and values consistent across all social media platforms. Chapter 12 talks more about brand.

- ✔ **Maintain crisis protocol.** Consumer complaints will arise and legal issues will surface. A social media pro may even deal with a consumer mutiny. The team should have an action plan and a strict chain of command to effectively deal with the crisis. Chapter 19 talks more about what a decision tree should address.

Getting Assigned Projects

Social media can amplify messages, target particular people, and distribute information different ways. Therefore, the social media team may help with projects related to sales, public relations, marketing, traditional media, or customer service.

These kinds of projects may come your way:

- ✔ **Aiding a traditional media campaign.** If a brand is running a national marketing campaign on television, radio, newspaper, or magazine, social media might supplement the brand's efforts. Smart brands use the traditional outlet as a call to action and encourage consumers and businesses to extend the conversation to social media via a direct response mechanism such as a *landing page* (a one-page website used to collect email addresses), hashtag, or visiting a specific social media platform.

- ✔ **Promoting a new initiative.** Social media often promotes a brand's new philanthropic effort, product, service, or seasonal campaign. These initiatives might only last for a few days but, depending upon its success, the initiative could be ongoing and need to be added to the social media team's responsibilities. See Figure 9-3.

- ✔ **Customer feedback.** Brands use social media to get performance feedback. The company might use platforms to gather metrics or couple social media with traditional surveying and feedback mechanisms. The company entity may run a customer feedback campaign about a particular company aspect, product, or service. Social media's especially helpful because it can gather information by specific keywords and phrases.

- ✔ **Customer acquisition campaign.** Because brands constantly ask for a return on investment for social media, an acquisition campaign is often considered the Holy Grail of assignments. During such a campaign, a company tries to get new customers. They may be a "two-day blast" or they may last a quarter.

- ✔ **Consumer appreciation blitz.** Customer retention, rather than acquisition, may be the focus. During a consumer appreciation blitz, the company lets current customers know they're appreciated. These campaigns may last a few hours or a quarter. We believe this should be an every single day deal, but do appreciate brands that consider customer retention.

Campaign and project duration vary greatly. Average projects typically last a fiscal quarter to a full fiscal year. The social media team meets weekly to review progress and make future decisions about the project's time, effort, and capital.

Project timelines are typically organized into a flow chart like the one in Figure 9-4; that way everyone knows what everyone is working on.

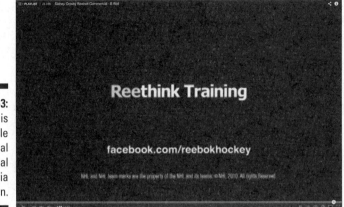

Figure 9-3:
This video is an example of traditional and social media integration.

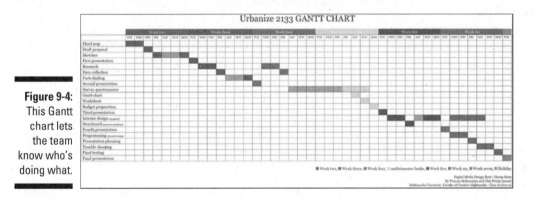

Figure 9-4:
This Gantt chart lets the team know who's doing what.

Being Part of a Business Unit

If you're a single social media professional floating among departments, you'll face some particular hurdles:

- **People don't understand social media.** Employees probably won't understand how to apply social media to business. You might struggle to explain not only social media's validity in a business context but how it impacts the different business parts.

- **People don't like change.** Some employees will throw up barriers or create unintentional resistance. Educate the business segments about social media and emphasize how it will make their lives easier.

- **People are busy.** It's difficult to explain new policy and procedural changes to professionals who are already working on their own responsibilities.

If you know what obstacles will be faced then you will be more prepared to overcome the potential setbacks and know what to expect. The next aspect that needs to be addressed is how to deliver massive value and ensure that the team or business division understands what social media brings to the table.

When you're added to a team, it's important to understand how your department works, who you'll be working with, and who you'll report to.

Communicating Across Business Silos

Communication between different business departments must be efficient. If internal communication isn't streamlined, you lose valuable time with consumers and across departments.

Most companies already have emergency and crisis plans, but it doesn't hurt to be aware that these situations will arise. Make a plan if one doesn't exist. Any company that doesn't have a plan will be impressed.

For example, if a product makes a consumer sick and that consumer makes the company aware on social media, you can nip the issue in the bud. You might need to let the legal department know, alert the finance and accounting departments to pay for the hospital bills, and ask the customer service department to send the customer a gift on behalf of the brand.

However, if the company or social media department doesn't have a plan for communication across departments, this same situation could cause negative public relations or a costly lawsuit.

Some easy ways to transmit communication between respective departments are

- The company's intranet
- Mobile and web-based communication apps such as Yammer
- Email-based chat systems such as Gchat or Google Hangouts
- Computer software such as iMessenger

Quick communication is important because your job is easier when you know who to ask for help or who can answer a question.

Delivering Results

When you're part of a business unit, keep in mind the following:

- ✔ **Avoid the naysayers.** There will be some team members that will never understand the value of social media no matter how it is explained. However, wasting time and energy trying to convince these team members of anything otherwise is not worth it. As such, it's important to be polite and cordial but only utilize the efforts of these team members when absolutely necessary.

- ✔ **Find out what the team thinks is important.** Always consider the thoughts and ideas about what the various team members value. The easier you can make the team members' jobs and the better that you can make them look in the eyes of the superior; the more enjoyable your role will be.

- ✔ **Make the team intricate in your plan.** It's imperative that social media pros make the functional team an important piece of the social media efforts to make them feel more vested in how social media enhances their department.

In addition, social media requires that you set realistic expectations, be quantitative, under-promise, and over-deliver.

See Chapter 16 for more information on those topics.

Chapter 10

Living on the Edge with a Start-Up

In This Chapter

▶ Knowing what type of start-up companies fit with social media

▶ Developing a new social media presence

▶ Facing start-up realities

A *start-up* company is a temporary organization designed to establish a scalable and sustainable business operation. Start-up life means being in the trenches with your friends and hustling to make it bigger than anyone could imagine.

Social media has lots of opportunity within the start-up space — but you have to sacrifice time, security, money, energy, and relationships. You have to get elbows deep in the most monotonous tasks while making strategic decisions that could make or break the company. But this difficult road can be the most fruitful.

In this chapter, you discover what types of start-up companies are likely to have social media in their culture, how to build a successful social media presence from the beginning, and the pros and cons of being a part of the start-up movement.

Knowing Whether You Have What It Takes

If you don't like risks, prefer stability, and aren't willing to put everything on the line, don't pursue the start-up life.

Take a hard look at yourself. For this to be a good decision, you have to be extremely motivated, open to change, laser focused on key performance indicators, able to make bold decisions, and lead confidently.

The opportunity for money doesn't trump your overall happiness, so go confidently in the direction that makes you feel purpose filled.

Start-Ups with Social Media in Their DNA

Newer companies have an advantage over more established companies when it comes to social media:

- ✔ **Start-ups can make quick decisions.** They're typically smaller and more nimble.

- ✔ **There are no set rules.** Start-ups don't have set forms of advertising, marketing, and communication.

- ✔ **Social media takes time rather than money.** Start-ups are typically short on cash; however, they need growth, which social media helps you do.

- ✔ **Start-ups have fewer shareholders.** There's less pressure from outside sources that are demanding a return.

This isn't to say that traditional, more established businesses can't be successful on social media — they absolutely can. This also isn't to say that start-up businesses are automatically great with social media. We're suggesting that certain kinds of start-ups are more likely to succeed via social media for the preceding reasons.

The following sections discuss start-ups that have lots of opportunities for social media pros.

Entrepreneurship idols

Entrepreneurship is often glamorized. People idolize business icons such as Mark Cuban, Tony Hsieh, and Mark Zuckerberg. The public buys their books, attends their speeches, and buys anything that they endorse. Why shouldn't there be this level of emulation? Entrepreneurs have it all. Being your own boss allows you to make your own rules; you'll see the big money and have the freedom and autonomy that we all dream of.

Crowdfunding companies

Crowdfunding is when a large group of people financially support a business venture. This practice typically happens via the Internet, but it can certainly happen offline as well.

Crowdfunding sites are looking for social media pros who understand how to promote campaigns. The funded companies need top people to grow the concept via social media.

Notable crowdfunding platforms include

- ✔ Kickstarter.com (See Figure 10-1.)
- ✔ Indiegogo.com
- ✔ Gofundme.com

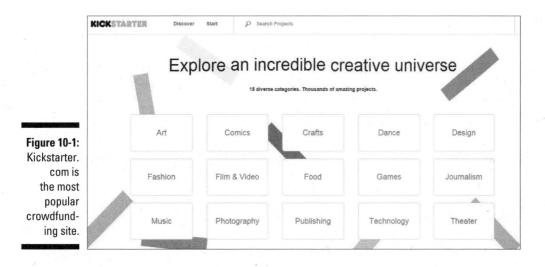

Figure 10-1: Kickstarter.com is the most popular crowdfunding site.

Crowdfunding is mixed with social media because every campaign or project that's up for funding needs help getting the word out. Social media is the best way to spread the word. All crowdfunding sites make it easy to share campaigns on different platforms.

For example, Brooks has been on the small team that built a crowdfunding platform from scratch called ENDcrowd.com (see Figure 10-2), which helps organizations that fight human slavery. By using a WordPress content-management system website platform, a crowdfunding template, and some WordPress plug-ins, the site was ready to launch and collect funds within a few months.

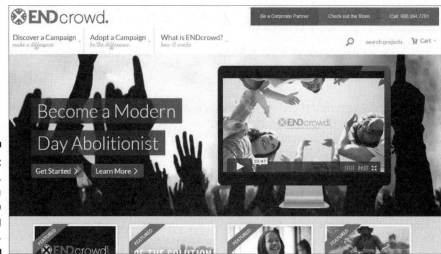

Figure 10-2:
ENDcrowd.
com is a
start-up
crowdfunding
site.

E-commerce

Electronic commerce firms are prime candidates for social media pros. Sales and acquisitions, via their websites, are their number-one goal. Most e-commerce start-ups would rather invest time (with social media) than money (traditional media) if they can to grow their brand.

Smart e-commerce companies start with a wide range of activities: email marketing, *search engine optimization (SEO),* pay-per-click ads, and social media.

Software and SAAS

Software and *Software as a Service (SAAS)* companies are prime candidates for start-ups in need of social media pros. Software and SAAS companies typically focus on how to solve problems and make life easier for consumers or businesses. They can discover what those problems are by watching what people talk about on social media.

Software and SAAS are also constantly evolving and trying to figure out how to find subscribers and users and fill their needs. As such, social media offers the perfect opportunity to find data, use feedback, and continually improve the company's products. No other form of communication can reach current and potential users at a scale that social media can. Software companies are aware of this.

Take Jet.com, for example. When Jet launched, thousands of people shared the site via social media. Top social media influencers were promised early access, a trial product, and equity in the start-up. People didn't even know what Jet.com did. Regardless, it became a household name. See Figure 10-3.

Figure 10-3:
Jet.com launched via social media.

Social media management firms

A *social media management* firm handles another company's social media platforms. This seems like an obvious choice, but social media management firms' needs have two parts. Obviously they serve client needs, but the firms themselves need social media for client acquisition, retention, and community management.

Social media management companies are always looking for social media pros to serve as contractors.

To find agencies in your area, search for **social media agency** along with your city, state, or zip code.

Marketing and advertising agencies

The marketing and advertising industries are constantly looking for social media pros. Because advertisers are used to traditional media, they have to reinvent their offerings.

Bootstrapping a Social Media Team

Bootstrapping means completing a nearly impossible action. In terms of start-ups, that means a lack of manpower and financial resources.

The lack of cash, brand equity, and resources is another reason social media is crucial for start-ups. Social media is virtually free with the exception of effort and time. You can build sales, data, and a customer experience with your social media expertise.

If you're working with a start-up, as quickly as possible establish your responsibilities and the time associated. Don't overwork yourself if you can request a larger budget and more time to take the load off yourself. Put in the necessary work, but bring in the right people. See Figure 10-4.

Most people in the start-up environment believe that working hard all of the time is the only way to be successful, but it's also the quickest way to burn out and self destruct.

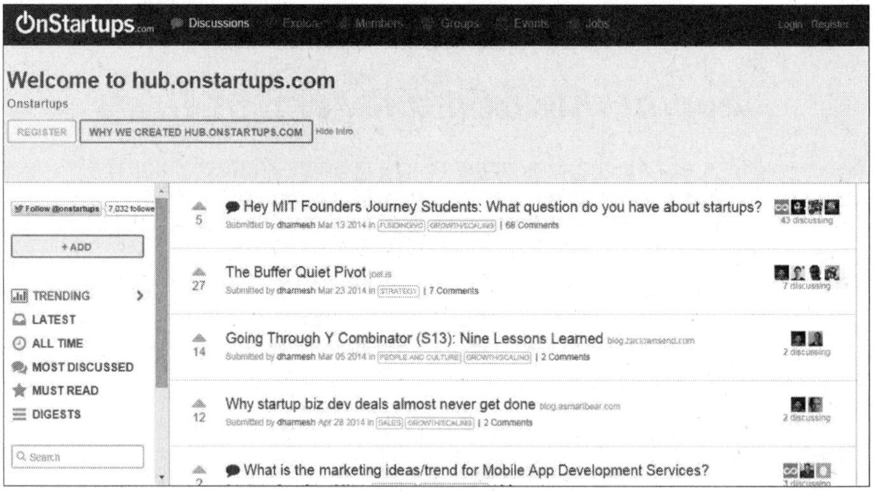

Figure 10-4:
OnStartups.
com is the
premiere
start-up
blog about
entrepre-
neurship
and start-up
entities.

Clearly defining social media roles

Roles vary from company to company, as do the resources that you have.

What's important is to be a part of the start-up team and fulfill the roles and responsibilities that have been delegated to you. If you have any sort of manpower at your discretion, use these best practices:

✔ **Build a list of roles and responsibilities.** Explain each position's roles and responsibilities throughout the hiring and onboarding process. Document the responsibilities and sign off on them via an employee contract. Also make sure to carefully explain your standards and expectations throughout the documentation; sign off on rewards and repercussions as well. Chapter 4 delves into roles and responsibilities in more detail.

✔ **Explain, show, watch, and refine.** Don't guess whether your team members understand the tasks you've defined. *Explain* to them how you expect tasks to be completed, *show* them exactly how you want it done, *watch* them perform the task, and continually *refine* the work.

✔ **Hold your team accountable for results.** At a minimum, spend two minutes in the morning discussing the previous day's results, today's work, and any resources your team might need. Hold a weekly one-on-one where you review each team member's overall progress. Provide praise, consequences, or rewards during this time.

Wearing multiple hats

In the start-up world, every day is new: new projects, new challenges, new customers.

That might scare some people, but a start-up social media pro embraces that constant change. You might have to wear these hats:

✔ Organizational management

✔ Marketing, advertising, and sales

✔ Customer service

✔ Information technology

✔ Financial and accounting management

Focus on your key performance indicators (KPIs) and goals, but remain open to changing circumstances and pitch in at a moment's notice. See Chapter 16 to find more information on KPIs.

You'll have to take on responsibilities that fall outside social media and require working after hours, but you're getting valuable business experience. Furthermore, great start-ups reward people who were there in the beginning. Brooks has answered phones as a customer service representative, signed off on a major purchase decision, created a Facebook advertising campaign, and developed a hiring plan for warehouse workers — all on the same day!

For more information on what it takes to be a successful entrepreneur, consider reading *Start-up Hats* by David Gardner. The book details the skills and abilities that entrepreneurs must master before they can reap the benefits from a start-up business.

Doing whatever it takes

To be a successful start-up, you must be willing to fail constantly, perform unfamiliar tasks, and sacrifice in just about every way possible.

As always, you have to decide what makes you happy. Ask yourself the following questions:

- What will I have to sacrifice to be a part of this start-up? Is there an *opportunity cost* to me? For example, if you work at a start-up for $30,000 a year but my market rate is $90,000 per year, then the opportunity cost is $60,000 per year. In other words, what potential monetary compensation am I giving up to work here?

- What's the return for building this start-up? Will this experience help me create my own start-up? Will I get what I need to take care of my family?

- What are the main reasons I should put all my stock into this start-up? What are the main reasons I shouldn't? Is there any way for me to hedge my risk?

If you choose a start-up, give it all you've got. Don't second-guess yourself. If you're curious about what you're getting yourself into, Entremanureship.com was created by entrepreneurs about the realities you'll encounter in the startup world. See Figure 10-5.

Focusing on direct response deliverables

Since start-ups are typically lean when it comes to manpower and resources, every revenue-driving activity and expense is carefully looked at. As such, social media is asked what its ROI is. If your answer is, "We're building a lot of good will with our fan base," then you're setting yourself up to be stripped of resources, or worse — fired.

This is exactly why tying down organizations to their objective goals is so important. Focus on sales and acquisitions first. Let the long-term benefits supplement your efforts.

Figure 10-5:
Entrema-
nureship.
com is
about start-
up realities.

Start-up entities are looking for these types of deliverables:

✔ **Direct response sales:** Track every promotional post on social media, including the link that you post, the landing pages, and the ultimate websites that you lead them to. How many clicks, impressions, and sales do you get? Have as many metrics as possible that are related to ROI and costs.

✔ **Permission marketing variables:** Marketing is easier if you have contact information for your current and potential customers. You may have heard Internet marketing gurus emphasize, "The money is in the list." This is true. You might not make a sale today, but you can build a relationship with someone, and ultimately, sell them products and services. This information may take the form of email addresses, physical mailing addresses, and cell phone numbers. This data feeds other top-line building programs such as email marketing, direct mail, and SMS (text message) marketing.

✔ **Customer data:** Having contact information is great, but knowing what touches the hearts and minds of your target consumers is better. *Customer-relationship management (CRM)* databases such as `Nimble.com` or `Salesforce.com` can easily hold your intangible information. Chapter 7 reviews Nimble in more detail, and Chapter 4 reviews Salesforce; see Figure 10-6.

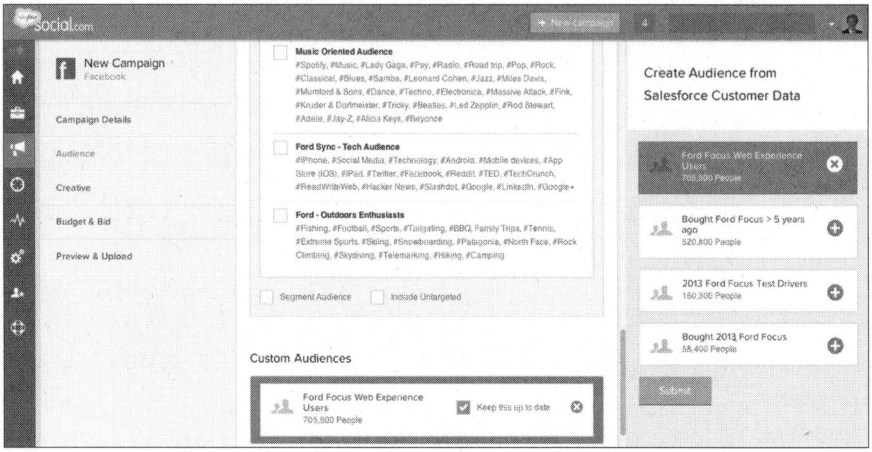

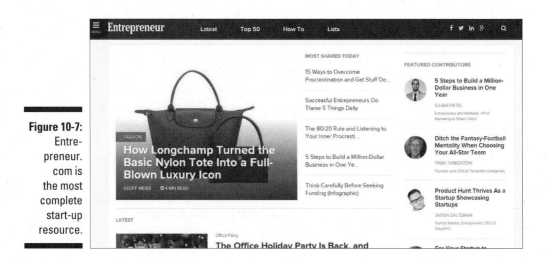

Figure 10-6:
Salesforce is a social media CRM.

Pros and Cons to Start-Up Life

Imagine coming and going as you please. Focusing on what's most important to you. Hiring someone to do work for you. Hiring a manager to manage those employees. This is a possible reality if your start-up makes it. Even better, you might get taken public or be bought or merged with another company. There are no guarantees that this will ever happen, but if this is your ideal, becoming part of a start-up is a chance to make it. To get the full scope on entrepreneurship, read `Entrepreneur.com`. See the site in Figure 10-7.

In the meantime, a social media pro faces lots of pros and cons in a start-up.

Figure 10-7:
Entre-
preneur.
com is
the most
complete
start-up
resource.

Pros

Consider a start-up if you're a grinder or a hustler. The key is staying focused on providing value and doing activities that yield the best results. To stay motivated and engaged with the start-up community, spend some time over at www.EpicLaunch.com and connect with other entrepreneurs. See Figure 10-8.

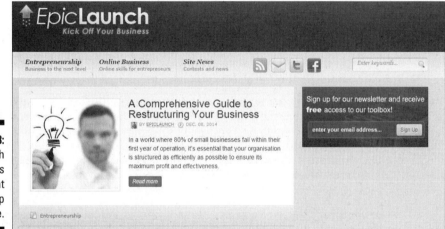

Figure 10-8: EpicLaunch provides great start-up guidance.

Start-ups are a good fit only if you're a proactive leader who manage his time well. If you aren't excellent at focusing on specific results, then the rest of the benefits aren't worth the risk.

Potential equity

What start-ups can't afford in terms of salary, benefits, or perks, they can make up for in stock options or a percent of ownership. The best part is that once you've worked for a time, you've earned that percentage for the rest of your life.

To get the most out of a start-up and its equity positions, do the following:

✔ **Ask early and often.** Right out of the gate, ask if and when equity and stock options will be available to employees. The start-up should have contracts that outline when equity vests, but clearly establish that you're interested in equity. *Equity vesting* means that you'll have a contract to work for a specific amount of time before you can earn your shares or ownership percentage.

Check with your superiors about your opportunity to earn equity on a quarterly basis and always ensure to get these conversations in writing. Otherwise, you'll risk having to prove a verbal or implied promise rather than having something definitive in writing.

✔ **Know your return.** You need to know if sacrificing a salary today is worth the weight of equity and stock options in the future. For example, do you feel confident that your start-up can get a $100 million dollar valuation and sell for twice that? The best indicators will come from valuations that are provided by investment firms during capital raises and your financial reports. See Figure 10-9.

If there isn't consistency between what the entrepreneurs are saying and what the financials are saying, steer clear.

✔ **Get it in writing.** Implied contracts are great for building trust with your employer, they're also a quick way to lose the equity that you're after.

Always get your equity and stock options in the form of legal documentation. You and the start-up should sign off on it. The agreement should review the equity percentage, vesting periods, limitations of your sale of stock, and any provisions that could hinder you from your claim to equity and stock options. For more information regarding these financial terms, visit investopedia.com.

Figure 10-9: A valuation calculator can help you figure out how much a start-up is potentially worth right now.

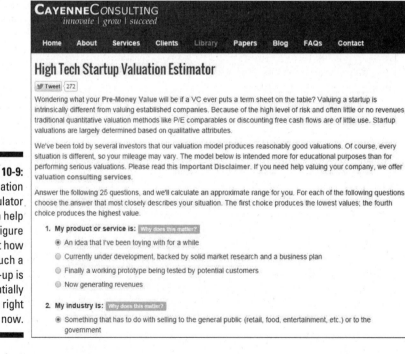

Every day is different

Some people consider the day-to-day at a start-up absolutely crazy: hardly any rules, no set standards, and pursuing a completely different social media direction on a whim. Brooks has been in charge of marketing departments and had to jump into customer service, operations, hiring, and programming all in the same day. Even if you don't know exactly what you're doing, a start-up demands that you figure it out. Embrace the fast-moving change.

Broader scope of responsibilities

Start-up responsibilities can't be matched in any other business phase. You'll expand your skills and knowledge at a start-up. Your daily responsibilities may vary from accounting, finance, forecasting, human resources, information technology, management, or marketing.

Organizational influence

Arguably one of the largest advantages of a start-up is the influence you have. It's almost like being an in-house consultant since the team will value your opinion so heavily. There's no upper management to shut down your ideas, and you have free reign to begin initiatives. Even if you didn't start the company, you can become part of the ownership. Treat the start-up like your own business and create the type of culture that you like.

If you want a guaranteed paycheck, we recommend the start-up route, but if you're looking to completely own the profit, the consultant route is for you.

You also create your budget, responsibilities, expectations, and timelines. Attract and hire people you want to be around. If there's anything about your department that you aren't satisfied with, change it — you're in charge. For more thoughts and ideas on how to become a standout leader in a start-up, check out Derek Lidow online; see Figure 10-10.

Creativity and passion

Start-ups are notorious for their ability to encourage, foster, and reward significant creativity and passion. In no other environment can you take these kinds of risks or start so quickly. In a start-up environment, passion facilitates thinking and action. Established companies are typically more conservative.

Challenge yourself to take action with your creative ideas; be prepared to fail fast. If you try ten ideas, you might find one worth keeping around.

Cons

Being in a start-up offers some good things, but there are negative factors to be aware of. However, we're not here to lambast start-ups. In the following sections we discuss the potential downsides of being in a start-up. But we also give you another way of looking at the supposed shortcoming.

Figure 10-10:
Derek Lidow
focuses
on start-up
leadership.

No name recognition

When you're a part of the start-up world, no one is going to know who you are. The lack of brand equity and impressions can make it difficult to grow the business.

These challenges are obvious when you're negotiating with vendors, trying to sell to your target consumers, and raising capital.

However, we challenge you to look at the lack of brand awareness with the following viewpoints:

- ✔ **Make yourself a household name.** You can build the good will and reputation necessary.
- ✔ **Every person matters.** When no one knows who you are, every single person you communicate with is important.
- ✔ **You set the tone.** If no one has heard of your company, you can clearly explain your offering and you decide how your story should be told.

Lack of stability

If having a guaranteed salary, benefits, retirement, or perks are crucial, then a start-up environment isn't for you.

Start-ups don't pay well and typically offer stock options and equity instead. If you have children or other dependents to support, then the start-up environment is one that you have to carefully weigh.

We've gone unpaid or provided just enough to stay at the poverty line. Not only that, but our retirement and medical benefits were entirely our responsibility. There's no beating around the bush when it comes to this topic: Start-ups can make you very uncomfortable financially. However, if you choose that path, stick to the decision and remind yourself to stay positive and to have faith in where you're headed.

Never quit a full-time job with benefits if you can't afford to go months or years without a steady paycheck.

Probability of failure

What's the likelihood that a start-up will fail? It's pretty significant. But a lot of them succeed. For an idea of what it takes to truly make it, check out the tech-centric investment group at www.ycombinator.com. More successful startups come out of this business incubator than anywhere else, and the folks freely share their knowledge and experiences through their website. See Figure 10-11.

Businesses that focus on building better products and services, genuinely serving people, and solving problems are those most likely to make it.

And suppose that your start-up does fail. At least you'll have knowledge and skills from the experience that you can take wherever you go.

Extremely hard work

All the rumors you've heard about long hours and mountains of work are true. If you're all in at a start-up, expect between 60 and 90 hours of work a week. You'll have to sacrifice time that you'd normally spend with friends, family, and interests. If you let a start-up life consume all your time, then it will.

Start-ups are notoriously bad at focusing on end results and putting their efforts toward what matters at the end of the day. To get everyday, monotonous personal and professional tasks done, use a website like www.TaskRabbit.com. This site, shown in Figure 10-12, connects you to local people who have the skills to get time-consuming tasks (such as data entry) done for you very affordably.

Determine the roles and responsibilities for your core team members. Don't duplicate efforts.

Figure 10-11:
Y Combinator is a start-up accelerator.

Constant chaos

If you're comfortable with the same routine every day, stay out of a start-up.

Information flies and decisions are made fast. Our suggestion is to turn the chaos into something positive. Harness the energy. Challenge yourself to improve.

If you have trouble with change, we recommend *Who Moved My Cheese?* by Dr. Spencer Johnson. This short read teaches you about the four typical reactions people have when there's change at work.

Figure 10-12:
TaskRabbit can handle everyday tasks.

Chapter 11

Starting Your Own Social Media Company

*H*ave you decided that working for The Man isn't for you? Congratulations and welcome to the wonderful world of entrepreneurship.

The tools and services you need to build a business from the ground up are abundant, ever improving, and affordable.

Giving You a Heads Up

We know that you're excited to get started, but keep three ideas in mind:

- ✔ **Hedge your risk.** Unless you're independently wealthy, don't quit your job and go after an entrepreneurial venture. Build an income and *ease* into the entrepreneurial world.

- ✔ **Partner whenever possible.** Don't try to do everything yourself. Find established professionals and agencies where you can build good will and help one another. Establish mutually beneficial value.

- ✔ **Solve problems and facilitate needs.** Focus on the imminent pain and problems that your target clients have. Study your market, figure out the needs, and combine those needs with your proposed offering.

Brooks entered social media by writing a book and creating a web TV show called "Triple Your Tips." The premise was simple: Teach full-service restaurant employees how to have more fun and make more money. Though the company ended up making money and helping Brooks land consulting gigs, the market wasn't interested in the original content. The restaurant industry was more intrigued by leveraging social media to attract and keep restaurant customers. This led to Brooks's social media consulting firms.

Establishing Your Offering

Though your agency's direction might be ever-changing, strictly define what your offering is to your marketplaces.

For example, maybe you start in the general social media market. Then LinkedIn ads became your passion, and you know the biggest need is advertising for lawyers that specialize in DUI cases in the city of Chicago. That sounds extremely detailed, but owning that sort of sub-niche can be lucrative and relatively easy.

Don't chase money when you're establishing an agency.

Just because companies are paying big bucks for Instagram content that you don't understand (or care to) doesn't mean your business model should provide it. Instead, ask yourself questions like these:

- ✔ What makes you unique?
- ✔ What are you excellent at doing within social media?
- ✔ What could you happily do all day?
- ✔ Can you make a decent living doing this? How do you know?

The first three questions help you find passion, which we delve into deeper momentarily. The last question comes down to your financial viability.

Defining your scope of work

Do what you enjoy. When you start an agency, it's smart to offer between one and five services in which you're an expert.

It's better to specialize in something no one else can offer rather than offer a little bit of everything. For example, consider these two service offerings:

Agency 1: We offer every single social media service that you can imagine. We can manage ads, develop websites, develop creative, write sales copy, and much more for all social media platforms.

Agency 2: We offer full-scale management of Instagram accounts for women's handbags.

How can one person possibly be the best at all of the things listed in the first ad? The second example is laser focused both in terms of offering and their target market. For a good example of laser focus within social media advertising, visit `jonloomer.com`, whose website is in Figure 11-1.

✔ **Get as specific as possible.** When you're developing your offering, focus on your skills and what you enjoy.

✔ **Never stop studying your marketplace.** Spend time each day reading articles, connecting with people in your industry, and working in the trenches.

✔ **Add services over time.** Add services only after testing and you're positive you handle the scope and delivery of the work.

✔ **Outsource whenever possible.** Have a list of other vendors who you might be able to refer work out to or *white label* (they do the work; you represent the work through your brand so the client doesn't necessarily know that the work was contracted). Farming out work creates good will in your industry and may entitle you to premium prices; you can mark up the services.

Figure 11-1: Jon Loomer focuses on advanced Facebook advertising.

Designing your ideal workday

Having your own social media agency should allow you to do only the things you want to do. The whole point of starting your own social media agency is designing your ideal workday, and even your life, the way that you want.

Imagine your perfect work day — no limitations. Write out the answer to this question:

If there were no limitations, describe your perfect workday that you could live repeatedly for the rest of your life.

What time do you get to work? What tasks do you perform? Do you work with any employees or contractors? What's your relationship with your colleagues? Who are your clients and what's your relationship with them? What do you see, feel, think about and experience throughout a day?

Envisioning your ideal client

If you own your agency, not only should you work on projects you like, but you should work for the clients you like, too.

To help find your ideal clients, answer this question:

If there were no limitations, describe your perfect client that you could work with repeatedly for the rest of your life.

Here's why this activity is so effective:

- ✔ It reveals what your clients are looking for and how you can provide it. Happy clients mean repeat business and strong recommendations.
- ✔ You'll know how to strengthen your client's business.
- ✔ Your marketing collateral will speak to your potential clients because you can hone in on their needs.

Your ideal client may change as you progress. You'll learn what you enjoy the most about working with clients and what you don't enjoy. We can't emphasize enough the joy and purpose that you'll feel when you genuinely enjoy the people that you serve.

Creating the "ideal day" for yourself and your "ideal client" may seem a bit hokey, but the exercise helps give you clarity and focus.

Making It Clear How You'll Compete: Your USP

Be crystal clear about who you are, what you offer, and how you're different from every other provider. Your *unique selling proposition (USP)* is the core reason you're different from anyone in your market. Answer why your target customer should do business with you instead of anyone else.

For instance, if your social media services build sales and impressions, then you have to know why your agency is better than direct mail firms, television, radio, pay-per-click advertising, and other, similar entities.

Chapter 3 talks, in detail, about forming your USP.

Beware of two pitfalls when picking your USP:

- ✔ **Don't offer all unique selling propositions.** You can't have the most services delivered the quickest at the lowest cost with the absolute best customer service imaginable. Pick one of those selling points and run with it.

- ✔ **Don't try to compete solely on price.** Price isn't a sustainable business model; it's too easy for a competitor to undercut your prices. Price has no customer loyalty associated with it.

Handling Legal Matters

Protect yourself. Handle legal stuff first after you start your business.

If you own a business, you're going to get sued.

We don't mean to scare you; but anyone can sue anyone at any time and for any reason. As long as you provide excellent service, take care of people, and put your legal ducks in a row, then you should be fine.

Legal services and business incorporation used to be wildly expensive. Thanks to the Internet, almost anyone can become a small business owner in less than an hour and at a fraction of the cost.

LegalZoom

`LegalZoom.com` offers business services and documents. You can legally establish your business, establish copyrights and trademarks and so forth.

Work with the customer service agents at LegalZoom to establish what sort of entity you're establishing. Take their recommendations about what you absolutely need to get up and running. This process takes about an hour and cost you somewhere between $300 and $500, depending on your products and services.

LegalZoom, shown in Figure 11-2, also provides a directory of attorneys and members get flat-fee legal plans. These attorneys, who are reviewed by LegalZoom members, give you an objective view of their services and abilities. Similar legal help is much more expensive and may lack the same credentials.

Every state and country has different fees and requirements, but you can have nearly everything you need legally to start a business for under $500.

Figure 11-2: LegalZoom.com can help you set up.

SBA.gov

The Small Business Administration (SBA) is a U.S. government agency that services entrepreneurs and small businesses through the three Cs: capital, contracts, and counseling. Though the SBA is mainly known for offering government-backed loans, it also provides exceptional legal services to new businesses. Consider the pro bono assistance. For more information or to begin the process with the SBA, visit `sba.gov`. You can see the site in Figure 11-3.

Figure 11-3:
SBA.gov offers small business guidance.

Banking

You need to have a safe place to keep all that cash that you'll be raking in, and underneath your mattress isn't safe. After you're established as a business and have legal protection on your side, figure out where you'll be collecting, saving, and investing your money.

Small business account

When you go to start your business, you'll probably be walked through the process or given an invitation to establish small business banking accounts.

At a bare minimum, set up small business checking and small business savings accounts that are completely separate from your personal banking accounts.

We both use Bank of America small business services and their free online accounting application called Wave.

Here are three of the best banks for small businesses:

- ✔ Wells Fargo
- ✔ Bank of America
- ✔ Citizens Bank

We recommend these banks because they offer lots of different services but have dedicated account reps. You may want to explore a small-to-medium–sized local banking institution or credit union; they typically go above and beyond and have a significant vested interest in keeping your business.

Minimum standards

Once you have your small business checking and savings account, you're almost ready to open.

Small business banking has a lot of nuances, but these suggestions will help you stay legally compliant and get the most out of your money:

- ✔ **Avoid transactional fees**. Get and compare quotes from at least three different banks. Which offers the most complete customer service and takes the least?

- ✔ **Let consumers pay how they want.** Some clients will prefer to pay via ACH, Google Wallet, or PayPal, while more progressive companies may want to pay using Snapcash, Venmo, or Apple Pay. Ask your current and prospective clients how they want to pay.

- ✔ **Keep everything transparent.** For example, your fraud radar should go up if a brand-new client insists on sending and receiving money via wire transfers. Your bank is on your side, so stay in touch with them about how to accurately and thoroughly keep all your banking straight.

Accounting Best Practices

Accounting in your new business can be kind of a pain, but accounting haphazardly can result in fines and significant legal trouble. You have to pay taxes on all your earnings.

You might as well have an excellent system in place. At a bare minimum, file your taxes quarterly or yearly, depending on the state and tax classification that you chose when you incorporated.

The good news is that proper accounting helps you save more money, establish more tax-deductible expenses, and stay organized. Excellent accounting standards help you make decisions.

Wave

Wave is a completely free service that offers cloud-based software and tools for small businesses. Wave specializes in invoicing, accounting, payroll, payments, and personal finance services. To find out more, see Figure 11-4 or visit `waveapps.com`.

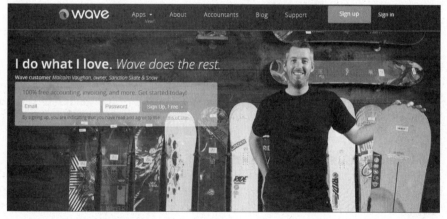

Figure 11-4: Wave is free small business accounting software.

QuickBooks

One of the best small business accounting software programs comes from QuickBooks (`quickbooks.intuit.com`). QuickBooks costs you anywhere from $8 to $40 per month, depending on the number of services that you want. The software helps you prepare your quarterly and yearly state and federal tax returns, track your deductible expenses, create proposals and invoices, and download all your bank transactions. See Figure 11-5.

We both use QuickBooks to run our businesses and recommend it to anyone who's brand new to social media consulting.

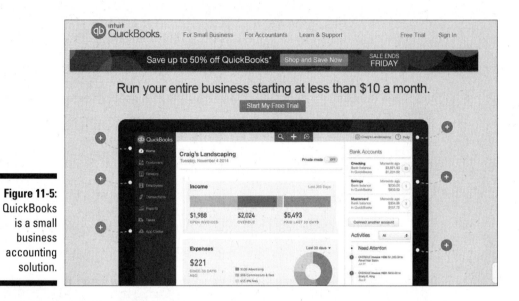

Figure 11-5:
QuickBooks
is a small
business
accounting
solution.

Local sources

You might want to consider full accounting services or consider hiring a part-time controller or *chief financial officer (CFO)*. Generate revenue before making this decision! Your financial and accounting costs should be somewhere between 5 and 20 percent of your total costs.

If accounting and financial management aren't your strong suit, consider offering equity or some other type of ownership to a local firm in exchange for top-notch assistance. Search online for **part-time controller** or **part-time CFO** along with your city, state, and zip code. After you find a few reputable options, compare the services and costs of three firms.

Graphic Design

It's worth your time to invest in a decent graphical representation of your brand. Having an attractive, unique style that brands your entity without spending a fortune is extremely important. You can pay for more advanced graphic design down the line when you have more income.

A graphic design background is an advantage. Even if you don't, you can find online resources (that can become even more valuable if you start offering web design or graphic design).

Paying thousands or tens of thousands of dollars for a professionally crafted email signature, business card design, or logo is a waste of money. Design creative on a shoestring budget that will appeal to your current and potential clients.

Chapter 12 talks more about brand creation and design ideas.

Fiverr

Fiverr.com is a global marketplace where people are willing to provide products or services for five dollars.

1. **Search for a gig (such as** graphic design**).**

   See Figure 11-6.

2. **Sort the results to find the most reputable and accomplished service providers.**

   The service providers will dictate exactly what they can deliver and how long it will take them.

3. **Buy the gig for five bucks through PayPal.**

4. **Tell the service provider exactly what you want.**

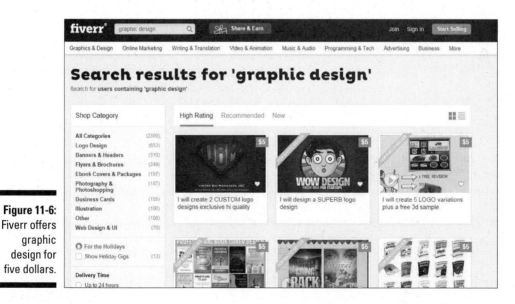

Figure 11-6: Fiverr offers graphic design for five dollars.

Though the base pricing is only five dollars, many of the vendors offer add-ons and premium services such as faster delivery, higher quality, and multiple completed projects. If you love the work that the vendor does then make sure to keep in touch with them and offer your vendors more projects directly so that communication can be streamlined.

We start work through Fiverr and then take the job to a platform where the graphic designers are more vested. We describe 99designs.com, which is just such a site, next.

99designs

This site is a step up from fiverr.com in terms of quality, but 99designs.com is still much cheaper than an advertising agency.

With 99designs, you'll pay a few hundred to a few thousand dollars to showcase a project and explain what you're looking for. Graphic designers compete and create designs for you to choose from. You get to pick from dozens of designs; send those you like through a few rounds of selection and give feedback before a final round.

When you're starting, go with the lower bronze packages. You don't need the premium features until you start turning a profit.

oDesk

oDesk.com is the world's largest online workplace. Although oDesk hosts different kinds of freelancers, some of the world's best graphic designers are here because of the site's size. See Figure 11-7.

Figure 11-7: oDesk is a freelancer marketplace.

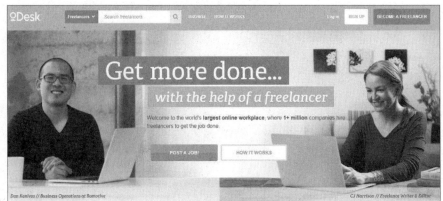

The same sort of formula applies to oDesk as Fiverr and 99designs: Post a job, hire a graphic designer, track their progress, and pay them via credit card, PayPal, or bank account. oDesk typically falls between 99designs and Fiverr pricewise, but it depends on the work and the vendor.

Developing Your Company's Website

Your website, your home, is where you showcase leads, content, and company information. It's worth your time to make it attractive and functional. If your website isn't aesthetically pleasing and doesn't complete the *call to action (CTA)* that you need it to, try again.

Although you should explore other best practices, and things certainly change over time, we firmly suggest following these rules:

- ✔ **Make it responsive:** This format automatically sizes your site for the device it's being viewed on, so it looks attractive on a laptop, tablet, and a smartphone.

- ✔ **Use a content-management system:** This platform allows you update via HTML. The CMS platforms like WordPress are common. To save a lot of time, money, and headaches, your web platform must make most of edits.

- ✔ **Capture leads:** You begin collecting email addresses from day one. People buy from those they trust. Emphasize data collection and provide value to your target consumers through email marketing. We prefer `iContact.com`, `Pinpointe.com`, and `GetResponse.com`, which work nicely with websites and have automated emails.

- ✔ **Make your content rich:** Search engines prefer activity. Websites that answer questions like human beings are great for *search engine optimization (SEO)*. Write content or blog about topics that your current and potential clients ask you about.

- ✔ **Integrate social:** Have plug-ins, or widgets, or whatever else you need to make it easy for people to share your site across multiple social networking sites. Bring attention to your presence on social media and encourage visitors to connect with you on these platforms.

From here, you need to get a website address, set up hosting, establish an email marketing vendor, and start creating awesome content.

Buying a URL

Picking a name either means absolutely nothing (and your service becomes synonymous with your industry) or your name tells consumers exactly what you do.

Whatever you do, don't spend too much time thinking about your name. Spend more of your time developing an awesome product and taking care of your clients.

✔ Don't spend hundreds of dollars on a website URL.

✔ When you have a name, search through a few domain-purchasing platforms for the address that you want the most.

✔ Expect to pay between $10 and $50 for the URL and between $30 and $60 per year for hosting.

✔ Buy a website domain from one of these sites, which have top-notch online business pros who help you:

   • `1and1.com`

   • `Bluehost.com`

   • `GoDaddy.com`

✔ Don't let a service provider upsell you on dedicated servers, SSL certificates, and site masking. Make a bit of money first and *then* bulk up your online features.

You can buy multiple URLs and

✔ Redirect them to a single website.

✔ Position the websites around different strategic focuses.

For example, if you're a social media manager named Tom Allen in Wake Forest, then you might want to brand your company with your name: allensocial.com. However, to help people understand what you do and to appeal to local clients, you might want to grab another URL: wakeforest socialmediamanagement.com. The latter could redirect to the former. That second web address doesn't roll off your tongue, but people will know where you are and what you do!

Strikingly

This emerging web-development platform is an easy way to throw up an attractive response that requires no programming knowledge. Just pick a template, type in the content, and upload your pictures. `Strikingly.com` is only $20 per month and allows you to create five websites. It isn't as flexible as other CMS platforms, but it does let you insert custom Cascading Style Sheets (CSS) and additional programming.

WordPress

WordPress is by far our top recommendation for a website platform. It's flexible and affordable, and it works well with search engines. You can customize it, and even though it might cost a few extra bucks to hire a programmer to customize your website, WordPress offers almost unlimited tools.

The free blogging platform is at wordpress.com; get more information at wordpress.org.

Don't use a system that you can't change yourself. Save some money — try to make manual changes yourself before hiring a web developer to do it.

Client Acquisition

Most new businesses ask this question: How do I sell my stuff to people? Find a common need, apply your skills, and fill the need.

Beyond that, these methods work for getting clients:

- ✔ **Elevator pitch.** Chapter 8 tells you how to get it right.

- ✔ **Creating and promoting quality content.** You have lots to consider. Don't post the exact same content on multiple platforms. Search engines don't like duplicated content. Chapter 3 helps.

- ✔ **Answering questions.** Look for opportunities via social media to answer questions and solve the problems that others are having. Giving a little now can turn into a huge opportunity later. Chapter 3 details this idea.

- ✔ **Contacting people you know.** Chapter 12 talks about networking in detail.

Chapter 8 tells you more about how to close the deal with a client.

Part IV

Becoming a Top Social Media Pro

Get rid of any doubt that you're dressing professionally after reading the skills and hints at www.dummies.com/extras/gettingasocialmediajob.

In this part . . .

✔ Network, on a schedule, with people you already know.

✔ Decide what your brand includes.

✔ Write a killer, up-to-date résumé.

✔ Get familiar with different interview types, get help anticipating questions, and read advice about following up.

✔ See more at www.dummies.com.

Chapter 12

Building Your Network and Your Brand

*T*imes are changing. You know it. You feel it. You see it everywhere. Companies are figuring out needs, costs, and investments, just like individuals are. People are beginning to decide what really has value and they're looking for positive attention.

Social media runs on information. The flow is constant, large, and easy to access; you have to identify what resonates with you. Social media's appeal is that you can self-censor rather than leave it to the media to set agendas. When you watch TV news, program directors and production people — not you — decide what you learn about.

Social media gives you control — control of your voice and look.

Understanding the power of social media is simple: Be open to receiving and sharing information. That's it. If something strikes you as informative or interesting, pass it on.

Hop on board and use social media to help expand your network — people who have interests similar to yours. Those people know other people. Connecting with the larger network increases your chances of hearing about job opportunities and finding new people in common with companies you're interested in.

In this chapter we tell you how to make the most of your existing network, how to expand your reach, and how to launch your personal brand.

Have We Met?

A million networking sites are available today. Some are casual, while others are more professional. They all work pretty much the same: You create a profile and the system finds people you have contact information for. They're your *followers* or *connections* or *contacts.* Start with the contacts you already know (in email address book, Gmail contacts, Facebook friends, and so on).

Networking sites allow you to introduce yourself to people you may not have ever met otherwise. The sites help you get out there and be found. Say you just moved. As far as your contacts know, you're still living in your mom's garage trying to launch your social media company. Social media lets you announce your move to your friends and family. Professionally, social media allows you to announce your presence in the new city, and can help you establish new connections.

If you want to limit your network, you can create a group. Creating a group allows you to limit access, without limiting the ability to connect. This may make sense if the group is comprised of people with specialized skills. Members who don't have the specialized skills could be distracting to the core audience.

Networking Effectively

Connections can help drive viewers to your profile. Industry connections and circles of influence enhance your credibility.

Don't do it: Most people that establish themselves as social media pros are quick to go into business circles looking for job opportunities or trying to sell their social media skills. To network effectively and set yourself up for success down the line, you absolutely must resist the urge to do this.

People know that you're excited and eager to help, but you must get to know business people personally and professionally before ever asking them for anything.

Instead, focus on the relationship and prove your merit. Promote your contact or the contact's company. Use your social media prowess to share news related to the company — not stock price, but the things that humanize the person (or company): community event participation, charitable donations, and volunteerism.

Download the Networkr app (www.networkrapp.com) to meet other professionals in your area who share interests. This app, shown in Figure 12-1, is especially useful at networking meetings, conferences, and other large gatherings. It's a social media tool that helps people connect in real life, too.

Figure 12-1:
Network-
rapp.com
allows you
to share
interests.

How can you network effectively and get where you want to go?

- ✔ **Establish target connections.** Make a spreadsheet of your most important contacts and those that you want to connect with. Who are the 20 most important people in your life right now? And what 20 people could effectively change your life if you were in their good graces? Add all these people to your list, along with their contact information and anything that you know about them, professionally and personally.

- ✔ **Make a daily action plan.** Knowing who you want to talk to and keep in constant communication with is vital, but absolutely nothing is more important than making daily progress (connecting with new people and identifying potential connections). Software such as nimble.com reminds you when and how to contact your key people (people you already know).

  Make and maintain at least ten relationships per day.

- ✔ **Give before you ask.** This seems obvious, but it's extremely important to provide value up front before ever asking for anything in return. Figure out how you can help others, and don't be afraid to ask for their help over time when you need it. What you're attempting to do is to build goodwill — but not solely giving just to receive something in return.

✔ **Be interesting.** If you have a professional or personal interest worth talking about, then make sure to share this with others! People are always willing to learn, so make sure that you educate others on a topical area of interest — or better yet, invite them to participate. We've found that expertise in fine wine, craft beer, and up-and-coming sports such as FootGolf and Pickleball are always intriguing.

✔ **Focus on people, not positions.** Breaking into the world of top executives is quite difficult. However, connecting with people who influence the decision makers is much easier. Every connection matters; always try to connect with driven people who appear to be on the rise.

✔ **Beef up your profile.** Profiles should be complete. Pay attention to how you word things; mention specific accomplishments instead of using general terms. For example, instead of saying, "Increased website traffic," say, "Increased website traffic by 10 percent, *month over month (MOM)*, by using direct email campaigns to engage audience." Include work-related experience, training, certifications, groups, and recommendations. Include a picture of yourself! (Your LinkedIn profile is 11 times more likely to be looked at if you include one.) Photos *(avatars)* should be clear and professional.

Try these ideas for making the most of your profile:

- • Create a distinct landing URL for your profile on a networking site.

- • Include your Twitter ID.

- • Add at least two professional recommendations from people you've worked for or supported.

- • Join groups on the site. (LinkedIn allows you to join up to 50 groups.)

✔ **Establish clear objectives.** Define a targeted number of comments each week that you intend on making. Commit to a set number of new introductions you will make each week. Allot time each day, and be consistent. Ask questions, comment on posts, and respond to polls. Earlier, we explored making a daily action plan for connecting with people you already know. This content refers to setting goals for reaching out to new people and for establishing a targeted number of comments made on others' posts each week.

✔ **Identify specific target audiences.** Use the app's Advanced People Search to find people with whom you'd like to connect. Search by zip code, industry, job title, or company name. Start with people you already know, but expand your search to include people that work for companies you admire, too.

✔ **Communicate professionally.** Keep your initial communication brief — no more than 200 words. Introduce yourself and share why you're connecting with the person. Offer yourself as a willing and available networking contact. Encourage the person to learn more about you by directing her to your profile.

Say "Cheese!"

Employment branding and social media influencer Jason Seiden explored different types of profile photos to determine which type grabbed the most attention on LinkedIn. He looked at how many people visited his profile, how many reached out to connect, and how many asked him to work with them. Jason suggested testing a variety of photos over three to six months to see what works best for you. He did discover that photos showing a person in action can resonate with viewers. The action infers passion, energy, and enthusiasm.

Focus on igniting the same level of engagement when you're seeking new job opportunities. Start by putting others first.

✔ Use social media to share information that you find of interest, or you believe will benefit others.

✔ Share research, articles, blogs, tips, and opportunities that may appeal to others in your network.

✔ Push information that you believe can help enhance others' experiences.

✔ Answer requests for information, participate in surveys, and attend networking events — even the local ones that are casual and not industry specific.

Using the Big Five to Your Best Advantage

It's impossible to be familiar with every social media outlet; there are too many of them. The good news is that you only have to be intensely familiar with five networks and may end up using even fewer in the future. We go over the best practices, cultures, types of information, and tips for each network to help set you apart.

Hone in on the Big Five networks, which are the first five listed here. When you can be found on the big boys, build a presence on industry- and occupational-specific sites. (See Chapter 7 for more.)

- LinkedIn: 300 million
- Twitter: 255 million
- Facebook: 1.3 billion
- YouTube: 1 billion
- Google+: 300 million
- Instagram: 200 million
- Pinterest: 70 million
- Quora: 2.9 million

You may have heard that many of these networks are becoming less relevant, but we assure you that isn't the case.

Having a strong base with the most prominent networks is essential for your success. Ultimately, it's important to focus on using these networks for building contextual relationships, promoting your content and establishing where your optimal audience is.

Focusing on Facebook

Facebook is the most powerful network. As of late 2014, over 1.23 billion Facebook users exist, and over 757 million members are active at least daily. Over 60 percent of its user base logs in daily.

The behemoth platform mainly is a casual networking tool. People of all ages, backgrounds, industries, and occupations use Facebook. It's a viable tool for your job search. Be aware of the information you share on Facebook. Followers typically don't want to be bombarded with professional posts.

Create two accounts on Facebook:

- Personal account
- Business account

Your personal account has to maintain a professional image and clearly tell others what you do.

Some people leave their personal page completely separate or even hide themselves from search results. We recommend using the incredible power of Facebook's *page rank* (Google's ranking for the validity of websites) for search engine purposes and revealing who you are personally.

To carefully decide what information the public sees, follow these steps:

1. **Go to** facebook.com/settings.

2. **Choose the Privacy tab.**

3. **Control who can see your page, who can contact you, and who can look you up.**

The most important section of your personal Facebook account to use is your Workplace and Work History. To edit this information, go to your personal About section and add all your pertinent work experience. Highlight your knowledge, skills, and abilities and quantify your impact through KPIs whenever possible. Always think about what your immediate benefit to potential employers is and clearly communicate what you bring to the table.

You can set up your business page at `http://facebook.com/business`.

✔ **If you already have a consultancy or other type of relevant business,** choose the Company, Organization, or Institution business classification.

✔ **If you're personally branding yourself as a social media professional,** select Artist, Band, or Public Figure and classify yourself as a public figure. Supposing that you're starting from scratch, then you'll want to select the Public Figure section and identify yourself as a Business Person. You're prompted to fill out the following information:

 • *About.* Add a few sentences about who you are and what you offer. Include your website and choose a Facebook web address (`facebook.com/yourname`). Use your About section as your "hook," where you make onlookers feel compelled to find out more about you. Use a few strategic keywords to increase visibility on Facebook and on search engines: *social media strategist, social media manager,* or *social media community manager.* Resist the urge to use cute terms such as "social media enthusiast" or "social media maverick;" they don't tell others exactly what you do. For example, look at the two following examples and notice what makes the second option stand out:

 Brooks Briz has been a social media maverick since 2007 and offers a wide variety of marketing services.

 Brooks Briz is the "social media ad guy." If you want instant social media results and substantial ROI, then you've come to the right place. Call 805-PROFIT-4 for a free 15-minute consultation now!

 The first About is rather boring and isn't nearly descript enough to really entice your ideal audience. The second clearly brands the page, uses a number of strategic keywords, tells the onlookers exactly what value they can get, and has an immediate call to action.

Take your time to craft a killer About statement and try to use those few sentences whenever promoting your services!

- *Profile Picture.* Upload a picture of yourself that's at least 180-x-180 pixels. Make sure it's a bright, high-definition picture of yourself: Don't use a logo! Remember: People do business with *people* rather than logos. See Figure 12-2.

- *Add to Favorites.* This option lets you keep your page prominently displayed in your Favorites section, which is in your left column.

- *Reach More People.* This section lets you advertise your new business page and promote your page to get Likes and engagement. Though the advertising part will become very important down the line, it's important now to build thought leadership content and a relationship with your target audience.

Figure 12-2:
Facebook
has pre-
ferred
image sizes.

Knowing why they're there

The single most important aspect to consider is *why* people are on Facebook. Then give them what they want.

Your prospective business page fans are there to learn from you in ways that will help them personally and professionally. Your prospective employers are there to analyze your knowledge, and abilities, and to ensure that you're a good fit for their organization. Your job is to focus on their needs and how you can best solve their pain and problems.

The other aspect to consider is your intended actions. In other words, when you get someone paying attention, what should they feel compelled to do? Try to be in tune with what your audience wants. When you provide value, you increase the odds they'll share your content.

Facebook has an internal algorithm that's based on shares, comments, Likes, and comment Likes that will determine the likelihood that your content will be seen in a user's feed. These metrics are in direct proportion to the size of your audience and is most heavily weighted by sharing.

Creating high-performance content

Facebook is a *thumb streaming platform,* meaning that people are constantly passing through their feed and only stopping to pay attention to content that truly captivates their attention. As such, Facebook relies heavily on images.

On Facebook, images and short videos typically are the most engaged with in the forms of clicks, likes, comments, and shares.

- ✔ **Images** should be big and bright and have limited text. Your pictures should have clear branding and limited, attractive typography. Pictures that show smiling women, animals, babies, or landscapes and are odd or quirky tend to get the most clicks. One of the best ways to create these types of images without a graphic design background is through a medium such as www.pagemodo.com.

- ✔ **Short videos,** when uploaded directly to Facebook, play automatically (to keep users on Facebook rather than leaving). Videos that perform the best tend to be 5 to 20 seconds long.

Once you've captured their attention, ask for an immediate action and provide a link to click for more information, if applicable. The *action* is typically sharing the content, but will vary based on your audience.

Trying unconventional methods

Try some unexpected ways of reaching out and getting information:

- ✔ Offer helpful advice, step-by-step guides, and information in the form of wall posts, comments, and direct messages on other business's pages.

- ✔ Pay attention to Facebook Insights. Insights, shown in Figure 12-3, gives you metrics to better understand your audience. It helps you optimize your content, target advertising, and improve your overall *return on investment (ROI).* You can better profile your target audience and see what works best.

- ✔ Use an action button. Services like www.ActionSprout.com allow you to create custom tabs on your Facebook page. By using ActionSprout, your fans can take immediate action — donating to charity or providing their email address — without leaving Facebook.

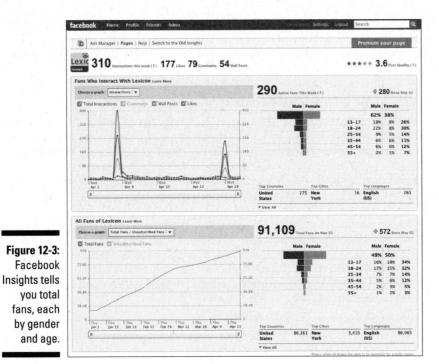

Figure 12-3:
Facebook
Insights tells
you total
fans, each
by gender
and age.

Creating conversation on Twitter

Twitter (www.twitter.com) is a great venue for short bursts of information
with links to more in-depth articles.

Twitter lets you to send 140-character messages called *tweets*. *Retweeting*
(reposting someone else's post) and mentioning the person who initially
shared the information is essential.

Retweeting not only allows you to push helpful information, but it helps the
initial poster see you. This is a pay-it-forward tactic. Do for others before
asking for something.

Twitter profiles are brief. Use words to describe yourself, not just your job
title. Include a link to your LinkedIn page. This *reciprocal* linking helps build
your network, since most viewers will look at each of your profiles if you
make it easy for them.

Twitter is about sharing based on what you're currently up to. It brands
itself with the slogan, "What are you doing?" Twitter is described as the
"SMS (short message service) of the Internet" because messages have to be

short, like text messages on cell phones. The network is often said to be the "purest" because it allows conversations between people at any time and for any reason. In essence, you can communicate with people all over the globe, from your best friend to the President of the United States.

Twitter is one of the best ways to establish and maintain relationships in an *open environment* (where virtually anyone else can communicate, collaborate or comment on your discussion). Watch Twitter discussions through hashtags (#).

People insert the hashtag symbol before a specific keyword or phrase to categorize their tweets and make them easy to search for. If you click a hashtagged word in any message, you'll see all other tweets with that keyword. Using a platform such as `search.twitter.com`, `www.hootsuite.com`, or `www.tweetdeck.com`, you can simultaneously

 ✔ Watch your Twitter *feed* (all the tweets from people you follow).

 ✔ See direct messages sent to you.

 ✔ See new followers.

 ✔ Monitor keywords of your choice.

For example, we watch Twitter keywords including our names, companies, and commonly used terms through all social media platforms. We can jump into conversations at a moment's notice and constantly build our networks. See Figure 12-4.

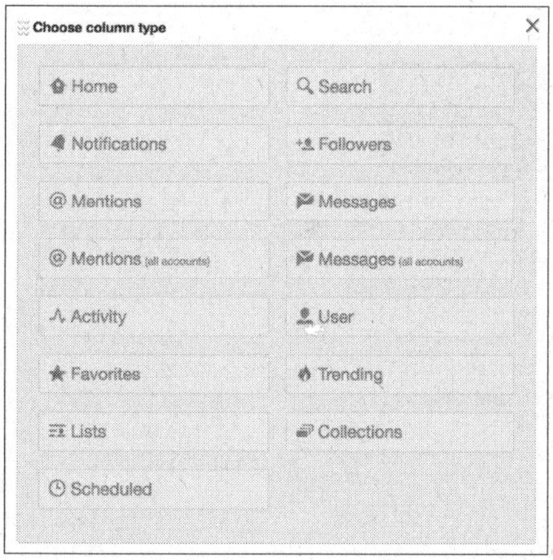

Figure 12-4:
Tweetdeck columns help you keep an eye on things.

Choose column type	✕
⌂ Home	🔍 Search
🔔 Notifications	+⚊ Followers
@ Mentions	⚑ Messages
@ Mentions (all accounts)	⚑ Messages (all accounts)
⋀ Activity	⚊ User
★ Favorites	◈ Trending
☰ Lists	⚎ Collections
⏱ Scheduled	

Discovering best practices

Despite its simplicity, Twitter is full of faux pas. Remember the following to ensure that you are able to get the most out of Twitter:

- ✔ **Don't blatantly sell.** Twitter is full of self promoters who use the platform to distribute their content and retweet positive comments about themselves. (See a good example of bad use in Figure 12-5.) This tactic is overaggressive for the Twitter culture and turns off many users. The only thing you should "sell" is the content and services of people and companies you trust, and your own content and services — and even then, selling between 5 to 20 percent of the time. For example, if you tweet 20 times per day, it's acceptable to promote a piece of content between one and four times during the day.

- ✔ **Keep tweets short.** You get only 140 characters to begin with, but it's best to keep tweets as short as possible. The best length is 100 characters; it lets other users retweet your content and add their original thoughts — an additional opportunity to build your relationship.

- ✔ **Stick to what you know.** Tweet about topics that you're an expert in. Being a thought leader around strategic topics works best when you participate with hashtag chats. *Hashtag chats* are prearranged discussions on Twitter and based around a specific hashtag. Thought leaders often agree to meet and share information with one another.

- ✔ **Be human.** Look for opportunities to be a friend and interact like a human being at all times. People are friends who talk; they aren't blatant salespeople. Building business relationships occurs naturally over time after people trust, like, and respect you.

Figure 12-5
Poor Twitter usage by a company.

Merging content and context

Above all else, Twitter is where sharing helpful content and building tremendous context is absolutely essential. Though one or the other is a significant advantage, a healthy blend of the two is how you make the most out of Twitter.

Though sharing helpful content is great, your reach will be limited without the relationships that can help you distribute the content. To combine content and context seamlessly, make the following part of your strategy:

- ✔ **Retweet:** Aim to share the tweets and links that your target market puts out. The more often you commit this action for others, the more likely they are to be willing to return the favor.

- ✔ **Favorite:** Twitter users are big fans of "getting love" on Twitter. The best ways to give love are to retweet and favorite tweets. By doing this habitually, you're letting other users know that you like them.

- ✔ **Direct messages:** Also known as *DMs,* you can send these messages only if you and a particular Twitter user follow one another. DMs are great for congratulating someone or sharing something more personal.

Creating art on Instagram

Instagram launched in October 2010 and is a photo- and video-sharing social network that boasted over 300 million users in 2014. Facebook bought Instagram in 2012 for over $1 billion and has grown in leaps and bounds over all other social media platforms.

Its essence is to give users a group of photo-editing tools to create artwork and share with the Instagram community, known as *Instagrammers*. To compete with the rise of micro video social networks such as Vine and Snapchat, Instagram added a video feature that allows 15 seconds of stop-action video.

Stop-action video allows you to pause the video and continue it whenever you please, rather than just shooting one continuous video. This type of technology allows for video manipulation and effects that have been made famous through claymation pictures.

Instagram is the epitome of a thumb-streaming social network whose users zip through their feed of users that they follow. The objective of an Instagram marketer is to get users to comment or "love" their photos and videos. As such, Instagram demands that users capture and create genuine works of art that compel users to stop in their tracks.

Instagram constantly evolves, adding features regularly — allowing users to send images directly to users that follow them, for example. Perhaps the most unique feature is hashtags, which is the most common way Instagram users find and discover new content and users. For example, #TBT (Throwback Thursday) and #Follow exploded in 2014, allowing Instagrammers to discover new users and creativity.

Mastering the tools suite

The Instagram world has a number of nuances and tools, but you absolutely must use a few specific tools to get ahead:

- ✔ **Profile:** Make this part engaging but clearly explain who you are and why you're worth paying attention to. Let people know what type of work you do and include some of your personal interests. Check out `instagram.com/michaelacton` for a great example. Don't forget to add your website! See Figure 12-6.

- ✔ **Editing:** First, you'll want to take interesting photos and pictures that give others insight into your personal and professional interests. After taking your video or picture, you're prompted to use the digital photo filters and editing functionalities. The *filters* change your photo's brightness or tint and inject different color shades. Try playing with all the different filters, including 1977, Inkwell, and Amaro. You can also use the Lux functionality to enhance light and exposure, which is especially important for outdoor shots. Figure 12-7 gives you a look at filters.

- ✔ **Search:** This is by far the best way to find new users and connect with others. Search on a daily basis by keywords and phrases to find users who share your personal and professional interests. When you find related users, show them attention by Liking their content and leaving thoughtful comments on their posts.

Figure 12-6: This is a sample Instagram profile.

Figure 12-7: Instagram filters are your friends.

If you want to make remarkable content, buy a camera lens that you can attach to your smartphone. eBay and Amazon offer all kinds of deals for **cell-phone lens** packages that include cool products such as fish-eye lenses, macro (close-up) lenses, and much more. The more time and attention you give your photos and pictures, the more people notice you!

Uncovering uncommon methods

After you have a basic understanding of how Instagram works, check out the expert tips; they'll make you stand out from the competition. Stay updated with Instagram best practices on sites like `Mashable.com` and `TechCrunch.com`. Test any new tools these sources mention as often as you can. We find and test new Instagram tools on a biweekly basis. Some don't work or add significant value.

Some of the top tactics and tools take your Instagram usage to the next level:

✔ **Hashtagging:** Use hashtags with your content and use them to find new people who share your personal and professional interests. On other social networks, hashtags are typically limited to three terms. Anything beyond this number is a faux pas — but not on Instagram. Because users search mainly through hashtags, always attach as many relevant hashtags as possible to your pictures and videos. Even the larger Fortune 500 brands average five hashtags in each one of their posts.

✔ **Tagging:** One of the best ways to get more eyeballs on your profile is by tagging other users. Precede a user's name with an @ mention in either your Content Description or Comment section. Be wary: Don't use tagging to spam. Only tag friends or people who would genuinely be interested in the content that you're sharing.

✔ **Integrating other platforms:** You can easily share your Instagram photos on Facebook. Use the built-in sharing app or Facebook's Instagram feed tab, which is at `apps.facebook.com/Instagram_feed` and shown in Figure 12-8. You can also share your content on platforms such as Twitter, Tumblr, Foursquare, and Flickr. In your Instagram profile section, let your followers know on what other platforms they can find you.

Figure 12-8: Facebook has an Instagram tab.

FEEDS

Feature your best content on Facebook

Show your own photo feed and/or one hashtag feed of your choice.

Define the order of your feeds so that your most important content is displayed first on your Page Tab.

★ Premium plan: Display up to 5 hashtag feeds at the same

✔ **Using other tools:**

• **Instac.at,** a cool web-based app, allows you to search for Instagram content based on hashtags and keywords. (Instagram only allows for this on the mobile and tablet app.) Instac.at allows you to seamlessly like, comment on, and share the stuff from other Instagrammers on multiple social media platforms.

• **Iconosquare** offers advanced analytics that show any user you're connected to or any public profile, including the person's follower count, number of photos, total number of Likes, and so forth. This gives you insight as to who Instagram users are connected to and what touches their hearts and minds. See Figure 12-9.

- **Instagrille** is a desktop Instagram app that's identical to the mobile app with the additional benefit of your being notified when someone you follow posts new content.

Key metrics about
your Instagram account...

Get your total number of likes received, your most liked photos ever, your average
number of likes and comments per photo, your follower growth charts **and more advanced analytics**.

...to share with your community!

GET YOURS

25%
OF FOLLOWERS ARE
FROM **UNITED STATES**

23% RUSSIA
9% SWEDEN
5% FRANCE
5% ITALY

305   2,82

Figure 12-9:
Use
Iconosquare
with
Instagram.

Crafting a professional LinkedIn presence

Two new people join LinkedIn (www.linkedin.com) every second. Professionals go to LinkedIn for sources of education, information, business networking, and news. This active professional networking tool is a great place to gain attention from prospective employers and hiring professionals.

Use LinkedIn often; timeliness could mean the difference between getting an opportunity and missing one.

LinkedIn is an opportunity to

- ✔ Expand your network.
- ✔ Uncover opportunities to better serve your community.

 ✔ Find decision makers who align with your objectives.

 ✔ Find top-notch talent for your organization.

 ✔ Provide value for local business leaders in a professional context.

LinkedIn is a professional social media platform. It isn't the place for pictures of your kids or cats. For more casual content, try Facebook or Pinterest. It's okay to show a personal side to yourself while in the job hunt, but never post anything you wouldn't want your mother to see.

If you provide value — sharing insight about your graphic design, research, or copywriting skills, for example — up front when connecting, or providing status updates on your business page, you can connect with more people. Word about your generosity will spread. You could use this method of paying it forward to get exposure from news sources and local celebrities, networking with other influencers or strategic partnerships with other local charities.

Constantly be thinking about what the LinkedIn users are looking for and what they value.

Exploring networking opportunities

LinkedIn offers lots of opportunities to connect with others. You can send connection requests to virtually anyone at any time, you can converse via comments, you can send private messages to people you're directly connected to, and so forth.

Look for opportunities to start or grow relationships. Here are areas where you'll find the biggest return on your networking:

 ✔ **Groups:** Use LinkedIn's search function to find professional and personal groups that interest you. Hover over the Interests subheading and choose Groups from the menu that appears. From here you can search existing groups by keyword, select a category, or click Groups You May Like. Request to join these groups and try to provide value whenever you can by sharing helpful resources and providing your insight with content pieces that others share. If they're local, make their meetings whenever you can. Finally, if you can't find the type of group you're looking for, create your own group and invite other people to join. Being a group administrator proves to others that you're a thought leader in your field. See Figure 12-10.

Try these LinkedIn groups:

 • *Social Media Marketing,* moderated by experienced social media leaders, is ideal if you crave new insights. Get weekly announcements, resources, and webinar information, in addition to lively discussion. Visit www.socialmediopolis.com.

- *Social Media Today* focuses on social currency, brand advocacy, and the overall value of social media in society today. Visit www.socialmediatoday.com.

- *Digital Marketing* is professionals working in web, mobile television, mobile marketing, marketing 2.0, social media, online advertising, interactive, and digital media. Visit marketingtechnews.net.

✔ **InMails:** Be open to accepting and responding to InMails, and be open to sharing information with others. InMails (see Figure 12-11) are part of LinkedIn's subscription service, and they help you communicate with people you aren't otherwise connected with. You can review free and paid options in the Accounts & Settings tab after creating an account and logging in.

✔ **Connections:** Stick with your daily plan for interacting with your direct network, as well as finding new connections. Don't connect with people and hardly ever speak to them again.

Send at least a message per day to someone you know. Ask what they're up to and if there's anything that you can do to help them. It's even better to research your connection and figure out how you might help them before you reach out.

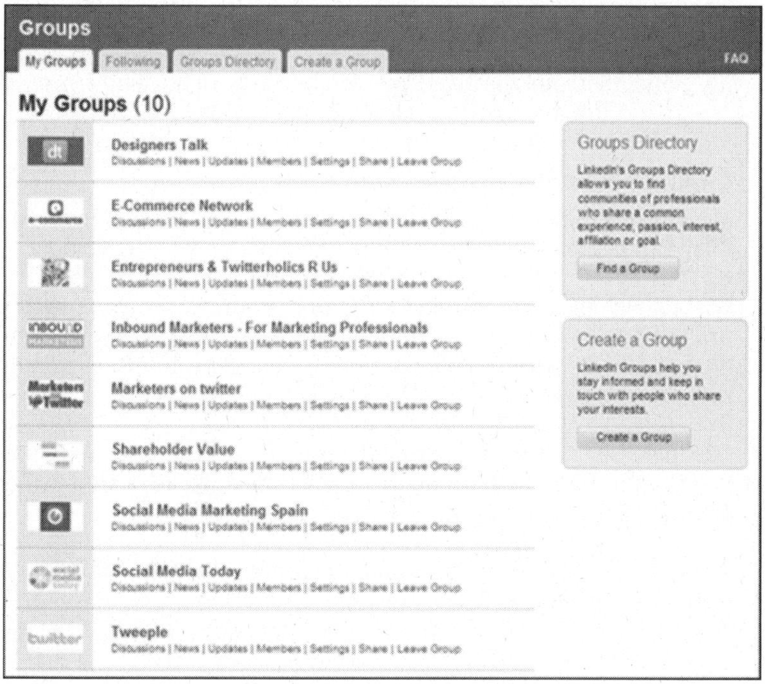

Figure 12-10: Use LinkedIn groups to your advantage.

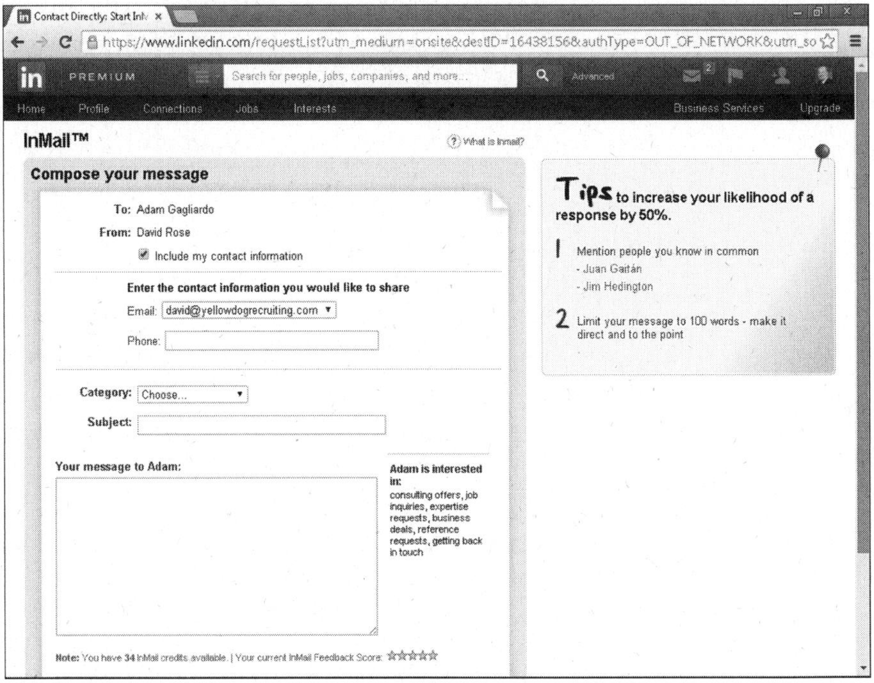

Figure 12-11: InMails allow you to communicate with people you wouldn't otherwise. Notice the people it points out in common.

✔ **Content promotion:** Produce and promote your own content to your immediate network and groups. Being a creator and a promoter gets you in front of more eyeballs and creates goodwill.

Establishing a professional appearance

Many people believe that LinkedIn should be only for professional purposes — that your personal interests should never be present there.

We believe that it's possible to integrate your personal life with your professional appearance, and that people are actually more keen on doing business with people who reveal insight about their personal and professional lives.

The logic here is that common interests in business and personal lives can build rapport and help others decide if they'd like to start a project with you or even offer you a job.

When it comes to crafting a top-notch appearance on LinkedIn, we recommend the following:

✔ **Headline and industry:** At the very top of your profile, underneath your name, briefly describe who you are and what you do. Your headline should have at least one keyword or phrase that you would like to build your career around, such as *social media ad consultant.* Choose an industry from the list LinkedIn provides. Social Media isn't an option, so you'll have to find an industry related to your particular expertise, such as Graphic Design or Marketing and Advertising.

✔ **Summary:** Give a quick snippet about who you are as a professional. Craft an overview that's succinct and that prompts readers to take immediate action such as visiting a website or getting in touch with you. Challenge yourself to create a piece that makes your knowledge, skills, and abilities come to life and makes others genuinely interested in what you do.

✔ **Additional info:** This is where you list your personal and professional interests and give advice for contacting you. List all your contact information and let people know why you want to connect with them. For example, you might tell headhunters that you're currently looking for opportunities and are very receptive to particular types of positions.

✔ **Experience:** This is essentially your resume. List your positions, companies you've worked for, how long you were there, and what your responsibilities were. Summarize your impact and the key performance indicators that you accomplished while at each job. If you have any multimedia examples of your work — videos, periodicals, documents, and so forth — share these pieces of work within each applicable position. Use keywords in your position titles and throughout your descriptions.

A prominent group of people on LinkedIn are called *LinkedIn Open Networkers (LIONs).* If you mention within your profile or title that you're a LION and an **open networker**, then you'll get a lot of connection requests. Any other LIONs will accept your connection request.

The theory behind this movement is that the more connections you have, the better it is for your overall network regardless of whether you do business with one another. Additionally, LIONs believe in giving and receiving favors and gladly give out recommendations, make introductions, and so forth. See Figure 12-12.

Diving off your platform

LinkedIn is one of those networks where the more you give to others, the better your long-term results.

If you concentrate a majority of your job-search efforts on one platform, LinkedIn is a wise choice.

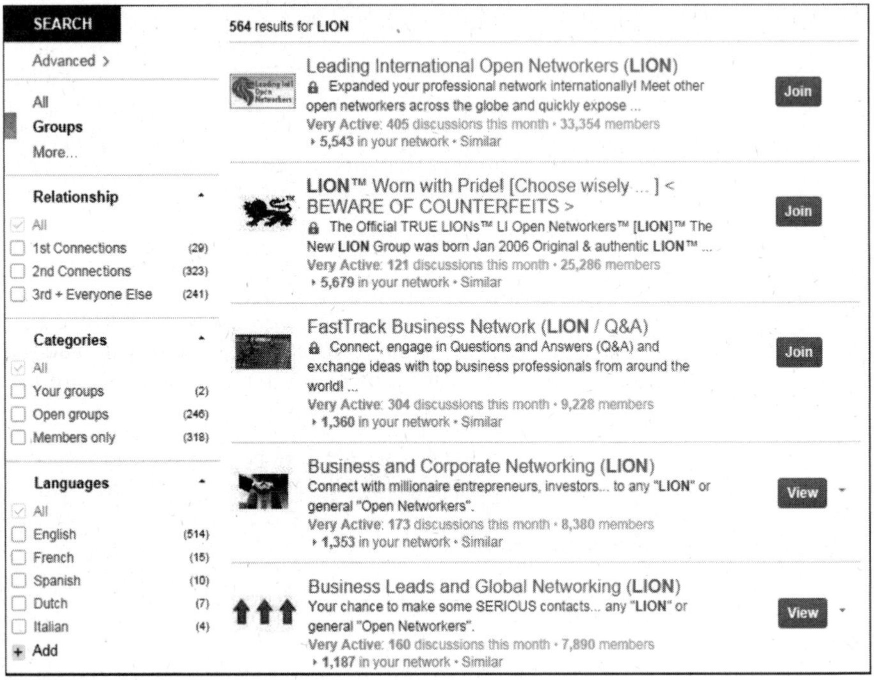

Figure 12-12:
LinkedIn
LIONs
groups lead
to connec-
tions.

With that being said, we think you can set yourself apart:

- ✔ **Add experience content.** As we mention earlier, have proof of your expertise with all your positions. The trick is to use as much high-quality information as you can get your hands on and offer a variety of formats. LinkedIn allows you to upload spreadsheets, PDF documents, presentations, videos, and so forth. Try to upload as many kinds as you can to both your individual jobs and to your overall summary.

- ✔ **Give recommendations and endorsements.** Recommendations are located after your individual jobs and they serve as testimonials for your work. The Skills & Endorsements section lists knowledge and skills that people within your network confirm that you have. Give out genuine recommendations and endorsements to others without looking for anything in return. People within your network will be so pleasantly surprised that they'll gladly return the favor, and you'll have built goodwill with them.

- ✔ **Proactively connect.** Make time on a daily basis to look for people who you'd love to connect with. Use LinkedIn's search feature to find people based on their title, company, or experience. If you're connected through a mutual acquaintance, ask that person to introduce you; or you might connect with the person directly (only if you're a Premium member). Think how you can be of value to them and explicitly state why you're connecting with them.

✔ **Complete all profile sections.** Between the summary, education, experience, volunteer experience, and awards sections, LinkedIn's profile is quite advanced. Don't skimp on any section. Remember to use keywords associated with your profession or that demonstrate your knowledge in other fields.

✔ **Publish content.** Create high-quality content that you share as an individual and also with a company page. (Position yourself as a consultant, author, or speaker.) As you begin connecting and creating useful, actionable advice, people will subscribe to you.

✔ **Give video recommendations for your contacts.** Upload them as Unlisted on YouTube. Email your contacts the link and advise them to add the video as a content piece within their job descriptions or overview. They'll want to return the favor. All the sudden, you have video testimonials on your behalf and virtually no one else on LinkedIn does.

Riding the Google+ momentum

Google+, also known as Google Plus, is a social networking site that markets itself as an identity service. In essence, Google+ enhances many of its online properties (such as Gmail and YouTube). In addition, Google maintains that Google+ is different from all other social media sites because of its authorship tool that associates web-content directly with its owner. See Figure 12-13.

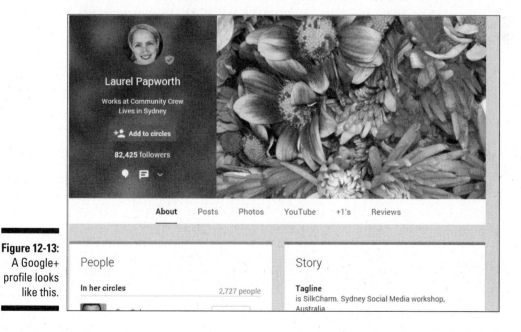

Figure 12-13:
A Google+ profile looks like this.

Anything Google related is worth paying attention to. Period.

Google requires that all Gmail and YouTube users also set up a Google+ account. Also, the social media network works well with search engines and can be a huge part of your job-searching strategy despite that the network doesn't have the engagement that it is aiming for as of 2014.

Here's why Google+ is worth paying attention to:

- ✔ Search is changing. People are starting to get their news from Twitter and Facebook rather than from television or even websites. Think about that for a moment. How often is trending local news initially coming from a Facebook post? Watch a breaking story on ESPN and you'll find that the original source frequently comes from a player, coach, or owner's tweet. It's only a matter of time before Google+ is integrated into that equation and search results favor news that's posted there.

- ✔ Search results on Google will begin to prefer content posted on Google+ more and more and will almost *always* outperform your website or other types of new sources. When you search on Google, sometimes a picture of a person is underneath the search result title. Clicking the picture might lead you to a Google+ profile. Google+ profiles are consistently getting prominent placement since they're playing by Google's rules. Why not use Google's power?

- ✔ Google+ has diverse types of content. Your post updates can include video, text, images, hashtags, website links, and *animated GIFs* (a combination of images that act as a short video). No other platforms allow this versatility; it lets you connect with a broad range of audiences.

- ✔ Google+ allows the highest-quality images among all social media sites. You'll instantly notice the stunning photographs in your Google+ feed. Use this opportunity to capture more eyeballs.

Connecting may be slow at first, but this platform has a huge potential upside for you. Our advice is to stick with the platform and commit yourself to contributing significant value. In essence, it's relatively easy to position yourself as a mover and shaker on Google+. When the rest of the world catches on, you'll be way ahead of the game.

Contacting People You Know

Having a history with an individual will help you to capture attention sooner. People who know your quality of work are more likely to help directly, or refer you to others who may help.

Connecting with people you already know is a great start, but it's limiting if you don't link up with new people too.

Who do you interact with each week? Who have you lost touch with?

- On the personal side, you have neighbors, your mayor, and your religious leader to speak to. Hairdressers, bank tellers, office managers, and school principals are all connected members of your community. It's your job to uncover how the people they know can help you. Friends and family are also part of this pool. Don't overlook fellow alumni, conference participants, and group members.

- From a professional approach, target people with whom you have previously worked directly or indirectly. Leaders, direct reports, colleagues, project teams, and affinity group members can act as eyes and ears throughout your job search. And don't stop there: Try college alumni sites, alumni groups, fraternities/sororities, and company employee sites. Many companies host sites that can only be accessed from inside their company portal. Often, those sites highlight employees, former employees, and activities. These are prime places to find new leads.

Making a spreadsheet

Create an electronic contact list. A simple Microsoft Excel spreadsheet is sufficient.

Alma mater

Your school's alumni association will provide great discounts, support, networking events, conferences, and other benefits, usually for a nominal annual membership fee. Once you contact them, take advantage of the information provided in the alumni magazine and online. Alumni groups are designed specifically to help alumni connect and to establish business relationships.

This format allows you to sort your data as you get more information. List each contact and include headings for

- ✔ Name
- ✔ Job title
- ✔ Company
- ✔ Contact information
- ✔ Relationship: personal or professional
- ✔ Notes: Include dates and times you left messages, sent emails, or spoke with the person, in addition to details about that interaction

Use the spreadsheet with your calendar of choice. Tools like Microsoft Outlook connect to your email, calendar, and folders. Yahoo! Calendar or Google Calendar are fair options. Use the tools you're already familiar with.

By linking your calendar and spreadsheet, you can block out time for activities, review your availability, and schedule reminders within one system.

The tool you use isn't as important as the consistency of the tool.

Keep easy-to-understand, concise notes from the beginning of your search effort. Do so the whole time you're looking for a job. It's a good habit to get into. By tracking your activity, you feel a sense of accomplishment. More importantly, you are developing a job search methodology. With good tracking, you'll be able to revisit your activity and re-establish relationships with people in the future. Just because someone couldn't help with your job search this time doesn't mean he won't be able to help in the future.

Keep a scheduled time to contact the people in your network, even when you have a job. (For more detail on tracking job search data, see Chapter 14.)

Engaging people

Everyone has an opinion and a bias. Experience, culture, and relationships affect perspective. During transitional times, people get charged up, motivated to take action. It's during these times that people are forced to consider all possibilities. You find your passion and leap right in. There's a trigger; something impacts you and immediately changes your course of action.

People connect, but *engagement* is how you build a relationship. When you're passionate, you're completely in the moment. You're present. It doesn't feel like work. You're not doing it because you have to, but because you want to. That's *engagement*.

Consider the time you afford others. Who has taken time throughout your career?

Social media is for spreading a message or communicating an idea. The true benefit of socially driven tools is *the exchange of ideas,* not the means by which the ideas are delivered.

Getting in touch

After you make a contact list, go through it making introductory calls or emails. Mix it up. Call some people. Email some people.

1. **Review your contacts. All of them.**

   Check your address book, connections, followers, and friends. While it's smart to organize contacts in one place, professionals use many different systems to communicate. Often, specific communication tools are used to connect with certain people or groups.

2. **Once you have a total number of contacts, divide that number by 50.**

   The result is the approximate number of your contacts for whom you should be contacting each week.

3. **Identify the appropriate communication tool.**

   Don't let too much time pass between touch points when you're solidifying relationships. A phone call may be appropriate, but an email, text, comment on a blog post, or even a tweet may also be effective means of communicating. Besides, who has time to call all their contacts each week?

4. **Communicate with substance.**

   Ask interesting questions. Listen to the answers and engage your contact. Be genuinely interested in the success and well being of the person with whom you're speaking.

   • **Be clear that you are open to, and seeking out, new options.** Let the people you are contacting know that you value your relationship with them. Confide in them. Be brief. Don't speak ill of your current or former employer.

   • **Ask for support.** Ask your contacts to think about their own networks, particularly the people and specific job opportunities they believe would be a fit for you.

   • **Request an introduction.** Explain that you aren't asking your contact to get you a job. Rather, be clear that you're investing in your future and hope to broaden your network. If someone introduces you to someone, the person is vouching for you. It's a first-level prescreen.

5. **Follow up and make sure to use your calendar or scheduling tool.**

Keep these things in mind, too:

- ✔ **You can use a particular communication tool for the next interaction.** That tool will become clear as you get more comfortable. See Chapter 7 for a review of tools.

- ✔ **As you work through your list, schedule follow-up communication.** If you left a message for Bob Smith on Monday, follow up with another call or email on Wednesday. If you don't get a response by the following Monday, schedule another call or email on Tuesday. Give it another try on Thursday. Then, let things lie.

- ✔ **Sometimes people fall behind.** Give the person a chance to catch up. One week later, start the cycle again: Monday, Wednesday, Tuesday, Thursday, take a week off, and repeat. Your contacts will begin referring you to other people, and your call list will grow. Making a plan that includes frequent touch points will make you a known commodity. Over time, your name will become familiar and you will stay *top of mind*.

While these steps may seem calculated, it's about strategic planning. By breaking a large group into smaller, more manageable groups, you can target your communication.

Don't forget the people who already connected with you. Schedule touch-base calls and emails in the future. One-month, three-month, and six-month intervals allow you to remain in the forefront of your contacts' minds. Because the job landscape is constantly changing, this periodic base touching helps you to stay on top of new options.

Each day has 24 hours. On average, people sleep eight hours, work ten hours, and spend time on personal endeavors the remaining six hours of the day.

Being disciplined during unemployment

When you're searching for a job, keep these tips in mind:

- ✔ Use the time that used to be for personal interests looking for a job. It's the right move to use that time, even if it disrupts your normal routine a bit. Passing up a good night's sleep isn't in your best interest, from a health and wellness standpoint. Your body needs rest.

✔ Get out of bed at the same time every day whether you're employed or not. If you're out of work, keep consistent patterns of activity. If you're working, managing your time will require a greater level of attentiveness during a job search. You don't want to slack on your current job responsibilities.

✔ Block out time throughout every day to focus on your job search. Give yourself 15-minute, 30-minute, and 45-minute windows of time to devote solely to communicating with your contacts. How much time you allot is based on how busy you are. Spend as much time as you can afford; just be consistent. Keep at it. Break each day into parts. Consider making calls mid-morning and sending emails in the evening. Because of smartphones, people rarely disconnect completely. An evening email may have a greater chance of being seen versus one sent during the busy day.

✔ Use the data and analytics available to you. Many great social media monitoring and reporting tools are available; some are explained in the next section. You may have even used a monitoring tool in a previous job.

Picky posting

As a social media pro, you understand the importance of listening to your audience. Just as you tune into how an audience receives a brand, you must approach your job search with the same ferocity. Savvy candidates know their reputation and understand they have a greater chance of making an impression with different social tools at different times during the day.

Social media enthusiast, storyteller, and designer Dustin Stout (http://dustn.tv/about) did some research to determine the best and worst times to post on social networks. His findings are as follows:

✔ **LinkedIn:** 7am–9am or 5pm–6pm (Best), 10pm–6am (Worst)

✔ **Facebook:** 1pm–4pm (Best), 8pm–8am (Worst)

✔ **Twitter:** 1pm–3pm (Best), 8pm–9am (Worst)

✔ **Google+:** 9am–11am (Best), 6pm–8am (Worst)

✔ **Pinterest:** 2pm–4pm or 8pm–1am (Best), 5pm–7pm (Worst)

Beyond timing, don't forget content. What you share must be relevant to your overall goal of finding a job. Stick with industry- and job-related posts.

Going with the Pros

Because formal social media degree programs are in their infancy, most social media pros hold degrees in business, communication, marketing, or a related field. These individuals become subject matter experts (SMEs) by continuously focusing on improvement and by participating in

- ✔ Ongoing training
- ✔ Professional networking groups
- ✔ Peer-to-peer discussions
- ✔ Online forums

Networking with the pros is a surefire way to expedite your success. Think of it this way: Why read a case study when you can talk directly with the person who accomplished the feat?

Several *thought leaders,* or experts in their field, have been recognized by their peers for being innovative social media thinkers:

- ✔ **Todd Defren** is a social media and public relations lecturer. He founded Shift Communications and is online at `http://about.me/tdefren`.
- ✔ **Sarah Evans** is a digital correspondent for brands like PayPal, Cisco, and Cox Communications. See her site at `www.sarahsfav.es`.
- ✔ **Jason Falls** is an author and is known for his blog, Social Media Explorer. Falls is at `www.socialmediaexplorer.com`.
- ✔ **Seth Godin** is a thought leader with a particular emphasis on social media market. See his site at `http://sethgodin.typepad.com`.
- ✔ **Amanda Hite** is co-founder and Chief Change Officer of BTC. She's at `http://btcrevolutions.com`.
- ✔ **David Houle** has consulted and advised thousands of business leaders. He studies trends that are changing society, as well as how technology and connectedness are transforming the world. Check him out at `www.evolutionshift.com`.
- ✔ **Beth Kanter** specializes in social media for nonprofit organizations and is online at `www.bethkanter.org`.
- ✔ **Liz Ryan** is the founder of Human Workplace. She's a candidate advocate who writes and speaks about leadership, job searches, and personal branding. Her site is at `http://humanworkplace.com/whos-we`.

✔ **Mari Smith** is a highly regarded thought leader with an expertise in relationship marketing. She mainly uses Facebook to support socially conscious companies. Her URL is `www.marismith.com`.

✔ **Brian Solis** is an author, digital analyst, anthropologist, and a *futurist* (a social scientist who studies trends and predicts future possibilities). See what he has to say at `www.briansolis.com`.

✔ **Gary Vaynerchuk** is an author and one of the first and most successful entrepreneurs to use social media as a main platform for his business. Read more at `http://garyvaynerchuk.com`.

Contribute to other social media pros these ways:

✔ **Conduct research:** Both conducting and condensing information — taking the tens or hundreds of best practices for LinkedIn advertising and simplifying it into three bits of information that someone can take action on.

✔ *Bird dogging:* Take a request — an introduction, sales lead, or buyer — and find the solution for someone who needs help.

✔ **Make recommendations:** Maybe you're familiar with a resource or can fulfill a specific need.

✔ **Offer pro bono help:** Conduct research, write a blog post, interview an industry expert. You might not see an instant return, but you'll strengthen your skills and create goodwill.

Meeting Face to Face

Some of the advantages of building in-person relationships with other social media pros are as follows:

✔ Your relationships can lead to strategic introductions, joint ventures, referrals and an alliance within the industry.

✔ You'll get a clearer understanding of how to position yourself and your knowledge. By interacting with successful social media pros, you'll hone in on your messaging and make yourself more marketable. For example, Brooks originally presented himself only as an e-commerce expert. By spending time with established social media pros, Brooks evolved into "the social media ad guy."

✔ To find suppliers and solutions to your day-to-day problems. Not only can you improve operations, but you can help your employer (and others) solve the same problem that you had. This makes you look like a subject matter expert and establishes goodwill with others.

Tweetups

A *tweetup* is an in-person meeting or event that Twitter users organize. The primary benefit of a tweetup is to physically meet and connect with the people that you meet through social media and strengthen your relationships.

Tweetups are one of the best ways to network with other social media pros in your area.

Find local tweetups by searching for the term **tweetup** and your location. Ask Twitter *power users* (influential people who have a large, engaged followings) when and where the best tweetups are.

To get the most out of tweetups, we recommend doing the following:

- **Focus on the value that you can bring to others.** Always go into tweet-ups thinking about what you can do for others. Focus on them: their stories and passions.

- **Have an elevator pitch.** An *elevator pitch* is when you describe who you are and what you do in the time it takes to ride on an elevator with someone else. The pitch should be less than 30 seconds and have a hook. The hook captures someone's attention in less than 15 seconds. Here's what an elevator pitch sounds like, "Hey, I'm Brooks and I make social media ads that double ROI." That message starts a conversation and makes the listener feel compelled to find out how you're able to double a return on investment.

- **Volunteer at the tweetup.** Help make the organizer's job easier. Instead of asking *if* you can help, ask *what* you can do and/or offer to undertake some of the more time-consuming tasks.

- **Organize your own tweetup.** Become known as a connector in your local community. The more original and valuable the tweetup, the more fruitful it will be. To organize a successful tweetup, follow these steps:

  1. **Decide on a place to meet.**

  2. **Establish how food and drinks will be served.**

  3. **Organize a fun activity (such as a charity auction or cupcake-eating contest).**

  4. **Establish a guest list.**

  It might seem like a lot of work, but once you pull it off, you'll never want to stop! See Figure 12-14.

Meetups

Tweetup is a term borrowed from meetup.com — the original local connection. On meetup.com, you find people who're interested in different out-
doors activities, arts and crafts, sports — virtually anything else that you can
imagine. Focus on the social media and business networking professionals
that you can find there.

To join a meetup, follow these steps:

1. **Create a meetup.com account.**

2. **Search for groups by keyword.**

   For instance, you might search *social media* or *business networking*.

3. **Join a group.**

   You might have to request to join a group. Groups can sometimes be
   particular about the people they allow in, so you'll have to explain to the

group administrator briefly why you want to join. This process is very short and you should be accepted into the group within a day.

4. **Find out when and where the group meets.**

Most of the Meetup groups are free but in some cases you might have to buy a meal, contribute to a charity, or pay an entry fee. You'll always know what the group is offering ahead of time and whether you need to make alternate meal plans.

Go to a meetup before creating one of your own. It's always best to get a feel for how Meetup gatherings are run and to get to know other influencers in your immediate area first. When you know the flow and organization of a Meetup, you can make your own Meetup group and have complete control over the rules, expectations, and settings.

Don't worry about how many Twitter followers a pro has, or how many times they've tweeted. These numbers can't measure someone's influence. Instead of being fixated on numbers, focus on the strength of your connections.

Tapping Into Groups and Associations

People with common interests coming together is a part of the foundation of society. People need one another to advance. Whether in real life (IRL) or through social media platforms, the basic premise of sharing ideas, information, and deepening relationships remains.

These terrific social media tools bring people together:

- ✔ `Groupsite.com` aims to inspire social collaboration. This free, easy platform lets you communicate, share, and network. You can establish a group and make it public, semi-public (requiring approval), or private. See Figure 12-15.

- ✔ **The Marketing Executives Networking Group (MENG)** is a national network of top-level marketing executives. The organization, found at `http://mengonline.com`, is a professional group worth exploring. See Figure 12-16.

Figure 12-15:
Groupsite
encourages
social col-
laboration.

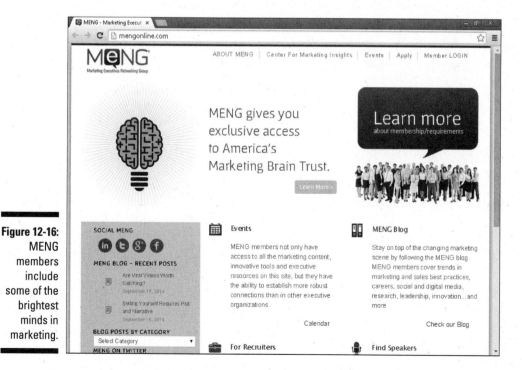

Figure 12-16:
MENG
members
include
some of the
brightest
minds in
marketing.

Keeping Tabs

As a job candidate, you're laser focused on your search and keeping tabs on anything you can control. That's the right play. Don't lose sight of your social media community, though.

It's easy to become self-centered during a job search. No one will look out for you better than you. But, your community never stops sharing new information. Scour your networks to see what's happening with the people and companies you follow.

Trolling your networks

Don't underestimate the time needed to establish your social media presence. Keeping track of all your contacts' activity on multiple platforms can be challenging, especially as you grow your network.

Tools can help you monitor, track, and calendarize activities, and give you a real-time view of your *stream* (your followers' activity in the social media space).

These tools maximize time and expose your brand:

✔ **Hootsuite,** at `https://hootsuite.com`, is one of the best free social media-management tools available, and it supports different networks, including Twitter, Facebook, LinkedIn, WordPress, Foursquare, and Google+. Hootsuite lets you monitor your different streams, including direct messages and mentions of you, and lets you schedule posts to a single network or multiple networks at one time. Spread your posts out during times where your audience is the largest. See Figure 12-17. The icons on the left are quick links to Hootsuite features — publishing, analytics, advertising options, team interaction, training, and theme options.

✔ **SocialBro,** at `www.socialbro.com`, provides daily reports on the best time to tweet. These reports show the days and times when the greatest percentage of your Twitter community is online (not just your followers).

✔ **Timing+,** at `http://timing.minimali.se`, is a very valuable tool for posting on Google+. Timing+ analyzes your past posts to determine what time of day has the most potential to have the greatest impact. See Figure 12-18.

✔ **Social Mention**, at `http://socialmention.com`, is popular among social media enthusiasts. It monitors over 100 such sites. Social Mention is probably one of the best free listening tools on the market, because it analyzes data in more depth and measures influence in the following categories:

- *Strength* is determined by the likelihood your brand is being discussed in the social media universe. The calculation is phrase mentions within the last 24 hours divided by total possible mentions.

- *Sentiment* is the ratio of mentions that are positive to those that are negative.

- *Passion* is a measure of likelihood individuals talking about your brand will do so repeatedly.

- *Reach* is a measure of the range of influence. It's calculated by the number of unique authors referencing your brand divided by the total number of mentions.

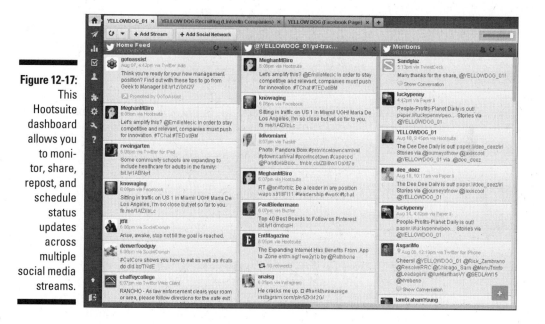

Figure 12-17:
This Hootsuite dashboard allows you to monitor, share, repost, and schedule status updates across multiple social media streams.

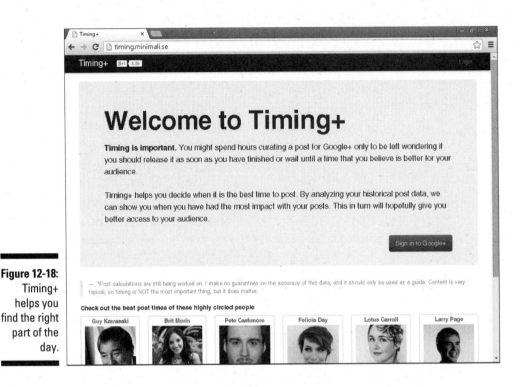

Figure 12-18:
Timing+
helps you
find the right
part of the
day.

Test out each tool. You may find that one, in particular, provides more value than another. Using multiple tools is also worth exploring. Some tools work for some actions, but not others. For example, if you're simply trying to build your social media presence, Hootsuite has a tool with some ability to analyze data. Social Mention, by comparison, lets you see which posts connect with your audience and which posts generate the greatest responses.

A successful job search requires you to remain flexible.

Who's worth following

Sites like the following provide insight and host debates about tools, platforms, companies, and personalities that are revolutionizing the way people consume information. Check out these great sources for top news in the social stratosphere:

- ✔ Social Media Today at `socialmediatoday.com`; see Figure 12-19
- ✔ Social Media Examiner at `socialmediaexaminer.com`; see Figure 12-20
- ✔ Social Networking Watch at `socialnetworkingwatch.com`

Figure 12-19:
Social
Media
Today
learns your
interests
and ten-
dencies.
Webinars,
ebooks,
and blog
posts are
available to
members.

Figure 12-20:
Social
Media
Examiner
hosts con-
ferences
and boasts
the world's
largest
online
magazine
dedicated
to social
media.

Major news agencies like NBC, CBS, Fox, ABC, Huffington Post, Fast Company, Bloomberg, Forbes, and US News & World Report all provide social media-related information as part of their daily reporting. These sites can help you keep current on trends. They help you track what's becoming more common in your business.

Building a Professional Brand Presence

Have you ever been watching a live news report and noticed someone waving in the background? It's often someone young or young at heart. For a few seconds, that person's sole objective is to be seen. The calm, professional reporter often moves seamlessly through the report. Of course, you might have seen reporters who lost their cool (search **reporter freaking out** on YouTube) only to recall that cameras are recording the entire scene.

While it may sound counterintuitive, think of yourself as the kid in the background, jumping around and flailing about. You don't need to be the center of attention to be seen.

In social media, being found in multiple places demonstrates your brand infiltration. Think about it: Social media pros pine after viral videos. They dream about creating that one video that grabs a million views. Perhaps creating a series of videos that capture a million views could be equally impactful.

Stay the course. Don't dream about views. Focus on the Four Rights: Getting the right information to the right people at the right time on the right platform.

Building Your Personal Brand

After deciding on your social media brand, it's time to make the most of that brand equity and set yourself apart from the crowd.

Brand equity within the social media space is by far the most valuable asset that you can possess and can't be taken away from you. Consider the long list of celebrities who have been found via social media: Kate Upton, Justin Bieber, Kim Kardashian, and Carly Rae Jepson, or even the resurgence of "washed-up" stars such as MC Hammer, Vanilla Ice, and Fred Durst.

Social media allows you to connect with people and build genuine relationships whether you're a "nobody" or a "has been." People have lost jobs because of inappropriate tweets or curse-laden Facebook posts. Social media gives people a chance to rebuild their personal brand and make great things happen if they put others first.

Designing your personal brand

The physical representation of a brand typically comes in the form of your name, icon, and design, with any communication materials and the content that you produce.

It's important to have a brand all your own. Your brand must

- ✔ Be aesthetically pleasing
- ✔ Encompass remarkable thought leadership content
- ✔ Be marketed to the social media landscape and beyond

Don't create your own graphics, logos, and so forth unless you're a graphic design professional. Get the help of a graphic design pro or use sites (such as fiverr.com or 99designs.com) to get top-notch work done for a fraction of the price.

Overall, to avoid branding yourself in a complicated, inconsistent, or unprofessional manner, follow these rules for creating your central graphical appearance:

- ✔ **Keep it as simple as possible.** Limit the design to a max of three colors and keep it as focused as possible.

- ✔ **Be memorable.** If a target consumer can't recall what your design looks like, then you're not nearly distinct enough. Show your design to five people you're close to. Ask them to recall your design; see how accurate they are. If they're having trouble remembering, or their explanations are inconsistent, then your design is too complicated.

- ✔ **Have a timeless graphic design base to work from.** There are times when a graphic design overhaul's in order, but great graphic design doesn't require many versions; the design stays relatively the same over time. For example, graphics for Coca-Cola, McDonald's, and Subway have stayed relatively the same for decades and hardly require any new elements.

- ✔ **Allow for versatility.** A simple design with up to three colors allows for surprising flexibility. For example, you may have some promotional materials that have a light background, a dark background, or consisting of only two colors. Your graphics should fit within these confines.

- ✔ **Be appropriate.** This refers to your color scheme, name, feel, tagline, and so forth. Your design needs to directly reflect your intended audience and speak clearly about who your target market is. For example, Toys R Us knows exactly who its target is. It would be inconsistent and inappropriate to use this imagery to sell software.

Assembling the elements

Many people argue that a personal brand doesn't need a logo. Some choose to brand behind their face (which is also a wise strategy). Whatever avenue you choose, you need a few assets to remain consistent across the Internet:

- ✔ **Social media branding:** If the platform allows a background or hero banner image, make sure it's attractive, consistent, and recognizable.

- ✔ **Email templates:** *Templates* are the design of emails that you send to your audience. You send those messages through an email marketing provider such as `ConstantContact.com` or `Bronto.com`. These messages should be instantly recognizable.

- ✔ **Blog design:** This is a dynamic platform such as Wordpress, Blogger, or Tumblr. Here's where your share personal or professional thoughts and attract employment suitors.

- ✔ **Website design:** This is your home. Your website will change less than your blog, but they're not mutually exclusive. Your website should overview your career, gather leads, and tell people how to reach you.

You don't need collateral such as business cards, brochures, flyers, pamphlets, and so forth. This is a waste of time and money.

What you *do* need to start with is something "good enough" that captures people's eyes, made by following the graphic design rules we mention earlier in this chapter, and that can be effectively branded over time. Even your name is something that can be branded with relative ease. Brooks figured out that positioning himself with his full name, Brooks Brizendine, was tougher than using Brooks Briz. Try ordering pizza with a name like Brizendine.

Your relationships and leadership are most important, but if you graphically brand yourself, then you'll be more memorable.

As you begin to define your personal brand, ask yourself the following:

- ✔ How do people explain who you are and what you do?
- ✔ What do people think about you as a person and as a professional?
- ✔ How do you make people feel?

If you're not certain what the answers are, ask your ten closest personal and professional contacts for their feedback. This information will give you a baseline for how you should brand yourself (and what kind of voice to use).

Use what your friends and colleagues have picked up on that helps define you. If you try to be someone you're not, you'll come across as inauthentic.

Pushing information

Being an information pusher is a great way to establish your area of expertise. You don't always have to create your own content. Articles, research, polls, and blogs related to your knowledge base enhance your credibility with your audience. Share the good stuff you find. If something interests you, it's safe to assume your audience may like it too.

Sharing job opportunities and information on companies seeking talent is a great way to show your value. Part of being in a prominent role means looking out for the people who depend on you.

Because you know the challenges of finding a job opportunity, because jobs are scarce, and because there is a lot of competition, job boards have lost luster. (They were designed to level the playing field by providing small and big companies alike with a platform to get their jobs in front of prospective applicants.) The volume of applicants has saturated the talent pool, making it difficult for anyone to distinguish himself from other candidates.

Because most interviewing and hiring processes have become technologically driven, and because the human element has been removed from a lot of stages, candidates must go the extra mile to separate themselves from the pack.

By sharing job opportunities with others, you help them speed up their search process and increase their chances of identifying new career paths. More and faster information increases the odds of getting a job.

Pulling information

Beyond sharing, start conversations and get attention by

- Asking questions
- Soliciting feedback from your network
- Following up with your followers and connections

Getting feedback isn't easy. Instead of criticizing, offer suggestions with a focus on improvement and solution. By reframing your message, you can ensure understanding in a respectful way.

You can refine your efforts and begin to solidify your *voice* — what you stand for — after you gather more information and develop a daily routine. Your professional brand develops as you gain comfort and confidence. Your voice, your experience, and your discipline act as the foundation for how others perceive you, and the way others perceive you is your professional brand.

You can

It's curious how people wind up in their chosen occupation. Many people have a clearly defined focus. They work hard with the intention of attaining a particular skill and, ultimately, stay the course towards their goals. Doctors, for example, don't just stumble into their profession. They work hard, from coursework and practical experience to interning and specialization, to reach a place where credibility and accomplishment collide.

It doesn't always happen as planned. Some people start on one path, only to find themselves migrating in another direction. Call it an entrepreneurial spirit or a "Squirrel!" mentality, many successful people identify ways to build and use their skills, and then take those skills across occupational or industry lines. It's no easy feat. Refining a particular competency or skill set until it's an expertise allows you greater career flexibility. When skills transfer, the individual increases his potential for opportunity, growth, impact, and influence.

Think about the expertise you need to hit a Major League fastball or to return a tennis professional's first serve. Consider the delicate touch needed to bake a soufflé. Experts make their expertise look easy, even when it's not.

Remember *The Little Engine That Could?* It's probably been a long time since you heard that title. It's a story of determination, motivation, and overcoming obstacles. A train tells herself, repeatedly, "I think I can, I think I can." The more she tells herself she can get over the hill, the more she believes it, and finally she tops the mountain. Besides the fact that the story is about a train that speaks, the resounding theme is that you can do anything you put your mind to. You just have to choose to do it.

Saying aloud what you can do helps you appreciate your abilities and accomplishments, and it helps enhance your confidence. Before any interview or meeting, a quick, internal pep talk can help you focus. "I can . . . " is powerful.

Try this: Write the words *I can* and complete the sentence. Repeat this exercise two or three or ten more times. Be creative. Take your time. These sentences will help you to drill down and better understand what makes you.

Here's a few to get you started:

I can write a press release.

I can develop a marketing campaign that uses multiple social media platforms.

I can engage an audience.

Through the course of your career, you have many choices. You can seize each opportunity as a learning experience or let failures get you down. You can choose to accept things the way they are, or you can make changes. It all starts with "I can...."

To help stay motivated and productive, try Remember Win (on iTunes for Apple users). The figure shows the app, which tracks your achievements and motivates you with reminders. Reflecting upon past success can help keep you inspired. Conveying confidence is a major component for any subject matter expert.

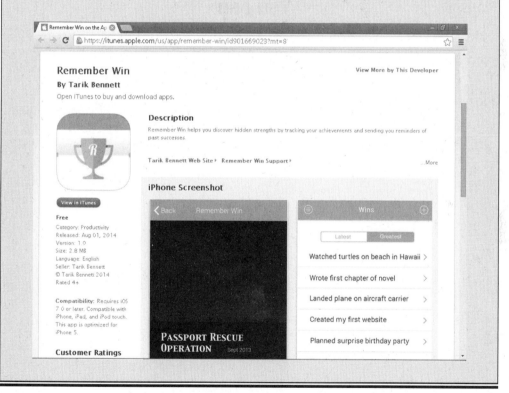

Participating

Liking, following, and poll participation are wise investments. When you get involved, you gain knowledge, meet new people, and have a chance to enlighten others. You'll develop a reputation as a subject matter expert if you consistently participate, promote, and share great content.

When you talk, you give information. When you listen, you gain information. As you listen to and engage your audience, you can cater your expertise to each member.

Contributing

Content creation is another key component in brand building. You must offer information that your audience finds useful, and you must leave them feeling that they will miss out if they don't continue to follow you.

Whether you're sharing something you found interesting, or something you created, be sure to cite your sources. Give credit to others for their work, and make sure to acknowledge any intellectual property. You'd want others to do the same for you.

Chapter 13

Creating a Winning Résumé

. . . .

In This Chapter

▶ Exploring résumé types, content, and layout

▶ Scripting cover letters

▶ Finding creative ways to résumé

▶ Understanding a recruiter's advocacy

. . . .

A résumé is the primary tool you use to introduce yourself, professionally. It features your work experience and defines job-related expertise. A well-written résumé gives an overview of your experiences and successes, and should be easy to navigate.

In this chapter, you take a new look at how to summarize your employment history, training, and relationships. You also see how to maximize the little time most hiring professionals spend reviewing your résumé.

You spend hours crafting, editing, manipulating, and deliberating over your résumé. You aim to construct a document that attracts the attention of a potential employer. You've even gone so far as to have your aunt's cousin's sister's friend, who was an English major, proofread your work.

Take a moment to rewind. Rethink how you want to present yourself. You aren't looking for any old job, you're looking for an opportunity that allows creativity and high-level communication.

Knowing the Basics

Your résumé should include the following: name, address, contact information, qualifications summary, work history, education, training, special skills and achievements, and any memberships or volunteerism.

- ✔ Use a font that's easy to read. Choose the right size for the font. Clean font types include Verdana, Calibri, Arial, and Century Gothic; points between 10 and 12 point work best.

- ✔ Stay away from columns, lines, and borders. They make it difficult for an application-tracking system that may scan the document. See Chapter 14 for more information about applicant-relationship systems.

- ✔ Use specific keywords and frame them with descriptive material that demonstrates experience and your familiarity with subjects.

- ✔ Focus on your last 10 to 12 years of work history; it's the most relevant experience.

- ✔ Proofread and pay particular attention to résumé substance and flow — the content you share, and the order it appears. It should make sense. Don't make the viewer search for information.

- ✔ Focus on accomplishments and provide real numbers or data points. Don't be afraid to **bold** that information on your résumé.

Defining Résumé Types

A résumé isn't an application. It's an introduction. It provides a snapshot of experience. Don't include your early career. Do highlight special skills and achievements.

Early career experience is best presented during an interview if necessary, not on the résumé. For example, rather than including a job dating back to 1999, on your résumé say something like, *Prior experience includes creative environments.*

Your résumé filename is a prime opportunity to stand out. Try saving your file as *Social.Media.Pro.John.Smith* or *Social.Media.Strategist.Jane.Smith.* Avoid just *John Smith Resume.* By saving the file this way, you reinforce how you wish to be perceived.

Traditional formats

Traditional résumés come in three types:

- ✔ **Chronological** résumés list work history, with the most recent position listed first, followed by previous work experience.

✔ **Functional** résumés focus on skills and experience, rather than on chronological work history. Career changers or people with extensive contract or temporary employment experience use this format.

✔ **Combination** résumés are just as they seem. It's a blending of both the chronological and functional formats. Typically, skills and experience are highlighted first, followed by a timeline of work history.

Producing portfolios, videos, and infographics

Creativity and innovation are being incorporated into how people present their employment history. Résumé format is evolving and can include *informational graphics* (infographics or infographs), videos, images, and QR codes. Links to online portfolios and projects are also becoming common.

Create a hub of information and drive your audience to that destination. Use *reciprocal linking techniques* (include a link, on all your profiles, that directs viewers to one site — ideally, LinkedIn). YouTube is the best place for your video introductions, presentations, slide shows, or online portfolios.

Old-fashioned, traditional Word document-style résumés are acceptable, but they can be a bit boring. To stand out in the crowd, you may consider incorporating a little creativity. Following are a few ways to incorporate technology on the cheap.

Enough about me. What about you?

About.me is a *vcard* (virtual business card) social media platform. Create a one-page profile at `https://about.me` and then provide links to your email, website, blog, and other social media platforms. This is an easy way to creatively show what you're all about. If you can't create a personal website for yourself, About.me is a great substitute. Because you can customize the end of your *URL* (unique resource locator or web address), it's very easy to share it with others. Having your name at the end of a web address will catch a viewer's eye and leave an impression. A customized URL reinforces your social media platform as a branding tool.

✔ Use **QR codes** for sleek, attention-grabbing, utilitarian purposes. QR Code Generator (https://www.the-qrcode-generator.com) is a free and easy tool for creating a unique QR code. Follow the simple steps to create the code, and scan it yourself to make sure it works before moving forward. A free barcode scanner app can quickly link a viewer to your professional profile. Dozens of scanner apps are available on iTunes or Google Play; try Barcode Scanner by ZXing Team or QR Barcode Scanner by WB Development Team. Add the QR code to your social media sites and print it on your business cards and marketing material. See Figure 13-1.

✔ A **portfolio** is a great way to group practical work experience and demonstrate your knowledge. It provides visual documentation of your skills and helps viewers understand your range. A portfolio is not meant to be a forum for all of your work. Instead, it should showcase your diverse accomplishments. A portfolio supplements your resume. It is not a replacement. Awards, big projects, community actions, and volunteerism are all samples of work that could be shared in a portfolio.

Figure 13-1: QR Code Generator helps get you set up.

For presentations and trainings, Slideshare (`slideshare.net`) works well with LinkedIn. It can help you compile your PowerPoint decks and share them publicly. Give participants the URL prior to the session; attendees can follow online, share the slides through social media, and save them.

✔ A **video introduction** is another attention-grabbing tool. A video introduction like the one in Figure 13-2 is similar to an elevator pitch — what you'd say to a potential employer if given the opportunity. It's an introduction that's as long as the time it takes to ride an elevator and allows you to show charisma, passion, energy, and enthusiasm. This vehicle provides you with a blank canvas to emphasize your creative talents while highlighting your communicative abilities.

Figure 13-2: This video introduction gets attention.

✔ An **infograph** provides a whimsical way to display your experience. In Figures 13-3 and 13-4 you can see content, design, and branding coming together to capture attention.

Re.vu (`http://re.vu`) is a site that creates an infographic résumé for you based upon your LinkedIn information. Improve your LinkedIn profile before you create your Re.vu account. This will save you a lot of time.

Take a peek at other peoples' visual résumés on Pinterest (`pinterest.com/search/?q=résumé`). A search for **résumé** uncovers dozens of work histories presented in eye-catching ways.

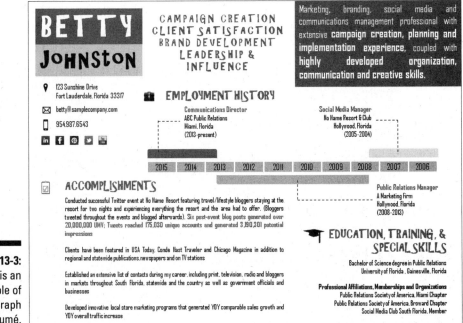

Figure 13-3:
This is an example of an infograph résumé.

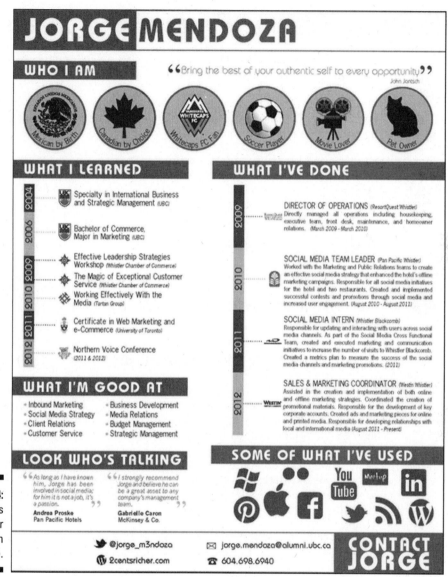

Figure 13-4: Here's another infograph résumé.

Spotting Résumé Content and Layout

People use abbreviations, acronyms, numbers, and characters in their daily lives while texting, tweeting, or commenting on blogs.

Employment-related communication requires proper grammar, spelling, and penmanship. There's no quicker way to be excluded from consideration than by poorly representing yourself with a slapped-together résumé.

Your name, address, email, phone numbers, and even your LinkedIn profile address should appear at the top of your résumé. Make it easy to be contacted.

Killing the objective

Listing an objective on a résumé has gone the way of the Saturn automobile and Jell-O Pudding Pops — they no longer exist. An objective is presumptuous. They're all about what you want, rather than what the employer wants.

Summarizing qualifications

Insert a quick list of key words or phrases, highlight your strengths and experience, in just a few sentences or bullet points. A well-written summary of qualifications prepares the hiring manager for the rest of your résumé; the manager sees you through that lens.

Think about your competencies here. *Competencies* are the measurable or observable knowledge, skills, abilities, and behaviors critical to successful job performance. They are what every company will look for in a employee or consulting partner.

The caveat here is that times are changing. Companies are seeing core competencies as outdated because they create *silos* (isolated areas) of skills and overlook talents. Until more companies evolve their thinking, include references to key phrasing. You have to act as a pro to be treated as a pro.

A strong summary of qualifications may look like these:

Example 1: *Marketing, branding, social media and communications management professional with extensive campaign creation, planning, and implementation experience, coupled with highly developed organization, communication, and creative skills*

Example 2: *High-energy, fearless leader with a creative edge. Proven adaptive ability to build, guide, develop, and inspire teams with a collaborative approach from project ideation to launch. Knack for setting clear vision and driving concepts to create innovative and interactive team experiences. Multifaceted, passionate, and innovative thinker with outstanding presentation skills, technical knowledge, and ability to have fun.*

Another key way to differentiate your résumé is to follow the wording with specific words or phrases that specify your capabilities. Use the words in the summary or list them as bullets under the summary. In either case, the words will capture attention, and that's what this is all about. Right? Some examples include:

- ✔ Campaign creation
- ✔ Client satisfaction
- ✔ Brand development
- ✔ Budget planning and adherence
- ✔ Sales development
- ✔ Leadership and influence
- ✔ Operational excellence
- ✔ Marketing program implementation
- ✔ Organizational skills

Highlighting accomplishments with data

Your employment history is the meat. Potential employers spend the most time reviewing this portion of your résumé. Maximize this space with details that capture attention.

1. **List your work experience and boldface your title and employment dates.**

    Start with your most recent experience first and work backward. Pay attention to tense here. It's not *oversaw;* it's *oversee* if you're currently working with the company. When you get to previous positions, write in past tense.

2. **On the next line, list the company name in normal font.**

    Don't boldface the company name. Bold captures attention, so use it to highlight you, not the company you worked for.

3. **Insert a one- or two-line description of the company.**

This is in case the manager, who may not know the company, can familiarize herself.

Use this space to call out what the company does and how large it is. *Lead a team within this global organization* isn't as profound as *Lead social media and marketing efforts for this global, $20M, industry-leading multi-media firm.* (And notice the boldface dollar volume.)

Boldface numbers, percentages, special projects, and high-profile activities or events.

4. **For each position, list accomplishments in bullet form beneath.**

Keep these guidelines in mind:

- Tie more accomplishments to more recent positions.

- Accomplishments related to cost savings and increased efficiencies are important because they demonstrate past success.

- Use -ed ending words like *created, developed, organized, planned,* and *implemented.*

For social media accomplishments, reference number of impressions, *unique monthly visitors (UMV),* or overall reach, for a campaign you managed.

Visit www.dummies.com/extras/gettingasocialmediajob for more résumé details and to see a video résumé.

Focusing on specialized skills and training

Specialized skills, training, and education demonstrate your commitment to your profession. Following your work history, include a section on your résumé for your formal and informal learning.

In order of appearance

- ✔ **List college degrees in full.** *Bachelor of Science degree in Telecommunication from University of Florida* is better than *BS from UF.*

- ✔ **Include your technical skills.** List your knowledge of Windows, Microsoft Office (PowerPoint, Excel, Access, Word, Outlook, and Publisher), Adobe Photoshop, WordPress, Apple iOS, along with any other specialized software. Include any links to your portfolios, presentations, or videos.

- ✔ **Reference any volunteerism, associations, or group memberships.**

Review previous learning and development material, certificates of completion, or industry certification program participation that you have completed. Include programs related to communicating feedback, situational leadership, whole message modeling, coaching models, diversity and inclusion, Six Sigma, and brand building if you've participated.

Crafting the Perfect Cover Letter

A _cover letter_ supports a résumé. Typically, cover letters provide detailed information about why you're qualified for the job. Effective cover letters explain the reasons for your interest in the specific organization and identify your most relevant skills and experiences.

Cover letters are often seen as a _pre-qualifier._ Companies that insist upon a cover letter often use the letter as a tool for insight into who you are professionally, and what you can do if you join their company.

Use proper grammar and spelling, and a clear focus, in your cover letter.

Defining the types of cover letters

Cover letters help you apply for, or ask about, jobs.

Types of cover letters include

- Send an _application letter_ or upload it with your résumé when you're applying for jobs. The job application letters you send explain to the employer why you're qualified for the position and why you should be selected for an interview.

- Send an _inquiry letter_ to companies that may be hiring, but haven't advertised job openings. Inquiry letters should contain information on why the company interests you, and why your skills and experience would be an asset to the company. Information on how you will follow-up and your contact information should be included.

- In a _referral letter,_ mention by name the person who referred you, and how you know that person. A referral can go a long way when you're applying for jobs. Hiring managers and recruiters are more likely to take a closer look at candidates who were referred by someone they know. Chapter 12 talks more about referrals and networking.

- Send a _letter of interest,_ also known as a _prospecting letter,_ to let companies know you're interested in jobs that may be open or become available in the future.

You can send cover letters as an email attachment or in the body of an email message, post them to a job site when you apply online, include them as a message on LinkedIn or other networking sites, or send them via mail.

When you're sending an email cover letter, follow the employer's instructions for how to submit your cover letter and résumé.

Components of the perfect cover letter

Customize your cover letter specifically for each position you seek.

When writing a cover letter, the layout of your letter is important, so it's easy to read and looks professional.

It's important to properly space the layout of the cover letters you send, with space between the heading, the greeting, each paragraph, the closing, and your signature. Single space your letter, and leave a space between each paragraph. Left justify your letter.

1. **Begin with your contact information.**

    This is the inside address, just like you learned in grade school. Your name, address, phone number, and email address should be included.

2. **Include the date you're sending the letter, followed by the employer's contact information.**

    Include the employer's name, title, company, and address.

3. **Insert the salutation.**

    This is a professional, yet friendly, greeting. *Dear Mr. or Ms.* is appropriate here.

4. **Write the introductory paragraph.**

    Keep it short and to the point. Hiring professionals have limited time to review your letter. Include the job title and information about the position you're applying for (or the person who referred you).

5. **Write the middle paragraphs.**

    The middle paragraph or two should describe what you have to offer the employer. Explain why you're qualified and discuss how your skills and experience translate for the specific position.

6. Write the conclusion.

Thank the employer for his time and consideration. Invite the person to contact you with any questions. Restate your interest in the organization. If you're bold, mention when and how *you'll* follow up.

7. Include a closing and your signature.

The closing should be something professional like *Sincerely* or *Respectfully*. If the letter's printed, include your signature followed by your typed signature. If it's electronic, simply use your typed signature.

Valuing Professional Recruiters

There are people with questionable motives in every profession. These opportunists are only concerned with themselves. You've encountered people whose pushy communication tries to force you to make a quick decision. In recruiting, the high-pressure, aggressive individual is a *headhunter*. A headhunter doesn't view people as individuals. A headhunter views candidates as a commodity.

Not all recruiters are headhunters.

Many types of recruiters exist. Some specialize in specific industries or occupations; some represent one or many companies.

Make sure you understand the different types of recruiters and how to communicate with your recruiter. However the recruiter communicates, respond in kind. (See Chapter 14 for interview tips.)

Corporate recruiters

Corporate recruiters are experts when it comes to their companies. They're knowledgeable about the hiring process and the intimate workings of the organization. Corporate recruiters are employed by the organizations they support.

Corporate recruiters' knowledge of the competition is based upon observation from afar. They can't provide objective feedback. Corporate recruiters are experts at buying time because they have to manage an internal process as well.

Work hard to connect and maintain the appropriate level of communication with corporate recruiters. Be cautious about how often you reach out.

Third-party recruiters

Many third-party recruiters have worked in the industries their serve. Their industry knowledge, and the people they know, make them good resources. Like corporate recruiters, *third-party recruiters* are paid by the company that employs them. However, third-party recruiters don't get paid unless a candidate is identified and hired. Because of that, third-party recruiters spend more time preparing and coaching you (and their other candidates) through the process.

David began his career as a radio personality. David conducted interviews with local and national celebrities, musicians, and entertainers before getting into recruiting with a firm specializing in the hospitality industry.

Third-party recruiters think in terms of milestones or steps in a process. The further along a recruiter can extend an interview process, the greater the likelihood the candidate will get a job offer.

You can speak more openly with third-party recruiters. By doing so, they can test the reaction to certain job-related information and discuss appropriate strategic responses with you. Remember, third-party recruiters want you to get hired, The more information you give them, the more easily they can guide you. For example, you may have had a difficult boss. Clearly, you shouldn't speak ill of anyone during an interview. A third-party recruiter can help you figure out the best way to anticipate and respond to questions related to that boss.

Your best bet is to always be honest and positive when speaking of other people or past employers.

Recruiters can shed light on the hiring process and help you understand how other companies approach hiring for the same (or similar) positions. Third-party recruiters analyze markets. They know the players and they study the perception of each. They understand the advantages and disadvantages associated with the competition. They can provide insight into culture, leadership, performance, compensation (salary, benefits, bonuses), relocation, and cost of living.

Because they're students of the industries they serve, and because they work with many people, third-party recruiters are terrific resources. They lend perspective. You should ask your recruiter specific questions related to companies, culture, market conditions, and the competitive landscape (like who else is hiring and how much they pay for specific jobs).

Chapter 14

Preparing to Nail Your Interview

- -

In This Chapter

▶ Researching and investigating companies

▶ Managing applicant tracking and assessment systems

▶ Understanding interview types

▶ Tracking interview activity

▶ Negotiating and accepting a job offer

- -

An interview process isn't easy. It's uncomfortable. It forces you to reflect and focus upon your career path. You're confronted with the reality that you may not have met your own expectations.

Then again, you may have exceeded all expectations and are uncertain how to navigate in a changing environment. Whichever scenario, a tactical approach to interview strategy is in order.

Using the 7-3-1 Principle

You can use an individual interview strategy or a good career strategy. *Career strategy* is big picture. If you're looking to apply your skills in a new industry, you may be willing to take an entry-level position. That's a career strategy. *Individual strategy* is more about targeting specific companies and focusing on the short term.

Changing career paths is a decision you make when your personal and professional needs, challenges, and desires come together at a particular time.

REMEMBER

Remain open to new options. You don't have to leave the path you're on to explore what's happening on other paths.

After you frame your career portrait and know the road you're on, figure out the best way to traverse the interview landscape.

The 7-3-1 principle is straightforward. Target 7 companies to interview with. Blow them away. Get 3 offers. Make 1 decision.

If you win every interview you go on, you increase the likelihood you will receive multiple job offers. One employment offer feels great; it's comforting to know a company is interested in you. More than one employment offer, however, gives you leverage: Now you have to make a decision.

Learning About Culture

Companies pride themselves on culture. It's a differentiator for them. They use their values, visions, systems, symbols, beliefs, and habits to attract talent to their organizations. Culture is the little red thread through any organization; a common view for all employees.

Understanding a company's culture, and mimicking its values and wording, can help you win the interview process.

- ✔ Make a short list of companies that you'd work for. Be realistic. You can't slide right in if you've never worked in the industry.

- ✔ See if the company's leadership, culture, and mission are in tune with your needs. Knowing what you're looking for in a company can help guide you.

- ✔ Identify the players. Review the impact or contributions they've made to the company or community, or to other institutions they're affiliated with.

Exploring the heart of an organization

Companies and roles that provide the support and environment you need are a fit. Fit is hard to find.

- ✔ *Companies that show commitment to supporting surrounding communities* often appreciate and value individual and team contributors as well. If you're an active community member, chances are these companies will provide flexibility and support the initiatives you hold dear.

- ✔ *Companies that embrace technology and innovation* may be more flexible about scheduling or telecommuting opportunities. These companies may also expect more production in exchange for the freedom they provide. Still, other companies may present more structure and have more stringent work expectations. However, companies that embrace tech may also provide great work environments and strong benefits, rewards, and recognition programs.

Locating mission and values

Mission and vision statements explain an organization's purpose and direction. When expressed clearly and concisely, they can motivate teams, or the organization as a whole, with an inspiring vision of the future.

Mission statements and vision statements do distinctly different jobs.

> ✔ *Mission statements* define the organization's purpose and main objectives. These statements are set in the present tense, and they explain, to members and to people outside the organization, why you exist as a business. Mission statements tend to be short, clear, and powerful.

> ✔ *Vision statements* also define an organization's purpose, but focus on its goals and aspirations. These statements are designed to be uplifting and inspiring. They're also timeless: Even if the organization changes its strategy, the vision statement stays the same.

Visit the company's website. Explore the About Us section, and investigate the company values. LinkedIn and Facebook company pages are also great venues for mission and values research. The streaming information provides a wide range of detail, from varying perspectives.

Perception

Perception is interesting. Cases in point: Today, ExxonMobil is the top performing American company in the world, surpassing Apple. Analysts have reveled in the company's steady performance on the stock market over the last 20 years. Investors squeal like robust pigs in poop about the potential of ExxonMobil's stock to outperform expectations.

Yet, public perception was very different in March 1989. Back then, the Exxon Valdez, an oil tanker bound for Long Beach, California, struck Prince William Sound's Bligh Reef and spilled 260,000 to 750,000 barrels of crude oil. The accident is still considered one of the most devastating human-caused environmental disasters.

As circumstances change, so does perception.

After years of top sales in the automotive industry, Toyota launched recall after recall in response to faulty equipment. Perception of the company diminished and Toyota addressed mechanical and technological concerns. Through smart pricing and a commitment to environmentally sound vehicles, Toyota is once again a top automaker.

Polaroid was known for its innovation. It inspired great ideas and fostered an environment where employees could create and improve constantly. Steve Jobs was known to admire the organization and its style of leadership. Instant photos changed the way people saw the world and inspired a generation. Today, technology (much of which was spawned by Polaroid), bankruptcy, and time have left Polaroid behind.

Beware. Perception is not always reality. It just takes time to understand.

Validating perception: Blogs

Even in an age of transparency, you still need to know how to extract information. Blogs are valuable tools in your job search arsenal because they go beyond a product or service. They provide information you can't find elsewhere.

Companies that do it well blog about community outreach and highlight their employees' successes. Some companies have multiple blogs for multiple audiences. Company blogs reveal how the organization operates. You can learn about affinity groups, charitable work, educational opportunities, tuition reimbursement, and health and wellness programs.

Beyond company blogs, search for personal blogs from people who work (or have worked) with an organization. Many of these blogs aren't directly affiliated with the organization. This information can be just as important as the company blog because you get a glimpse inside an organization without the corporate filter.

Reviewing these unaffiliated sites can help you uncover talking points during an interview process. For example, Ted Ryan, the Director of Heritage Communication at Coca-Cola, blogs about the rich history and culture of his company. Following his blog may help you better understand what makes Coca-Cola different than all the other cola companies.

Be cautious of rogue sites. Don't take every word as fact. These types of sites are often where former employees go to blow off steam.

Don't stop with blogs. Seek more information.

Validating perception: Testimonials

Friends, colleagues, and confidants can offer insight. If you don't know anyone within an organization, a *testimonial* (a personalized recommendation) can help pull back the curtain.

Companies use real employees to cast their message and build their brand awareness. By using existing employees to share a vision of life inside the organization, companies make employment more attainable while substantiating their claims. Testimonials also lend credibility because the people providing testimonials tend to be relatable to the reader.

Advice and feedback are only as good as the person providing it.

Take advantage of recommendations on LinkedIn. The site allows your connections to recommend or endorse you. Pay it forward for your connections too.

A simple Follow Friday (#FF) shout out on Twitter can drive attention to the profiles of the people you called out. See Figure 14-1.

Validating perception: Glassdoor and Career Bliss

The more information you have, the better you can target companies that match your needs. Some sites have feedback from current and former employees, in addition to what the companies and the communities they support have. Sites like Glassdoor and Career Bliss can make your investigation into a company more robust.

Glassdoor.com holds a growing database of 6 million company reviews, CEO approval ratings, salary reports, interview reviews and questions, benefits reviews, office photos, and more. Unlike other jobs sites, all of this information is entirely shared by those who have an intimate knowledge of the company — the employees. You can see pros and cons in company reviews, salary information, and interview experiences. Glassdoor offers a variety of reports, including Top Companies for Culture & Values, Top Companies for Comp & Benefits, Best Places to Work, Highest Rated CEOs, and more. See Figure 14-2.

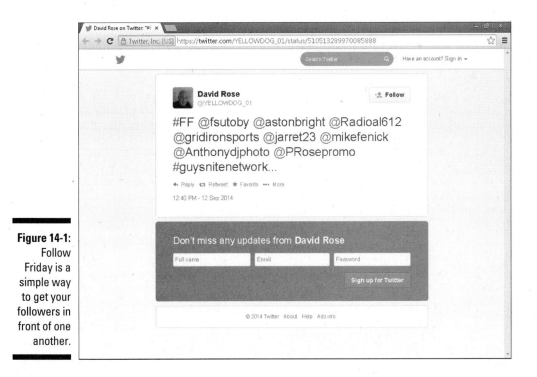

Figure 14-1:
Follow Friday is a simple way to get your followers in front of one another.

Figure 14-2:
Glassdoor
helps make
companies
transparent.

Career Bliss, at `careerbliss.com`, boasts millions of job postings, salaries, and company reviews. Its search capability is quick. See Figure 14-3.

Validating perception: Company websites

From history to segments served to open opportunities, company websites are full of information.

- ✔ Check out the About Us section for stock price, community news, talent on the rise.

- ✔ Seek out press material and announcements.

In a tight labor market, or when a company's hiring, you look for job links in plain sight. Typically labeled Careers, Jobs, Join Us, or Employment, look for the links in the top right or top left of the page. If you don't see it there, scroll to the bottom of the page — the next likely spot.

For help searching online for companies, visit `www.dummies.com/extras/gettingasocialmediajob`.

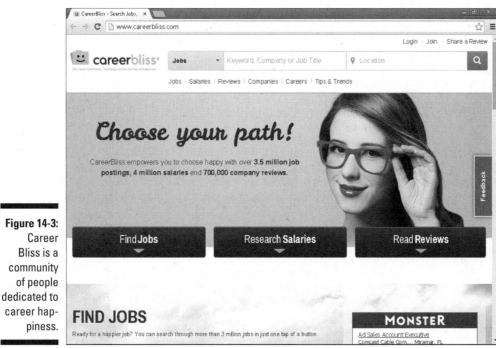

Figure 14-3:
Career Bliss is a community of people dedicated to career happiness.

Pay attention to the job posting's requisition number, the contact person, the job title and location for future reference. It's a good idea to keep a log of everything you do during the job search.

Online job applications run the gamut from company to company. Some companies want to capture your information briefly, while others request a great detail of highly personal information.

Expect to spend 10–25 minutes completing an online job application. Do so in one sitting. Often, the system gets tied up if you stop and try to return at a later time.

Plenty of candidates are overlooked because of an inability to connect with the interviewer. Uncover what the interviewer cares about. People are attracted to people they perceive to be like themselves.

Early in his career, David was interviewing for a company that had recently acquired another company. I knew the stock price, the companies that had been acquired previously, and who the division leaders were. I was prepared. A few weeks prior to my interview, an executive with the company died from a heart attack. He was young and it was unexpected. During the interview, the interviewer made reference to his mentor and, with teary eyes, shared that his mentor had recently passed away. I put two and two together, and knew exactly who he was talking about. I made a simple comment. I said the individual was well respected and would be sorely missed. I didn't think much of the comment. I just rolled with it. Months later, after joining the company, the interviewer told me that he knew I would be perfect for the job when I referenced his mentor's name. He explained that I was so well prepared that he knew details wouldn't slip past me.

Taking on Applicant Relationship Systems (ARS)

Spreadsheet, database, *applicant tracking system (ATS), contact management system (CMS),* and *contact relationship management (CRM)* are but a few of the ways companies gather, store, and track your applicant information. Some systems are simply reservoirs, holding data. Others let users pull information, search, and manage relationships.

Knowing how applicant relationship systems work can help you stand out from the crowd.

When you submit an online job application, the data goes into a database. Someone in charge of hiring is notified and reviews your data. You'll probably get an automated message letting you know they received your information.

Complete applications in their entirety. Don't hold off on sharing details related to employment or criminal history. What you say is reviewed for background verification. If your application doesn't match what the background check reveals, you'll be disqualified.

Finding multiple positions

ARS tools are only as good as the people using them. If the hiring person is astute, she'll refine her focus on a group of candidates. But the hiring person may be overworked or lack training. For example, maybe you've applied for one position and found another position that interests you in the same company. You may think that you're already being considered since you already applied. You're wrong.

If you find multiple opportunities available with an organization, apply to each one separately unless you're directed otherwise. You'll be linked to multiple needs and increase your odds of being considered for employment.

Resist the urge to apply for random positions just to get your name in front of the recruiter. This can make you appear desperate or unaware of what you are truly qualified to do. Many recruiters express frustration about job seekers who apply to every available position.

Thinking like the system does

Information is pulled into a profile from your résumé and online application. Each applicant has a profile that's searchable in the company's system.

Applicant relationship systems can be thrown off by borders, columns, lines, and alternative font. If your résumé has these elements, your information may not appear in search results. Chapter 13 explains résumé types, content, and layout.

After your data is entered, the company user (recruiter, HR manager, hiring leader, or the like) does keyword searches. He may use some code searches or use detailed search strings. However the approach, the point is to drill down to a pool of candidates. Recruiters, by the way, are evaluated for their performance. One of the criteria that is tracked and monitored is applicant-to-hire ratio. A typical applicant-to-hire ratio could be 18 to 1.

If you submit an application or résumé and don't get an acknowledgement, consider this:

✔ **Stay organized.** Check your email spam folder; automated messages often go there. It's very easy to mistake a message misdirected to a junk folder as a lack of communication. If you are a candidate, track the company you've applied to and add its email extension to your "safe-senders" list.

✔ **Second-guess your hold music.** Choose your tune wisely if your cell phone allows you to play music while callers are connecting. While the company representative may be a huge Sir Mix-A-Lot fan, he probably doesn't want to hear "Baby Got Back" when trying to coordinate an interview. (Apologies to Sir Mix-A-Lot.)

✔ **Second-guess your outgoing voice message.** Imagine how your outgoing message sounds to a potential employer. Review wording, how clearly you're speaking, and overall length.

Humility goes a long way. Stay away from "I'm your ideal candidate" statements. Don't presume that you're the best candidate that you've only read a job description for. Confidence can be good, but not in an environment where you don't have all the information.

Elevate others and accept responsibility for challenges. Companies are looking for these traits.

Realizing every company does it differently

Some companies use standardized interview guides with pre-established questions (and follow up questions) targeting particular competencies, while other companies simply develop a straightforward list of questions. Still, other companies expect you to participate in a job shadow experience, or want you to complete a small project.

Every company's process is different. Focus on what you can control. Keep clear notes on every company you apply to or interview with. Record names, dates, contact information, and take detailed notes for reference later.

Preparing for an Assessment

Many companies develop complex, secure systems for applicant information. In the hiring process, assessments are used to assist in selection.

Here are the basics regarding assessments:

- ✔ Assessments measure job fit over time, not intelligence.
- ✔ Companies have their top current performers take assessments. All applicants for a specific position take the same (or a similar) assessment.
- ✔ Assessments try to predict your performance and their own ability to retain you in the future.

Some companies disqualify candidates if they score outside a predetermined range, regardless of any interaction. Other companies hire candidates no matter the assessment results.

To prepare, keep these tips in mind:

- ✔ Eat a good breakfast; get a good night's sleep.
- ✔ Take and keep a copy of your resume nearby.
- ✔ Complete the assessment.
- ✔ Imagine yourself already in the role and respond to the questions accordingly.

Valuing Types of Interviews

Set yourself up for a successful interview by preparing according to the interview type:

- ✔ Telephone
- ✔ Video
- ✔ Live
- ✔ Meal
- ✔ Panel
- ✔ Working

Managing the phone interview

Many companies begin with a telephone interview. Don't underestimate the importance of this step: This interview will likely determine whether you move forward in the process.

- ✔ Make sure you have clear reception.
- ✔ Never disrupt a telephone interview to take another call.
- ✔ Eliminate all background noise and possible interruptions.
- ✔ Reference your resources.
- ✔ Have a copy of your resume, prepared questions, company literature, and notes in front of you.
- ✔ Pull up the company's website and the interviewer's profile on your computer.
- ✔ Speak clearly and enunciate.
- ✔ Stand or move around to keep your energy level up.

Find telephone interview tips on Twitter (search.twitter.com). Search **#phoneinterviewtips** for daily tips.

Embracing the video interview

Many companies use video conferencing to meet candidates. Approach this interview just as you would a face-to-face interview.

- ✔ Dress professionally from head to toe.
- ✔ Bring a note pad and multiple copies of your resume, and smile.
- ✔ Look at the camera when you're answering questions.

Try Skype (`skype.com`) in advance. All you need is a web camera or hand-held device with the app and to create a free account. See Figure 14-4.

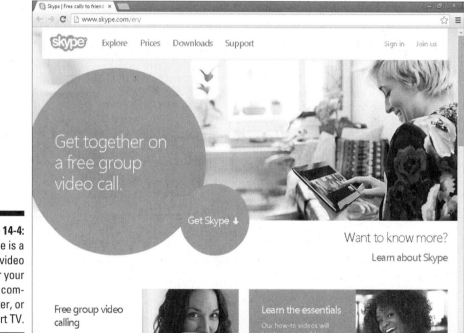

Figure 14-4: Skype is a free video tool for your phone, computer, or smart TV.

The real you shining through

Companies like HireVue (`hirevue.com`) have jumped into the video-interviewing stream. HireVue offers a tool that allows employers to see and hear candidates so they can gain deeper insight into personalities and abilities. The software allows candidates to demonstrate talents, share stories, and answer questions through digital interviews and skills-validation exercises.

Performing during the live interview

There are different types of live interviews:

- The *traditional interview* is most common. You meet with an interviewer, one-on-one, and you're asked questions designed to gather basic information.

- The *meal interview* is when an interviewer interacts with you outside the traditional work environment. Typically, meal interviews occur when time is limited. It can be in an airport lounge or at a Starbucks. It's often less formal, but as with any interview, never let your guard down. Stay focused on the conversation and order something that won't stick in your teeth.

Accepting the importance of the panel interview

In a panel interview, leaders (most often from other departments or group teams within the company), are brought together to participate in the hiring process. This lends alternative perspective, and ensures that all parties feel their opinions have been valued. Someone from the Benefits Department may sit in on an interview for a social media manager. The departments often work together when promoting an annual insurance rollout. While they aren't in the same department, they do work together. Panel interviews help build consensus.

During this type of interview, also known as *group* or *360 interview,* each person may ask you questions, and each person may use a different interview style.

Regardless of the type, close interviews by thanking the interviewer for his/her time. Let the interviewer know that the conversation was informative, and restate your interest in the opportunity. Ask about next steps in the process and when to expect to hear from the interviewer.

Mastering Interview Basics

The first 30 seconds of your interview are crucial. From there,

- Exude a positive attitude and pay attention.

- Clasp your hands as your speaking. Lean forward as you speak to increase the bond between you and the interviewer.

- Be a good listener.

✔ Represent yourself honestly; don't lie or deceive.

✔ Take notes.

✔ Don't speak inappropriately of a former company or supervisor.

If you're in a live or video interview, keep these tips in mind:

✔ Maintain direct eye contact.

✔ Be aware of non-verbal communication.

✔ Keep both feet on the floor and sit on the front edge of the chair.

✔ Sit on the tail of your jacket; it will force your posture upright.

Expect behavioral-based and situational-based interview questions.

✔ *Behavioral interview questions* focus on the past so employers can try to predict future behavior.

✔ *Situational interview questions* concentrate on future performance. The questions are similar to behavioral questions, but the interviewer asks you to envision a future scenario rather than asking you to draw upon past experience.

The interviewer will likely ask questions related to your career goals, current and past positions, your motivation, the qualities you possess, activities you've participated in that demonstrate initiative, why you're a strong candidate for the position, and why you're an asset to their organization.

Pause before responding. You don't want to begin answering too soon, only to find you didn't answer the question.

Speak about specific situations, actions you took, and ultimate outcomes.

Asking Questions

The research you did on the company will be obvious during the interview.

Strong candidates have questions. A lack of questions may be mistaken for a lack of interest. Prepare questions ahead of time.

Ask questions pertaining to the position, organization, or training. Make your questions insightful:

✔ What does the person in this job need to do to be successful?

✔ What's the biggest challenge that needs to be addressed right away?

Seizing the opportunity to interview

There's a reason people say that finding a job is a job in and of itself. But take any opportunity to interview. An interview is an opportunity to make an impression, to make a connection, to identify common interests and mutual connections.

The information you get during the interview process, coupled with your research, gives you all you need to consider. Don't make a decision until then.

> ✔ What kinds of resources are budgeted already?
>
> ✔ Why is the position open?
>
> ✔ How have you developed your team members?

If the interviewer isn't focusing on major accomplishments, ask the interviewer to clarify the position, responsibilities, and specific skills. It may sound something like the following: "I don't have a complete understanding of your real job needs. Would you please give me an overview of what the job entails and describe some of the key challenges in the job? Then, I'll be able to provide real examples of similar work or similar situations."

Close out the interview the right way: Draw an alignment between your skills and experience with those sought for the position.

Conveying your interest is very important. Many recruiters express the lack of enthusiasm or even lack of interest displayed by candidates. There should be no question that you're interested in the position.

Etching Out Areas of Focus and Executing

To get an edge, look for links between you and the interviewer. A brief, yet respectful, nod to someone's past demonstrates your desire to go above and beyond. That little extra bit of information can help set you apart.

Your research may have shown you a link. During the interview, scan for degrees on walls, certificates of completion, photos, and banners. Make sure the connection is worth pursuing; just because your friend graduated from the same university as the interviewer doesn't mean there's any value in mentioning it.

Identifying key competencies that every employer wants

Identify the key attributes for a particular position. For example, a company seeking a community manager may value customer-focused experience. Someone with that experience is likely to anticipate needs and ensure value is delivered.

If you're the candidate interviewing, talk about how you provided assistance or rectified a poor customer experience. Customer focus is a key attribute.

Provide responses that explain, in detail, your high-performing behavior.

Focus on the areas in Table 14-1 as well.

Table 14-1	Focus on These Areas in Interviews	
Areas	**What It Includes**	**What to Discuss**
Leadership and influencing skills	This is the ability to develop winning strategies while maintaining a broad business perspective.	Talk about consistent communication with clear and actionable goals. Discuss how you follow up, provide feedback, and measure performance. Think about how you impacted a person or team that didn't directly report to you.
Improvement and solutions	This refers to carrying out rational, systematic analysis to identify a problem's root cause. It's your ability to make sound judgments under changing circumstances, while driving innovation.	Share how you balance intuition and facts to make good decisions. Explore how you analyze and challenge the status quo.
Excellence	This is about personal and professional standards: ethics, integrity, high standards, determination, and resilience.	Talk about when you had to learn something difficult in a short period of time.
Time management, planning, and organization	This area emphasizes how you accomplish short- and long-term goals. It delves into whether you take personal accountability for achieving individual and shared goals.	Share how you set clear objectives, define measurable criteria, and establish tactics to complete all goals.

Areas	What It Includes	What to Discuss
Drive for results	This skill means adjusting to and overcoming obstacles. It's the ability to respond quickly, to persevere, to alter plans, and to capitalize on changing circumstances.	Talk about how you continuously seek contingency options and adapt plans. Discuss early preparation and tracking.
Communication	An appreciation for the ability to communicate is vital in all industries.	Emphasize your ability to establish and deliver a message and receive information. When you actively listen, you gather information.

Telling great stories can paint a picture

The ability to tell a great story is a major edge over your competition.

Preparation allows you to be flexible when an unexpected call comes in. Preparation gives you a chance to focus on behaviors and actions, and helps you feel familiar with the information you share. Familiarity begets confidence, and can help you capture attention.

To be a great storyteller, keep your audience wanting more. Use this framework:

1. Describe a specific situation.

The beginning is brief. It captures attention and lures the audience to the heart of your story.

2. Explain the action you took.

The middle of the story is the heart. Talk about data, statistics, accomplishments, and achievements.

3. Explain the outcome of the activity you described.

Just be sure to listen. You don't want to talk *at* the audience. You want to talk *with* them.

In addition to researching a company in preparation for an interview, do these steps:

1. Write down and refine your stories.

2. Identify the key wording you want to use.

3. **Read and re-read your stories.**

   Do it in front of a mirror.

4. **After several run-throughs, set the paper aside and tell the story, with a big smile on your face, to yourself in the mirror.**

Leaving the perfect message

Leaving a message for a potential employer is different than leaving a message for a friend.

When you leave a job-related voice message, keep it under 30 seconds. Clearly state your name and full ten-digit phone number, and mention the name of the person you're calling three times in the message. Calling the person by first name creates a more personalized interaction.

Hello [the name of the person you're calling]. This is [your full name]. I'm calling to follow up with regard to the résumé I submitted recently. [The name of the person you're calling], I am hoping for a few minutes of your time to discuss how my skills and experience may add to your organization. I can be reached at [XXX-XXX-XXXX] or via email at [me@abc.com]. [The name of the person you're calling], thanks for your time. I look forward to speaking with you soon.

Using social media to follow up with immediacy

Chapter 12 explains peak social media usage times and how to best use your tools. After an interview, shift your usage from information sharing to *tactical communication* — incrementally done to keep you top of mind.

Direct and instant messaging through social media platforms, in addition to texting, have become common communication vehicles.

Arm yourself with as many communication tools as you can handle during a job search. You want to be easy to communicate with. And remember, an interview process is private. Don't share who you're interviewing with on social media. You never know who's reading, and you never want to reveal confidential information.

Keep close to your tools:

✔ Choose instant messaging (IM) or direct messaging (DM) when communicating with a potential employer on social platforms.

✔ Set up reminders and notifications to follow up as directed, to explore new leads, and to reiterate interest.

✔ Check in on your platforms two to three times during the day. If you delay responding to a request, the employer will move on to the next candidate.

Tracking and Managing Submissions and Contacts

Interviewing can be a lot like an airplane arriving at its destination. The moment the plane stops, the bell dings and everyone jumps up. Everyone is antsy. It's a hurry-up-and-wait process.

From the start of your search, keep diligent records of your activity:

✔ The company

✔ Contact person

✔ Positions you applied for

✔ Date of contact

✔ Type of contact (phone, IM, text, email)

✔ Record action (left voice message, sent email)

✔ Any special directions

Long term, you can refer back and reflect upon your job search. You may even develop empathy for other candidates, which could make you a better leader in the future.

Noting actions and scheduling follow-ups

You may be responding to interview requests via email and through social media platforms more than through voice messaging.

Create wording templates for multiple scenarios like following up after an interview or checking on the status of your candidacy. Emails give you more space, but social sites and texting are limited by number of characters. Write a general introduction that you can change. This makes things faster and helps you reach a larger audience.

Thank you for your interest in me. I'd welcome a chance to further discuss my background, and to learn more about [company name]. I will make myself available to you at your convenience. Please let me know when I should expect your call. My number is XXX-XXX-XXXX.

Set reminders and schedule follow-up communication in your email or contact-management tool immediately following any interaction. The frequency of communication increases the further along you are in the process. In the beginning, follow up every three days unless directed otherwise. Later in the process, you may have to follow up multiple times in a given day.

Making the most out of contact apps and tools

Tools, especially contact relationship management (CRM) apps and programs, can help you be more efficient:

- ✔ **Android** users should try Google products and resources: Gmail, Calendar, Maps, Alerts, Forms, Docs, Translate, and more. Synchronize your information across devices. You're more accessible that way and you can be more responsive.

- ✔ **iPhone** users may want to explore Power Contacts (`https://itunes.apple.com/us/app/power-contacts/id476986356?mt=8`). This app lets you export contacts to and from desktop contact management applications, including Outlook, Gmail, Yahoo Mail, and Mac Address Book. Add a contact based on an email signature. Then send a LinkedIn invite from the app. You can also send out mass emails to multiple contacts, add calendar reminders to follow up with a contact, and view previous communication.

- ✔ `Plaxo.com` is a web-based CRM with a very specific focus on contacts. Like Gmail, the web interface means accessibility anywhere as long as you have an internet connection and a web browser. Plaxo syncs to tons of popular contact management apps, including Microsoft Outlook and Apple's Address Book.

- ✔ `Zoho.com` integrates productivity, business, and collaborative applications in addition to a CRM. A free version may be helpful to you, and you can access your account through the Zoho CRM app at the Google Play Store.

As your network grows, and as you communicate with more people, using a contact management system becomes an essential tool in your job search arsenal.

Negotiating an Offer

An employment offer feels terrific. It's validation: A company's willing to pay you for your skills and abilities. Ideally, you have multiple offers from multiple companies. This allows you to make the best decision.

When you get an offer, never accept on the spot. Thank the employer representative. Let the person know that you want to review the offer and talk with your family. Agree to follow up within 24 to 48 hours.

Compensation

Compensation is a topic that many people are uncomfortable to discuss. Most companies offer somewhere in the low- to mid range of their salary or grade scale. They allows you to grow within your role.

Throughout the interview process, ask questions about and validate compensation. And look at total compensation. Some companies offer great salaries with limited bonus potential. Others offer competitive salaries with very attainable bonuses. Total compensation includes salary, bonus opportunity, and benefits. Benefits could include discounted gym memberships, tuition reimbursement, and healthcare savings accounts (HSAs).

Applications and initial interviews include salary expectations. Focus on total compensation rather than base salary. Some companies offer stellar benefits with a mediocre salary, while others pay great salaries but no bonus.

Negotiating salary

When you follow up about an employment offer, be prepared to discuss salary. Negotiation is your right. It's the only point in the process where you have control.

It's perfectly acceptable at this point to ask if there's any room in the budget to increase the compensation. Be prepared with a specific number, but be realistic.

- ✔ If the job was posted with a salary range, make sure your proposal doesn't go over the initial range.
- ✔ Know what other companies are paying for the same or similar roles. Otherwise, you run the risk of being paid below your market value.

Reviewing wage data, surveys, and cost of living

You've invested time through the entire process. Don't get lazy now.

- ✔ **For wage survey information by area and occupation,** begin with the Bureau of Labor and Statistics (`bls.gov/bls/blswage.htm`).

- ✔ **For market conditions and the overall competitive landscape,** use tools like Payscale (`payscale.com`), Salary (`salary.com`), Glassdoor (`glassdoor.com`), and Transforming Data into Knowledge (`tdn2k.com`).

- ✔ **If the offer involves relocation,** know the cost difference between where you're living and where you'd be living. Bankrate (`bankrate.com/calculators/savings/moving-cost-of-living-calculator.aspx`) and CNN Money (`http://money.cnn.com/calculator/pf/cost-of-living`) provide a cost-of-living calculator to help you determine the impact on your lifestyle.

After researching, talk with people who influence you, and reflect upon your accomplishment. Getting an offer is an accomplishment. Now you have to make a decision.

Declining an offer

If, you decide to decline the offer, maintain your professionalism. Contact the representative. Thank her for the time invested in you. Be clear that you considered the opportunity but, while humbled by the offer, you don't feel it's the best fit for you and your family now. Reiterate your interest in the company, and ask to be reconsidered for future opportunities.

Accepting an offer

The decision to accept an offer is a weight-off-your-shoulders decision. Contact the company representative. Let the person know you appreciate the time afforded throughout the process. Confirm acceptance. Secure a start date.

Complete all new-hire paperwork and confirm details (arrival time, location, documentation, and with whom you'll meet) prior to your start date. Celebrate your success.

Chapter 15

Becoming a Star Employee

- -

In This Chapter

▶ Gaining insight and perspective

▶ Connecting and communicating with substance

▶ Devising a plan with a future focus

▶ Leaving a lasting impression

- -

*M*ost people just want to be happy. Identifying what makes you happiest increases your likelihood of finding success. A new job provides a terrific pivot point in your search for what makes you happy.

New opportunities provide you with a chance to refresh and reset plans for the future. A new job is a new opportunity to find job satisfaction. Seizing moments to reintroduce, reconnect and renew relationships, and not overlooking the people you encountered throughout the interview process, takes time and patience. In this chapter, we look at how starting a new job is also the beginning of a journey to become a stand out social media professional, all while finding job satisfaction. We'll explore how to get you there.

Satisfying Your Heart and Mind at Work

By understanding the components of job satisfaction, you can approach a new role with a clear focus.

To best use the talents of their employees, companies pay attention to team and interpersonal relationships, roles, responsibilities, and motivators. Simply put, companies want happy employees because happy employees perform better. People who approach their jobs with focus, dedication, and enthusiasm can receive new information more easily and they're more willing to see a project through to completion. As an added bonus for companies, satisfied workers feel and act more loyal, so retention rates are positively affected too.

As your productivity increases, you distinguish yourself as a star employee and new opportunities appear. Taking a job simply for the salary is no longer the status quo. People in the U.S. are looking for positions that provide a salary *and* overall satisfaction in their lives.

However, job satisfaction is *subjective* — people define it differently. Job satisfaction can mean flexible work schedules, being allowed to work remotely, and great benefits like on-site daycare, discounts with local businesses, pet insurance, or even "bring your dog to work" days.

Your life experience affects how you view your job and job satisfaction. How do you view it? The pieces of the job satisfaction puzzle include the following:

- **Evaluative:** You mull things over. You decide you either like or dislike your job, or can explain which parts you enjoy or don't enjoy.

- **Cognitive:** Is your work interesting and challenging? Your brain is in charge of cognition. Sure, evaluating requires thinking, but in this case the cognitive aspect means your brain is being challenged just right — not so hard you can't keep up, but enough to keep you learning.

- **Behavioral:** Your work ethic, including how reliable you are, influences how satisfied you are. The right job keeps you engaged and energized. It calls to you during off hours, when your mind wonders how to improve a system or find a solution. The right job fit makes it easier to alter your behavior. You'd get up earlier if you had a longer commute, and you wouldn't mind doing it if you liked the job you were going to.

Communicating, appreciating, and engaging

The ultimate variable — people — are a valuable resource. This network of professionals plays a major part in your early success.

- Having a presence is different than being present. Just being present physically isn't enough. You have to truly be there, in the moment, to really connect to the person with whom you're interacting. This is true in successful personal and professional relationships. When you talk with someone face to face, look that person in the eyes. Let him know that you're giving your undivided attention. Smile. Nod to convey understanding.

- Acknowledging and appreciating the time, support, and communication you get throughout the interview process is as important as any other action when beginning a new role. It sets the tone and lays a foundation for your professional persona. This simple act can have a tremendous impact. Write a thank-you note. Few people do this, so you can differentiate yourself by doing so. An email, text, or direct message, while less personal, also works. The important thing is to acknowledge the time, effort, and energy given to you.

✔ You're often asked to work together and accomplish goals with people you wouldn't even choose to have a meal with. If you enter a professional relationship, and truly, consciously, remain open to ideas, thoughts, beliefs, knowledge and culture, you gain so much. You gain perspective, understanding, and insight. And, with that, you can become more productive, efficient, focused, respectful and respected.

Try a few activities to initiate, appreciate, and engage with other people:

✔ **Introduce yourself to five new people each week:** Five is a manageable number. Make a point to request contact information, and to share your information. A business card comes in handy. Since you're a creative person, you may even see your business card as an advertising vehicle. Use it as an introduction tool.

Say hello and introduce yourself by name. Ask the person her name, and ask a question like, "Why do you go to work every day?" or "What are you passionate about?" These are great conversation starters. Request a business card before moving on. Carry a pen and note pad. If the person doesn't have a card, ask her to write her name, phone number, and email address.

Send an invitation to connect on LinkedIn or invite her to follow up on Facebook, Twitter, or Instagram. Based upon the relationship (or content of your conversation), you'll have to determine which platforms are appropriate: professional (LinkedIn) or more casual (Twitter and Facebook). You may find some overlap. Periodically reviewing your network is always encouraged. Chapter 12 gives guidelines for keeping in contact with people.

✔ **Take a walkabout:** Make time for two breaks each day. Quick walks are great ways to be seen. When David was the manager of talent acquisition with American Express, he got up from his desk in the middle of each morning and afternoon to make a loop. He walked around each floor of the six-story building. His objective was to greet each and every person. After a while, not everyone knew his name, but they all knew him as "the bald guy with a big smile on his face." It wasn't long before people were initiating conversation.

✔ **Ask the same question of multiple people:** By asking a consistent question of a variety of people, you can compare and contrast with your point of view. You'll see different perspectives or reaffirm your existing one.

Asking a question is a great way to get used to a new role, team, group, or company. It helps you understand culture, expectations, and maybe even the dedication of your new team. Great questions include: What keeps you up at night? What's your greatest challenge? What resources do you need to be successful?

✔ **Send a thank-you note:** Emails, texts, direct messages, and comments are all great vehicles to express appreciation. A handwritten note can also have great impact.

Re-connecting with the people you met along the way

No one is ever successful on his own. Everyone receives support and resources. Though some support is more valuable than others, anyone who offered help through your hiring process deserves to be acknowledged. Acknowledging people who supported you solidifies your network. By calling out your appreciation and willingness to be supportive in return, you establish a level of trust.

You may want to call upon these folks in the future for other opportunities.

1. **Make a list of friends, social media followers, and connections (new and existing) with whom you interacted during your job interview process.**

2. **Divide the list into three groups:**

    • Group one should include the people that inspire, motivate, and educate you. These are the people who shape your professional view; the people you most admire.

    • Group two is people you find interesting. You may need time to better understand their competencies and motivations.

    • Group three is people who act only in self interest. This group often steals time and lacks integrity.

3. **Review your lists. Then you'll know where to spend your time.**

    Spend the most time with Group One, but allow time for Groups Two and Three. Your purpose is to get to know your network better, and that takes dedicated time for conversations, callbacks, emails, and voice messages.

When people trust you, they're more willing to share information. That may come in handy when you're seeking new options down the road, during an interview process or when you start a new role.

See Chapter 12 for a step-by-step strategy for getting and staying in touch with your contacts.

Planning for Three Years from Now

Any longer than three years in a position, when you aspire to do more, leads to *stagnation* — all routine and little challenge. It's the point when you realize the company is no longer focusing its attention on your development.

When you're in a role for three years, a few things happen: Your competence has led to a comfortable place. The company isn't thinking about you any-more, and there's a good chance the company doesn't think you're as good at your job as you do.

After three years in a role, you're more valuable to another company than your current company. When fewer people are available, companies are chal-lenged to find candidates with the right knowledge and experience. People with specialized skills become sought after. Companies adjust their hiring tactics and entice candidates with higher salaries, greater earning potential, higher tier health benefits, and so on. After three years, some people will, fairly or unfairly, believe it's too hard for you to learn their systems. (Perhaps you're too set in routine?) You're an old dog not learning new tricks.

Squash speculation. Take control of your career with a three-year plan.

In addition to focusing on your health and wellness, try to meet the goals in Table 15-1 for your three-year career plan.

Table 15-1	Your Three-Year Career Plan
Year 1	
Months 1 through 3	✔ Build relationships.
	✔ Focus on the direction provided by people you've interacted with during your interview process. If someone gave you direction, encouragement, or insight during your interview process, let them know that you appreciate their support.
	✔ Always communicate clearly.
	✔ Define routines.

(continued)

Table 15-1 *(continued)*

Year 1	
Months 4 through 11	✔ Foster relationships by listening and asking questions.
	✔ Collaborate and increase confidence (your own and the confidence others have in you).
	✔ Read a book about time management, planning, or organization (for new ideas or as a reminder). See the sidebar.
Month 12	✔ Reflect and appreciate your accomplishments and the people who helped you along the way.
	✔ Pass on holiday greetings.
Year 2	
Months 13 through 17	✔ Join industry groups and professional organizations.
	✔ Set a target of five new introductions every week. (See Chapter 12 for networking help.)
	✔ Accept or request a project to manage.
Months 18 through 23	✔ Foster relationships.
	✔ Maintain knowledge of competitive landscape by following industry activity on your social platforms, and through your online and in person communities.
	✔ Seek out a recruiter or two and establish a relationship. (See Chapter 13 for more about recruiters.)
	✔ Become visible on LinkedIn and other professional media platforms.
Month 24	✔ Reflect and appreciate your accomplishments and the people who helped you along the way.
Year 3	
Months 25 through 29	✔ Request a project.
	✔ Schedule regular calls to your recruiter(s).
	✔ Investigate industry leaders, training, or certification programs. (See Chapter 5 for more about programs.)
	✔ Read a book about leadership or influence (for new ideas or as a reminder; check out the sidebar).

Year 3	
Months 30 through 32	✔ Complete training or certification program or course.
	✔ Update your résumé.
	✔ Explore internal opportunities.
	✔ Communicate more frequently with your recruiter.
	✔ Reconnect with people in your network that you may have neglected.
Months 33 through 35	✔ Explore external opportunities.
	✔ Increase communication with your recruiter.
	✔ Identify companies that you admire or are interested in.
	✔ Prepare for and participate in interview processes with multiple companies.
Month 36	✔ Reflect and appreciate your accomplishments and the people who helped you along the way.
	✔ Get ready for your new role.
	✔ Prepare your next three-year plan.

A three-year plan is a guide. Don't get down on yourself if it becomes a 40-month plan or more.

Reading recommendations

We recommend reading these books about time management and organization:

✔ *Who Moved My Cheese?* by Spencer Johnson

✔ *The 7 Habits of Highly Effective People* by Stephen R. Covey

✔ *Outliers* by Malcolm Gladwell

✔ *Tribes* by Seth Godin

✔ *Raving Fans* by Ken Blanchard

✔ *Good to Great* by Jim Collins

Part V
Your Day-to-Day Social Media Responsibilities

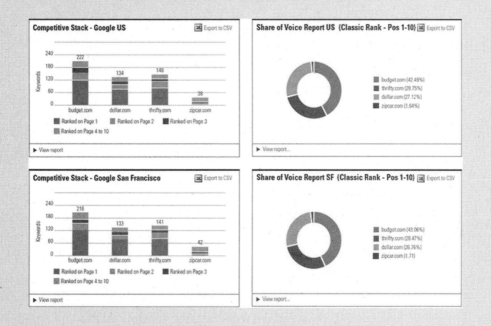

In this part . . .

✔ Getting an idea of what to expect in your social media job.

✔ Handling analytics and tools so you can show your impact and create reasonable expectations from your employer.

✔ Using online tools that will set you apart from other social media pros.

✔ See more at www.dummies.com.

Chapter 16

Creating Reasonable Expectations

· ·

In This Chapter

▶ Knowing what to expect in your new job

▶ Displaying your impact

▶ Setting yourself apart from the competition

· ·

Congratulations! You got your dream job and you're a full-fledged social media professional.

It's time to focus on your new job. Establish a relationship with your employer — especially your direct supervisor — that benefits both of you. For this to happen, you and your employer have to set reasonable expectations for one another: work performance, communication standards, timelines, and deliverables.

Working: No Average Day

Social media is such an exciting field because it's ever changing: new content standards, emerging networks, and algorithmic changes on platforms.

Your new colleagues might be skeptical about how this new medium works. Don't take this personally. Educate your coworkers about social media, but more importantly, deliver results and show your impact.

You won't have the same set of tasks and the same online conversations every day.

You can bank on having these factors play a part in your everyday work life:

✔ Quantitative and qualitative reporting

✔ Content creation

✔ Community management

✔ Data aggregation

✔ Strategy and accompanying recommendations

Focus most of your effort around these areas.

Knowing expectation criteria

You're trading your time and expertise for money and other compensation. Here are just a few of the expectations that you'll need to have both written out and signed by both parties:

✔ **Time:** What's the minimum number of hours per day, week, and month you'll put in? Where must you be physically located when putting in your hours?

✔ **Resources:** What sort of budget do you get per week? What process do you follow to request for additional money?

✔ **Labor:** What labor hours do you have at your discretion? What process do you follow for adding more labor hours and employees under you?

✔ **Communication standards:** How often will you communicate with superiors about your progress and deliverables? How often will you hold review meetings to get feedback? Chapter 17 reviews feedback meeting specifics and how to prove your merit in more detail.

Go into the onboarding process with a plan that overviews your expectations and review it with your superior.

Meeting company standards

Most of the company's standards are clearly defined through their employment agreement, employee handbook, *nondisclosure agreement (NDA),* and training manuals.

Don't take this stuff at face value. Follow these tips to make sure you're crystal clear:

✔ **Review everything.** Read everything that you're signing at least twice. You may even want to bring these documents to your attorney.

✔ **Communicate with superiors.** If you don't understand or have questions about something, talk to your superiors.

✔ **Ask for changes.** Make any necessary additions or requests before you sign the documents.

✔ **Keep copies.** Protect yourself legally. Sign multiple copies of employment agreements. File the originals as well as scan and save these agreements.

Abiding by the set rules and standards of a company is vitally important.

Establishing time commitments

Social media professionals can work from virtually anywhere in the world. Working remotely is possible, but make sure you're on the same page with your employer about daily hours. When you talk to your superior about this topic, have a plan about when you need to go into work and the advantages of doing so.

If you physically come into work on a daily basis, challenge yourself to under-promise and over-deliver when it comes to the hours you put in. If you're delivering results, and you're always the first one at work and the last one to leave, you're going to look like a rock star.

If working remotely benefits you, explain that benefit to your employer. Emphasize the benefits to the company in terms of production and results. Offer a trial of working remotely one or two days a week; make sure both sides are happy with the arrangement. Write up, sign, and have a copy of this agreement.

Juggling multiple responsibilities

Social media pros always have mounting tasks and additional responsibility — especially when their work is producing big results. To handle all of your responsibilities, stay organized and manage your time well.

It's easy to get caught up in positive company feedback online or carry on conversations with consumers via social media. At the end of the day, balancing multiple projects and deliverables requires planned discipline.

Here are a few best time-management practices:

✔ **Use calendar reminders.** Set up reminders every hour or two with an app like Google Calendar or iCal to help keep yourself on track. See Figure 16-1.

We use a calendar reminder every four hours that asks, "Are you doing what you're supposed to be doing?"

✔ **Set a contingency plan.** There will be interruptions but you don't have to let them slow you down. Prioritize your efforts to make the most of flex time.

✔ **Evaluate daily progress.** When you're documenting your daily results, always consider what you've done well and where you can improve. If you didn't finish everything that you wanted, plan accordingly.

✔ **Plan the next day accordingly.** Don't make the mistake of trying to schedule your day first thing every morning. Evaluate your results from the day before and make your schedule for the next day before you leave work.

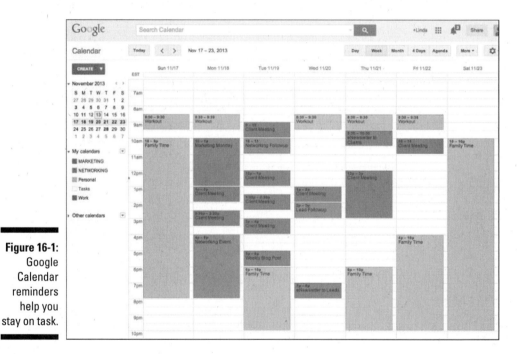

Figure 16-1:
Google
Calendar
reminders
help you
stay on task.

Typical Social Media Deliverables

Social media pros can have the bad habit of only emphasizing *qualitative* factors — the relationships that they're building with a company's fans and the positive feedback they get. While the qualitative results are important, the deliverables that most companies are concerned with equate to impressions, leads, and sales.

This chapter later explores how to present both quantitative and qualitative information, but you have to start by figuring out what results your employer is looking for.

When establishing the deliverables, consider asking your superiors hard-hitting questions such as:

- ✔ What does the company hope to gain from participating on social media?

- ✔ If you had to choose three deliverables from social media that are the most important, what would you pick and why?

- ✔ What would be a home run when it comes to the company's social media presence? Do you believe that you can necessarily quantify these results?

Armed with the answers, completing your daily deliverables is easier.

Types of social media reporting

The web is full of sophisticated reporting tools — but you don't need to spend $99 per month to understand how far a tweet will go, when all you care about is website conversions.

Our favorite social media reporting tools are listed here:

- ✔ `SocialReport.com` comes with a 30-day trial and is priced between $9 and $159 per month depending on your use and scale. Social Report has intensive reporting, monitoring, click-tracking, and conversion-tracking tools, plus team-management capabilities. You can even run reports that are branded specifically for your company. See Figure 16-2.

- ✔ `RavenTools.com` is a moderately priced reporting system that costs $99 per month for limited use and $249 per month for unlimited. Raven Tools comes with automated and branded reporting, over 20 different marketing tools, and a great social media monitoring tool, called Social Stream, that allows you to watch multiple social media feeds at once.

- ✔ `SimplyMeasured.com` is the Cadillac of social media reporting programs. It starts at $500 per month. Simply Measured offers advanced analytics, including analysis across your social media channels and click tracking from your social media links. It shows you how you stack up to your competition and focuses on how your social media use impacts your employer's effectiveness and ROI. See Figure 16-3.

Figure 16-2:
Social
Report
offers a
30-day
free trial.

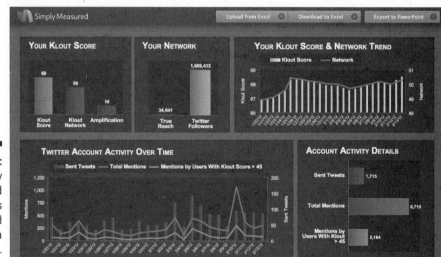

Figure 16-3:
Simply
Measured
offers
advanced
social media
reporting.

Disseminating data

Having data to show is one thing. Concisely presenting the most meaningful data is another.

Compile (put together) the report summaries so that a child can understand them. Emphasize the data points that are most important to your employer. The data that they'll be most concerned with are sales, impressions, and the upward momentum in these areas.

The best way to summarize the most important data points is in an executive summary that clearly illustrates the company's return on investment.

Most companies want to know this type of data:

- ✔ **A percentage increase:** These mainly relate to sales, brand impressions, and social media metrics such as shared messages. If the overall number increase is higher than your percentage increase in these capacities, then hone in on the overall numbers.

- ✔ **An overall number increase:** If you've made additional sales, impressions, or followers, then it's important to hone in on the numbers. If the overall number isn't very high, focus on the percentage increases instead.

- ✔ **Bottom-line efficiencies:** Any opportunity to build profit through management is important to illustrate. For example, compiling consumer feedback via social media about a product that isn't selling well is a prime opportunity to improve overall profitability.

- ✔ **Minimizing losses:** This can also be related to sales but if there is a particular product or service that has been stagnating, illustrating that your efforts aren't contributing to the hemorrhaging is a huge help.

When presenting the information, make sure you're clearly correlating how your efforts are tied to overall progress. Walk your superiors through how you got the most significant results and explain the process.

In our experience, investors and high-ranking company officials want a snapshot of your results rather than the entire picture.

Analytics for quantifying your impact

After you provide data (described in the preceding section) and explain why the numbers are important, it's time to show exactly why you're so valuable.

Track your results on a daily basis and show metrics in basic charts and graphs. Explain *how many, how much,* and *how often.*

For example, create charts that show the overall numbers and percentage increase on a weekly, monthly, quarterly, and even yearly basis. If there are extreme derivations either in terms of gains or losses, be prepared to discuss these fluctuations and have a plan accordingly to either alleviate the problem or scale results.

Table 16-1 has examples of what "how many, how much, and how often" look like in practice.

Table 16-1	Showing Analytics	
Show and Tell	**What to Include**	**How to Present It (and How Not To)**
How many	Detail how many units or deliverable numbers you're getting on a daily basis.	*Don't say this:* "I manage our social media platforms." *Say this:* "I post 74 times per day on nine different social media platforms."
How much	Typically top-line sales or profitability driven. Show how you've driven sales, retained customers, or saved the company a cost.	*Don't say this:* "Sales are going up and social media is doing well." *Say this:* "Sales have increased by $37,000 and sales have gone up by 11.3 percent."
How often	Emphasize the speed and scale at which you perform.	*Don't say this:* "I answer people's questions on Twitter." *Say this:* "I average the maintenance of 45 different customer relationships through conversations on social media per day."

Explaining Social Media Metrics

Hone in on numbers that the company finds important. Focus your metrics on what they're trying to accomplish.

The problem is that your company might be fixated on metrics that don't contribute to their *key performance indicators (KPIs)*. It's essential to know the difference between knowing what the stats mean and knowing which stats are meaningful. How do you determine?

Evaluate whether a metric can help you make decisions. If you look at a particular number and know what to do as a result, this is a good metric. If you look at the number and aren't sure how to proceed, this is most likely a *vanity metric* (the number looks great on paper but it won't make a significant impact as an asset, a top-line sales builder or bottom-line efficiency).

The information that you put on social media can typically be categorized into four segments:

- **Consumption** is the number and relative percentage of people who consumed your company's content. This is also known as *potential* and *real brand impressions,* which has a variety of measuring mechanisms.

- **Sharing** is indicated by a total number and its relation to your fan base. This concept has different names on different platforms (such as retweeting on Twitter) but the concept remains the same in that your fans repost your social media content on their own accounts. Measure how well this information resonates with your key people.

- **Lead generation** is how many people enter into your sales funnels based on what you have shared via social media.

- **Sales** indicate whether you make money and acquire or retain customers as a result of your social media participation. The only way you can accurately measure sales is by installing web pixels.

The following section not only identifies what stats are vitally important but also how to combine the longer term objectives, such as meaningful relationships, into a social media powerhouse.

Evaluating the most important numbers

The most important metrics are those the company says are the most vital to it.

You can explain until you're blue in the face why the company should put money into their employees and customers rather than advertising, but if they want immediate ROI, then that's where you put your effort.

Typically, larger companies are more concerned with impressions, engagement, and increasing *long-term value (LTV)* while smaller companies are focused on acquisition. Chapters 9 and 10 explain more about what life is like at large and small companies.

Most of the tools that we mention regarding social media management and measurement offer the following quantitative deliverables. Companies are fixated on these top quantitative figures:

- **Reach** is a measure of audience growth rate. Tracking reach helps you correlate increasing metrics with sales and profitability. For instance, focus on particular products or services to see how your reach directly relates to increased ROI. To help the overall growth rate, the total number of followers and overall growth of users in the social media platform should be considered.

- ✔ **Engagement** is a combination of reach, audience growth rate, and the number of users who have interacted with your brand in any way. These numbers become more valuable when this information is integrated into operations, customer service, and other areas of business. For example, feedback about your company's products and customer service is great information to have.

- ✔ **Acquisition** is most accurately measured through an individual visitor frequency rate to all your company's web properties. Acquisition is provided by your *click-through rate (CTR)* and impressions and leads to continuously improved targeting for your ideal customers.

- ✔ **Conversion** directly shows results in terms of sales and overall profitability. Conversion factors include overall impressions, the CTR, and engagement ratios.

- ✔ **Activity** is one of the most important aspects. Customer service savings are typically measured with the overall customer service costs and social media responses. This metric tries to establish how many customer service hours the company was able to save and contribute to the bottom line.

Combining quantitative and qualitative results

Qualitative data helps explain human behavior and the reasons they make decisions. This data defines your relationships with your consumers.

At the end of the day, quantitative results will reign supreme and qualitative factors will be an afterthought. However, combining the two elements demonstrates your immediate impact on the company and its long-term viability in terms of the brand equity that your company has built.

Qualitative results' impact can be summarized by three categories:

- ✔ **Target audience engagement:** Factors include ratings with brand loyalty, the sentiment of your interaction, and your overall influence.

- ✔ **Target audience reach:** Factors include new avenues, markets, and consumer segments that are reached.

- ✔ **Business results:** Results from an overall perspective include customer satisfaction ratings, the speed of your responses, and overall customer insight gathered.

Many disciplines fit within the confines of quantitative and qualitative results. Referral marketing is one of the most notable.

There are many referral marketing platforms. One of the most reputable, www.Friendbuy.com, is a prime example of merging quantitative and qualitative results. The site, shown in Figure 16-4, helps companies create tools so current and prospective customers can easily share the word about your company via social media and email.

In this instance, your company can use the relationships between consumers and the company (and the consumers and their friends), which are qualitative. Meanwhile, Friendbuy shows the messaging that your customers use to talk about the company, the social media profiles of all parties that share your company's messaging, and the interactions from the social media platform users toward the messaging. Analytics show clicks, the number of times the message was opened, and conversions for all of the messaging as well.

Figure 16-4: Friendbuy.com helps companies leverage their customers to refer their friends to the company.

Measuring Your Impact

Most people don't know where they stand with their company or how to value and prove their worth. Fortunately, you're reading this book. You know that to effectively measure your impact, you

- ✔ Define what you're measuring.
- ✔ Define how you'll measure desirable outcomes.
- ✔ Choose indicators that define your success.

Indicators define what has happened or changed as a result of your contributions. Excellent indicators can be defined by the acronym AIMS. *AIMS* stands for action focused, important, measurable, and simple.

Indicators are always one type or the other:

- ✔ *Quantitative indicators* answer questions that can be directly drawn from numbers.

- ✔ *Qualitative indicators* describe or explain the results that have occurred.

Getting to the point of choosing indicators takes some steps:

1. **Examine the organization's mission, business plan, values, and other defining characteristics.**

2. **When you have a clear picture how your company operates, ask the decision makers what outcomes they'd like to see.**

3. **Organize this information.**

4. **Start impact mapping.**

    Impact mapping is strictly defining what you're looking for and evidence that you're making a positive difference.

5. **Measure your desirable outcomes**

6. **Create a working plan for the future.**

    Chapter 17 helps you create such a plan so that you can get ahead!

With these parameters in place, you can do the following with ease:

- ✔ Develop or choose specific indicators that clearly show change happening or change that has already occurred.

- ✔ Organize your company's objectives and create more specific goals in the future.

- ✔ Choose the best ways to gather information. The way you get information is a direct trade-off between money spent on your compensation, time, and overall skills.

- ✔ Choose the indicators that define your success.

Get feedback from your superiors, and come to a weekly meeting that you set up, with a self-evaluation. Chapter 18 talks in depth about what to include in your weekly evaluation plan.

Improving continuously

It's up to you to remain disciplined and be accountable for your progression. Companies love to see people passionate about bettering themselves.

Brooks's process for continuous improvement gets broken down here:

✔ **Expectations:** Mutual expectations from you and your company. Expectations are clearest when they're succinct, demonstrated, and documented.

✔ **Training:** Knowledge, skills, and abilities that you gain through work and other resources. Share with your coworkers, and follow an educational timeline to work on new skills.

✔ **Assessment:** Measure through your weekly evaluations or with tests given by the company or with an educational product. Document and evaluate the results.

✔ **Reinforcement:** Break down results from assessment and overall performance into two areas: praise and opportunities. You should also get reinforcement from your superiors.

✔ **Systematic repetition:** After finishing a cycle with reinforcement, repeat this process consistently.

Establishing Your Secret Social Media Weapons

Armed with mutually understood expectations and the best social media tools (Chapter 7 talks about even more tools), you'll be as efficient as possible.

Though we fully believe in transparency, you might want to keep the following tools under your hat. They help differentiate you from the competition. If anyone asks what your secrets are, emphasize that they're hard work and focus. If your boss asks, then it's in your best interest to unveil the following suite of tools.

When you need software or an app to help make your job easier, it probably already exists. Search online by describing the product or outcome that you're looking for. You may also want to put the same search query into the respective Android or Apple app stores. Websites like 148apps.com and appadvice.com also can help you find tools.

Assimilating yourself with expert tools

What matters most to your employer? What results are the most impressive to your superior?

We recommend these tools:

- ✔ **Exacttarget.com** is a Salesforce email marketing product. You have to integrate social media efficiently with email communications, and exacttarget.com offers one of the best solutions.

- ✔ **Slideshare.com** is a fantastic solution if your company has killer presentations and top-notch information that needs to be spread quickly. Slideshare works seamlessly with social media and has extremely high SEO rankings.

- ✔ **Socialflow.com** is a software package that uses real-time data to let you know when to publish relevant content. If impressions, engagement, and leads are a top priority, then Socialflow is your answer. See Figure 16-5.

- ✔ **Demandforce.com** is owned by Intuit and offers comprehensive solutions to make marketing and customer communications easier. Demandforce integrates with social media to provide better systems for consumer communication, brand reputation and local search.

Adopt one program at a time. Trying to master multiple programs leads to potential disaster. Allow at least three months of training and use before moving on to the next option!

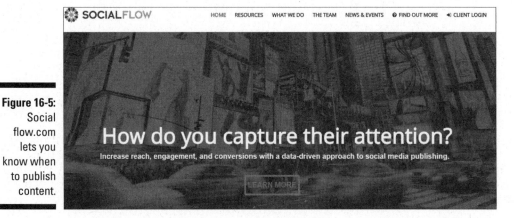

Figure 16-5: Social flow.com lets you know when to publish content.

Making yourself a shining star

Focus your energy on a few of your key talents and skills rather than constantly working on your weaknesses.

However, to become a shining star, educate yourself about all social media skills. Here are just a few resources that will help you:

✔ `Canva.com` is a simple graphic design tool that almost anyone can master in a matter of hours. If you're making quick designs for the web or print, Canva can help. The tool includes a free comprehensive graphics training program. See Figure 16-6.

✔ `Code.org` is the place for you if you have absolutely no idea what CSS, PHP and Ruby on Rails mean. Through simple, step-by-step videos, you can master computer languages in as little as an hour per day. The best part about the site is that it is completely free.

✔ `LeadPages.net` can help you make beautiful, responsive landing pages that capture leads. It also has products called LeadBoxes, a pop-up opt-in box, and LeadLinks, which allow consumers to subscribe to email marketing lists in real time.

✔ `Zirtual.com` is for you if there isn't enough time in a day. Zirtual has virtual assistants that complete your simple (yet time-consuming) tasks such as data entry and market research. Try the free trial, but by all means, sacrifice $100 per week — you'll get 16 virtual assistant hours per month. It's worth it.

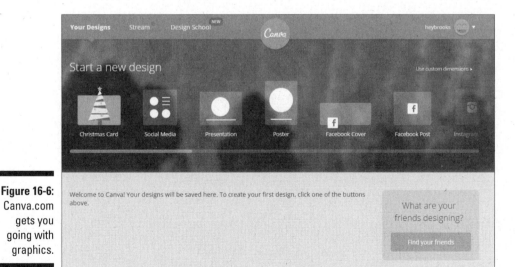

Figure 16-6:
Canva.com
gets you
going with
graphics.

Chapter 17

Getting Ahead

· ·

In This Chapter

▶ Making a plan for advancement

▶ Breaking it to the boss

▶ Uncovering freelance opportunities

· ·

S ome people want to blame their lack of job opportunity on the economy, on their boss, on the company that they work for — virtually any other factor they can think of. Some people let their employer dictate their path. Not you. You're controlling your destiny.

You know that getting ahead is on you.

Following the Steps

The best steps for getting ahead in your social media career:

1. **Figure out what you want.**

   When you're figuring out what you want, list specific accomplishments that you have to make in order — even if you don't know how to accomplish what you're going after.

   Chapter 4 talks about social media roles and responsibilities, and Part III gives you some ideas of different potential goals as well.

2. **Tell the right people.**

   Let the key decision makers in your organization know your intentions. More responsibility comes directly from your efforts and your superiors.

   Focus on how you'll benefit the company. Your career advancement is the long-term benefit.

3. Earn it.

Carry out your plan. Consistently under-promise and over-deliver. Build strong relationships with your organization's decision makers. Work longer hours, take on more responsibility, and do pro bono work.

If your company won't give you candid answers about skills that you need to advance, then you aren't working for the right organization. Great companies value their people and provide plans to help employees get where they want to go.

Telling the Right People

You can plan all you want, but without the help of your superiors, nothing is likely to happen. Explain exactly what you're trying to achieve and tie your goals into the company's objectives based on the feedback that you get from your superiors. This way your bosses are invested in your performance.

Ask for a 15-minute performance review at the beginning or end of each work week. The meeting should cover what you've accomplished, what you'll be working on in the coming week, and what you're working toward. The more objective driven your plan is, the more value you'll provide for the company.

Earning It

Don't just make plans for the future. Excel with your day-to-day responsibilities.

Keeping a daily results log

A *daily results log* details what tasks you accomplish and reviews the deliverables that you created during each work day.

Some people believe that a results log compromises the trust that a company has for its employees to perform their tasks. We believe that a daily results log proves your worth and gives your company documentation that validates results. As long as a results log doesn't interfere with the day-to-day operations, use it.

Here are just a few benefits that a daily results log offers:

- ✔ Quantifies your impact and demonstrates both your value to your specific job and to the company as a whole.

- ✔ Shows your initiative.

- ✔ Provides objective information for continuous improvement and job-evaluation purposes.

- ✔ Demonstrates an attention to detail and pride in work.

How detailed should you get in your report? That depends on your employer. Does she prefer the specifics of each task or are the end results more important? Does he value attention to detail? Refine your results log based on the feedback you get during performance reviews. See Figure 17-1.

Set up a weekly standing meeting with your immediate supervisors and other decision makers, and explain your results log. Chapter 18 describes what to include in this type of meeting.

Figure 17-1:
This is a
sample daily
SEO
performance
report.

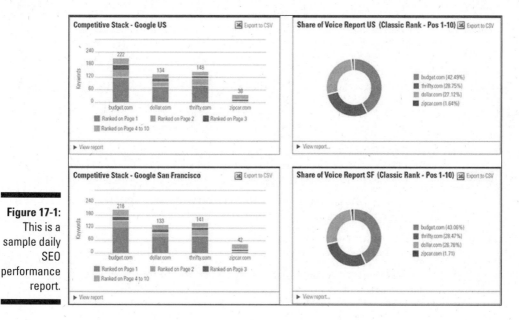

Setting SMART goals

Goals can't be vague or simply impossible to meet. Set SMART goals:

- ✔ **Specific** pertains to every aspect of the goal. All of the deliverables and outcomes must be as strictly defined as possible. State who, what, when, where, and why.

- ✔ **Measurable** involves the definitive criteria that will measure your progress toward your goals. This could be in the form of the end goal or a target that you hit along the way.

- ✔ **Attainable** means a quantitative number or outcome established that tells you when the goal has been completed. What is the action verb?

- ✔ **Relevance** can be the toughest aspect. It can be hard to say what's relevant (or irrelevant) in unchartered territory. You'll simply need to test your SMART goal with an educated guess about its relevance and continually improve your SMART goal setting.

- ✔ **Time related** means that all the objectives and outcomes will be delivered by a certain time.

Here's an example of a subjective goal that's doomed: *I will get us a ton of social media followers in the next few months.*

Now break that goal into the five SMART parts and put them back together for your final goal. Here's an example:

- ✔ **Specific:** I will add 2,000 Instagram followers over six months.

- ✔ **Measurable:** I will follow 100 target users per day, unfollow 30 users, and net at least 12 users per day. We will be able to sell at least one t-shirt per year to 10 percent of the users, which will net $2,200 in profit.

- ✔ **Attainable:** At least 12 Instagram users, approximately two per working hour, will be added per day.

- ✔ **Relevant:** Our company sells fashion t-shirts to 14–24-year-old boys whose main form of communication is through Instagram.

- ✔ **Time-based:** I will deliver all 2,000 Instagram followers within six months.

Developing Additional Social Media Skills

Social media says, "Always be learning (ABL)." The common knowledge, rules, and skills required for effective social media use are constantly changing.

Invest in educational programs, classes, and software that will keep you ahead. Chapter 5 talks about your options in depth.

You can probably convince your employer to pay for your education; clearly show what's in it for the company.

Seeking beneficial online education

A local college or university is an option, but they have a few drawbacks:

- ✔ The price is almost always going to be higher than an online course.
- ✔ Academia usually views business from a philosophical viewpoint.
- ✔ Social media's constant change requires the most recent information to be accurate.

Getting your employer to pay for development

Smart employers know that investing in their employees is cheaper than hiring consultants or contracting work. Even better, those same employers also have the long-term benefit of having an in-house professional who can complete tasks.

The best way to get your employer to pay for classes or conferences is by proposing a well thought-out plan that focuses on the value that your company will get. Show your educational value as objectively and quantitatively as possible when pitching to your employer. Show how you can build sales, improve efficiencies, or get rid of waste.

Talk to the people who can authorize this decision. Be concise and emphasize how the education will benefit the company. After that, offer to make up a proposal. That way, you make the decision as simple as possible.

Include these important factors in your proposal:

✔ Program specifics, including the knowledge and skills you'll get from the education.

✔ How long it will take to complete the education.

✔ The costs, including whether payment plans are available and if you're willing to be reimbursed based on your performance or grades (if applicable).

✔ A plan to incorporate some of your work time toward your education. Designate time blocks per day or week that you'll devote to your ongoing education.

Two main things may stand in the way of your company paying for your education: cost and value. An employer almost always looks at the educational cost as a line item. Your job is to clearly explain how the price is a short-term investment that solves a long-term, recurring problem.

Keeping Current

There are a ton of social media websites, forums, and chats full of self-promotional advertisements that don't add any actual value to the conversation. There's a sea of self-proclaimed "gurus" who've never spent any time in the trenches.

For the pros who think they know everything there is when it comes to social media, the exit door is to your right. No one knows it all. It changes too fast.

We only tell you about the individuals and resources that are on top of their game.

Premiere social media news outlets are another useful source for those who want to keep getting better. Chapter 22 lists ten of our favorites.

Subject matter experts (SMEs)

The following sections lead you to social media culture experts. They know its practical application. If you reach out to one of these sources, they may answer you. If you're looking to network and get involved with the big wigs, get right to the point and tell them exactly what you can provide for them.

SMEs understand how to use social media to accomplish strategic objectives and typically tend to be a bit more analytical or scientific when it comes to social media. These same SMEs often offer insight, analysis, and recent real-world experiences.

Here are some examples of the top social media subject matter experts:

- ✔ **Chris Brogan** was a social media consultant before social media consultants even existed. Chris is known for being the world's premiere social media marketing speaker and he has written a number of *New York Times* bestsellers. He's always willing to answer a quick question. Try buzzing him at `twitter.com/chrisbrogan`, and read his blog at `chrisbrogan.com/blog`.

- ✔ **Gary Vaynerchuk** rose to rapid fame through his web TV show about wine. He got ahead by making his show all about his fans; he teaches people at speaking engagements and with books exactly how he did it. Gary established a premiere marketing agency called VaynerMedia. Gary can be an erratic responder via Twitter, but try giving him a shout at `twitter.com/garyvee`, and definitely watch his newest web TV around business at `youtube.com/garyvaynerchuk`. See Figure 17-2.

- ✔ **Jay Baer** is a consultant, speaker, and author who runs his own digital marketing advisory firm, `convinceandconvert.com`, and his blog is the number-one rated resource for content marketing as voted by the Content Marketing Institute. Jay is excellent at addressing virtually every topic around online marketing but excels when it comes to social media. It's wise to follow Jay at `twitter.com/jaybaer` and to read his blog at `convinceandconvert.com/blog`. See Figure 17-3.

Figure 17-2: Gary Vaynerchuk is a top social media expert.

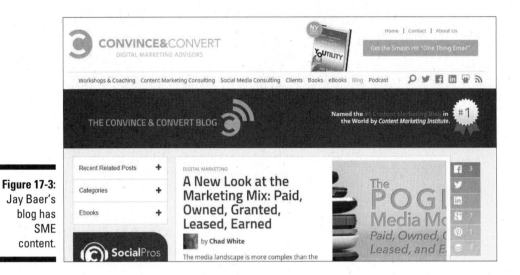

Figure 17-3:
Jay Baer's
blog has
SME
content.

Receptive resources

Though the SMEs in the previous section are receptive, they're also extremely busy. That means you might not get an answer back.

The following top-notch professionals will almost certainly be willing to lend a helping hand and point you in the right direction:

- **Mitch Joel** is a top author, consultant, and blogger within the digital marketing and social media space. Joel's blog through his consultancy, `twistimage.com`, will make you think bigger and challenge yourself. Try contacting Mitch at `twitter.com/mitchjoel` with your questions. See Figure 17-4.

- **Mari Smith** is also known as The Queen of Facebook. She specializes in Facebook marketing. Try to reach out via `facebook.com/marismith` or `twitter.com/marismith`, or drop her a line at `marismith.com`. She'll be happy to help you.

- **Mike Stelzner** is the founder of Social Media Examiner as well as the host of the Social Media Marketing podcast. Aside from his vast knowledge of everything social media, Mike also happens to be a heck of a nice guy. Any resource, question, or help that you might need is only a tweet away. Reach out to Mike at `twitter.com/mike_stelzner`.

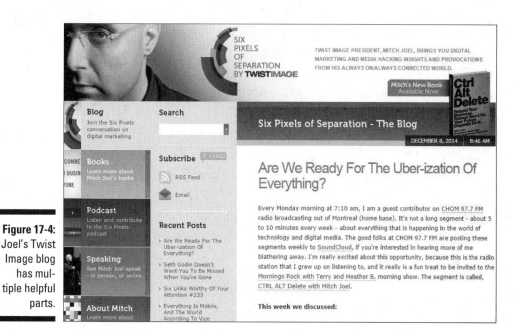

Figure 17-4:
Joel's Twist
Image blog
has mul-
tiple helpful
parts.

Building Freelance Work

If you're ambitious and want to get ahead — which we assume you are —
then explore freelance opportunities. Don't let additional work conflict with
your day-to-day responsibilities.

Brooks served as a marketing consultant with a restaurant chain while he
operated a restaurant. The only limits were that it couldn't be with a particular competitor and he had to put in a minimum of 60 hours of work per week
with his full-time day job. This agreement was in writing and both sides were
very pleased with the outcomes.

Ultimately, as long as you are not working with a competitor and you're
delivering excellence at your full-time job, most employers are open to you
working elsewhere.

Freelancing is advantageous for your career for many reasons:

✓ **Improves your skills:** You'll get more practice and more skills by working with other entities or in different industries. This benefits your
employer because you'll bring a fresh perspective.

✔ **Expands your portfolio:** Freelancing also lets you showcase your work. You can add every client to your portfolio, which will attract new clients.

✔ **Supplements your income and allows you to get paid:** Getting paid is certainly not something to scoff at. The best part is that for every job, you can demand a higher rate.

Increase your prices 3 to 10 percent after every job, depending on what type of value and the results that you can deliver.

Whenever you're pitching for freelance work, you're looking for a "Yes" from the potential client. You might not know exactly how to deliver what they need, but no matter! Make an agreement and figure out this part later. You can always find someone to farm work out to. `PeoplePerHour.com` is a great place for that, and for offering your freelancing skills. See Figure 17-5.

Finding opportunities

Where can you find freelance gigs? Use your established sources and — you know the drill — provide as much value as you can up front.

Brooks wanted to learn the Internet marketing industry during college, so he wrote a business plan and dropped the document in a box at the personal home of a world-renowned Internet marketer. It sounds crazy, but Brooks got a phone call from the professional the very next day and was invited to coffee. If you're serious about freelancing, be bold and ask for what you want.

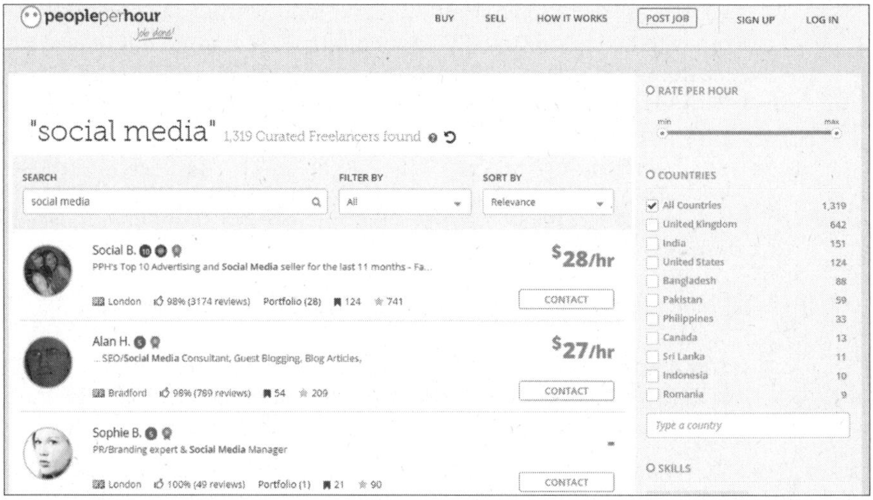

Figure 17-5:
I searched
for *social
media* on
People
PerHour.
com and
found
over 1,000
possible
freelancers.

You won't have to pound the pavement if you can offer your services to an established person or group. Not everyone will take you up on your offer, but someone will.

Our favorite methods for getting freelance work are explained here. Chapter 18 talks more about pitching to people and defining your value. Chapter 8 talks about other aspects of selling your skills.

Pro bono help

Approach other consultants, marketing groups, and agencies and state very clearly what you offer. After introducing yourself and asking them to keep you in mind for future projects, periodically check in.

Bird dog

Take leads you know of (through your network or who you've seen on social media) back to another consultancy or agency. From there, you can collect a finder's fee or, better yet, volunteer to be a part of or lead the project. The consultancy gets business that they probably wouldn't have been aware of and you get practical experience.

Social media broadcast

To get your freelance business started, tap into your immediate network on Facebook, LinkedIn, and other platforms.

Make your immediate and extended network aware of what you're offering without aggressively pushing it down anyone's throats. Offer something of high value, such as a free social media audit. An audit is an overview of the biggest opportunities that a company has, and the review is as transparent as possible. The trick is that most companies will understand the value and how to do the work, but would rather have a subject matter expert complete the job for them.

Guest posting

Create content on platforms whose users would be interested in your knowledge and abilities.

Approach blogs, periodicals, and websites with a content idea based on a need that you've identified or trends that you've seen in comments on their platform. Pitch your service offering in your author bio. If you're looking to master the guest blogging process from soup to nuts, Jon Morrow has created an amazing resource at GuestBlogging.com, shown in Figure 17-6.

We can't emphasize enough the importance of contributing value up front.

Figure 17-6:
Guest
Blogging.
com is an
educational
resource.

Presenting your offering

Too often social media freelance professionals focus on selling what they have to sell rather than offering a solution that prospects are looking for.

You have two jobs when it comes to effectively presenting to a prospect:

✔ Identify their need.

✔ Fill their need with what you offer.

Take these steps:

✔ **Practice your pitch.** Clearly state your prospect's need and what you're offering to fill this need. Prepare three elevator pitches —15 seconds, 30 seconds, and one minute long — that build on each other. Memorize these pitches and practice on your friends, family, and other freelancers to help you refine your sales pitch. The more that you practice pitching, the better you'll be.

✔ **Set a meeting.** Your best chance to close a freelancing sale is face to face. Make a face-to-face meeting your main objective when you're pitching over the phone, via email, in person, or across social media platforms. Present two potential times for your client to choose from. Offer to come *to* the client or use a webinar or screen-sharing service such as GoToWebinar or Google Hangouts. See Figure 17-7.

✔ **Break down objections.** Your prospect may have questions or concerns. Again, your objective is to get a meeting. Listen, address their objections, and ask for the meeting again. If you have to, offer even more value, such as pro bono consulting, and give a guarantee (such as offering to pay their company back) if they're not more than impressed with your results to sweeten the deal.

Closing the deal

During your meeting, it's essential that you

✔ Listen a majority of the time.

✔ Clearly establish what their challenges are.

✔ Offer the appropriate solutions accordingly.

Ask for the freelancing gig as soon as you identify their need and emphasize that you want to work with them.

Figure 17-7:
A Google
Hangout
session
works if you
can't meet
face to face.

Here's an example of a strong closing statement:

> *I want to earn your business and I am willing to offer you a 100 percent money-back guarantee if you aren't satisfied for any reason within my first 30 days of working with your entity.*

Because making a "100-percent money-back guarantee" is relatively unheard of in this type of negotiation, it's simultaneously bold and risky. Just ensure that your closing statement is strong enough where the contracting firm has little to nothing to lose.

You're clearly stating that you value their business and you're giving them an out. You've shown that you're prepared, you've gained their trust, and you've minimized their risk.

Here are a few more best practices that will help you stand head and shoulders above your immediate competition:

- ✔ **Set the stage for follow-up.** Set a time and date that a contract or any other deliverables need to be delivered to the client. If you need another meeting to finalize an agreement then ensure that you have two prospective dates picked out and gently prod the prospective employer to make a decision as quickly as possible.

- ✔ **Have your contract in hand.** If you want to close your agreement at your first meeting, take a working agreement (or a Request For Proposal [RFP]) contract that you've signed and dated. This contract should define the scope of work and timelines, which are discussed in Chapter 11. It might come off as presumptuous, but most of the time clients are impressed with your foresight and confidence.

- ✔ **Offer additional collateral.** This is *social proof* (testimonials and endorsements from other people) that can take the form of your portfolio, testimonials, and contacts that can vouch for your work and character. Send more than the entity requires and send it sooner than they expect.

- ✔ **Send meeting minutes.** Send your meeting notes, along with your recommendations, back to the prospective client. Make it clear that this is a gift from you whether you work together or not. The objective is to provide value.

If your gut tells you that the partnership won't be successful or that you don't care for the hiring party as people, then don't create an agreement. Your happiness is more important than a paycheck.

Chapter 18

Getting a Job Even if You Have One

Social media is valuable. Everyone knows that the information and communication that social media has to offer can make a significant difference within their organization but the fact of the matter is that most do not possess this skills set. Since the knowledge, tools and skills associated with social media are so new, it's almost impossible to have demonstrated results to contribute unless you are a full-time social media pro. That's the distinct advantage that you have over the decision makers who know that they need top-notch social media professionals but have no idea how to architect and execute a successful social media strategy.

This chapter mentions terms and concepts that might need further explanation. Please see the Glossary for definitions.

Making Opportunities

Opportunities exist while you're working your full-time position. Be aware of them.

You can create opportunities two main ways:

- ✔ **Expand your role with your current employment.** Your full-time responsibilities shouldn't limit what you accomplish.

  Always under-promise and over-deliver.

  The short-term downside to this approach is that you may not be compensated fairly for your time and effort. Brooks has volunteered his services and gone months without pay. It's hard work and it's easy to get discouraged. However, the long-term benefits are the goodwill you create with your employer and the skills you learn to become more valuable in the marketplace.

- ✔ **Take on consulting clients outside of your full-time job.** On the flip side, you can offer your talents to entities outside your full-time employment. This route guarantees that you get paid. It also helps set you up if you choose to go down the consulting route.

Brooks has chosen both routes simultaneously and it's been fruitful. He constantly looks for opportunities to develop his knowledge and take on social media projects as the marketing head for a restaurant chain and takes on other clients at night and on weekends.

Approaching with a Social Media Plan

Brands want to interact with you as little as possible; you are the proactive force that establishes exactly what needs to be accomplished. Many times companies don't know what they hope to accomplish from social media. It's up to you to focus on what they hope to gain. Chapter 16 covers quantifying your impact to your employer.

Companies are hedging risk in terms of time and money when they allow you to establish a social media plan.

Your social media plan must:

- ✔ **Be thorough** about what work you'll be doing. Your critical activities must be firmly mapped out so that the hiring entity knows exactly what to expect.

- ✔ **Be time-specific** about when critical activities, projects, and deliverables will be offered for approval.

- ✔ **Have an objective** for every aspect. Be as specific and concrete as you can when establishing what needs to be done, the manpower needed, and the hours that it will take.

Creating an excellent social media plan is much like writing a research paper. This process requires critical thought, planning, strategy, and research. The good news is that once you've created a social media plan, you can replicate it relatively easily for other employers.

If you're focused on the organization rather than yourself — if you effectively solve their problems — then you'll get more opportunities.

The following sections take you through the steps to creating a solid social media plan.

Asking what parts are most important

Meet with the decision makers to ask critical questions, take notes, and figure out exactly what the contracting organization needs.

Ask these kinds of questions to help make sure your social media efforts are put into a realistic framework:

- ✔ What do you hope to gain from this project?
- ✔ What quantitative numbers are the most important to you?
- ✔ How do the numbers you've laid out compare to comparable businesses? Are they fair and reasonable?
- ✔ What questions can I answer about the work that I'll be doing?

These questions

- ✔ Are open ended for broad responses (that the following sections hone in on).
- ✔ Emphasize quantitative results while putting these numbers into context with current operations.

Unrealistic employer expectations are often unintentional, because the decision makers don't understand what to expect. In other cases, unrealistic standards are created specifically to set up the program for failure. Some people want new initiatives like social media to fail so that a company can revert to its old ways. Asking these questions helps keep this from happening!

So your employer wants 10,000 Twitter followers? Follower numbers don't mean anything. You could go to `Fiverr.com` and buy as many social media fans as you want. Are 50,000 Facebook fans, while an impressive total, going to mean substantial brand equity or immediate top-line sales? Probably not.

Exploring the company's needs

After asking open-ended questions about what the company expects, get the specifics about what it truly *needs* rather than what it *wants*. The difference between these two words is significant.

- ✔ A *need* is something the company absolutely must have for its short-term survival or overall longevity.
- ✔ A *want* is something the company would like to have but it isn't a necessity.

Typically, decision makers lead with their wants. Continue to dig deeper.

For instance, you can determine a need with the following questions:

- ✔ If this challenge isn't met, could it impact revenue for the quarter or the year?
- ✔ If this solution is enacted, will it save immediate time, money, or other resources?
- ✔ Why must this critical activity happen right now? Could it wait? If so, what would be the appropriate timeframe?

Study the company's needs and be ready with definitive solutions; don't lean on the decision maker to offer up solutions. Your preparation will show, and you can choose the work you enjoy most.

Strictly defining the scope of work

After defining the company's needs, match those needs to your skills set.

Be self-aware while you match company needs to your skills. You don't want to agree to deliver work that you have no idea how to complete.

The most important part of defining your scope of work is breaking down three items in your agreement with the company:

- ✔ Deliverables
- ✔ Critical action plan
- ✔ Timelines

These elements are explained in detail later in this chapter, in "Closing the Deal."

Out on a limb

If you're already a contractor in social media, it's perfectly acceptable to say "Yes" to earn a job. But you have to know ahead of time how to contract out this work and ensure that you know how to manage a project efficiently. Make sure you have a manpower plan ahead of time — even if it's a just-in-case scenario in the future — and know exactly who and when you'll contact other social media pros. You can establish contractors through a simple agreement with your consultancy and IRS form 1099. For the specifics of how to start your own entity, please read Chapter 8.

Define exactly what you'll deliver to the company (deliverables), how you'll do it (critical action plan), and when the work is due (timelines).

Making this information as detailed as possible has benefits:

✔ You'll have a roadmap to follow.

✔ Companies prefer well thought-out plans and have more confidence you're proactive.

✔ You'll have standards that define how and when your work needs to be done. That way you know whether you're on track.

Contract your consulting work whenever possible to help with time, personal skill, or financial limitations. You can charge a higher hourly rate since you're managing other people. Not only will you make more money in the short term, but you'll build your network and get valuable contract-management experience.

Table 18-1	Sample Social Media Deliverables	
Deliverable	*12 Months*	*Comments*
Twitter updates	4 per day	—
Facebook updates	4 per day	—
Facebook poll	1 per week	—
Facebook contest	4	One contest per quarter
Facebook tabs/pages	4	Depending on new requirement, number can be increased
Facebook app	1	Game, quiz, etc. to engage with fans
Total Facebook fans	10,000+	Can be achieved by using Facebook ad platform
Total Twitter followers	6,000	—

Establishing valuable deliverables

Deliverables are by far the most important aspect that the company cares the most about. It's great if you're on the same page about how you'll get there, but results rule all.

Come to meetings with a good idea of realistic deliverables. You have to manage expectations; don't let the company expect too little or too much. You're the subject matter expert (SME); they're relying on your knowledge to dictate what to expect.

Here's an example of a poor deliverable:

> *We will have 10,000 Twitter followers next month.*

This deliverable is unrealistic, lacks a defined value, and has a vague time frame.

Contrast that poor deliverable with this good one:

> *ABC Company will gain 2,000 more Twitter followers by June 30, 2015 over a 19-week period and will generate $5,700 in sales.*

This deliverable is more realistic, sets a dollar amount, and strictly defines the delivery date. You can break down this deliverable by the strategies, too: how Twitter followers will be earned, how impressions will be achieved, how sales will be accrued, and so forth.

A deliverable summary in the contract holds everyone accountable for the performance. Set the terms yourself so that they're realistic and manageable.

Summary of Monthly Deliverables

4,500 fans on Facebook page

60 updates

20 reviews

Online reputation maintenance

Customer relationship maintenance

Chapter 3 covers these terms in much more detail.

Companies always want to see how the deliverables impact them. They emphasize the end results.

Concentrating on the Company

Companies and organizations typically care most about these objectives:

- ✔ **Sales:** The top-line dollars brought in for the goods and services that you provide.

- ✔ **Brand impressions:** The total number of times that consumers could have seen, or did see, your particular marketing message.

- ✔ **Bottom-line efficiencies:** Opportunities to save on costs and increase overall profits.

- ✔ **Aggregated customer data:** A list of your customers' quantitative and qualitative information.

Chapter 16 reviews these objectives in more detail.

Figure out how your services fit with what your employer is looking for. Your value will come later. If your skills aren't what the potential contracting company is looking for, find contractors to complete the work for you.

The answer is always "Yes." Then you find a solution to the problem.

Getting value in return

You can expect some primary benefits to all the work you're doing:

- ✔ **Compensation:** You'll get monetary compensation, but you might get other perks as well: a product, service, or paid day off. Ask during the negotiation process!

- ✔ **Valuable work experience:** You're refining your skills, which means you can more easily do this type of work in the future. If you're able to contract some of work, then you'll have valuable project-management experience as well.

- ✔ **A reference, recommendation, or a case study:** Of course the payment and work experience are extremely valuable, but showcasing your abilities and building your future business can be even better. Try to turn every client into three more clients.

- ✔ **Future opportunities:** After you finish your contracted work, will they hire you for additional work? While you're completing your agreement, talk about this factor. Try to get first right of refusal for future work whenever possible!

Tying objectives to your skills

Before you finalize your agreement with the hiring company, make sure you're on the same page with your employer about how you'll meet those objectives. From there, you can make decisions about the time, additional manpower, and resources that you may need to complete the objectives.

Consider the following objective:

> *ABC Company will create a Facebook advertising campaign.*

This very broad objective might make you feel lost.

A laser-focused objective looks something like this:

> *ABC Company will attain a 2.5% CTR, $16 CPM, and a $25 CPA with lookalike customers on a $1,000 budget per day via Facebook advertising.*

Closing the Deal

After you go through the negotiation, definitively convey that you want the work and ask for a final agreement.

To ask for the business, you can say, "I believe that this is a mutually beneficial partnership. Can we finalize this agreement now?" It's really that simple. Most employers have legal documents ready to customize. You and the company or organization need to sign and date the contract and receive physical copies. The contract also should be scanned and emailed to both parties.

Find out whether you or the contracting firm will produce the consulting agreement. In most cases, a simple contractor agreement and an IRS 1099 form will work fine. To see a sample social media contracting agreement, see Figure 18-1.

- ✔ **Deliverables** are your physical tasks and the quantifiable results that you'll provide. For example, a category such as a social media management should be broken down by the network that you'll be servicing, the amount of content that you'll produce, and how many hours it'll take you to perform the overall work.

- ✔ **Expectations** should outline what work you'll do and how you'll do it, and any rules that both sides should be aware of. Include all provisions, terms, and specifics about the agreement in this section.

- ✔ **Timelines** define when your work is due and how your employer will approve these deliverables. If the wording doesn't have specific dates or define the subsequent approval, you're setting yourself up for discrepancies in the future. The more detailed and concise the agreements are, the easier it is to avoid discrepancies.

✔ **Compensation terms** define whether you're charging billable hours, per project, or for-performance. Compensation for a single project may be broken into increments. Also, your compensation terms must define how expenses or reimbursement will be handled. The following sections details these options.

✔ **Future benefits,** additional perks, benefits, bonuses or opportunities: Put them in writing. These factors are typically related to performance and involve promises for future work, recommendations, or referrals.

Deliverables, expectations, and timelines are discussed elsewhere in this chapter. The following sections explain compensation and future benefits.

Figure 18-1: This is a sample social media consulting contract from docstoc. com.

Social Media Consultant Agreement

This is an agreement between a consultant and a company or individual for social media consultation services. The consultant is hired to provide the company with their best advice, information, judgment, and knowledge pertaining to mass exposure on social media websites. In addition, this agreement can be customized to include the specific duties or services the consultant will provide. This agreement can be used by small businesses or other entities that want to hire a consultant to help manage and market their social media accounts.

Getting paid

A general consulting invoice template works perfectly. You can customize the template to your work. See an example in Figure 18-2.

Make sure that your template has the following information:

✔ **Contact information** for yourself and the contracting company.

✔ **A list of your services.**

✔ **Listing of billable rate and hours:** List your hourly rate for all services, and multiply your hourly rates by the hours that you've put in. Charge in increments of 15 minutes.

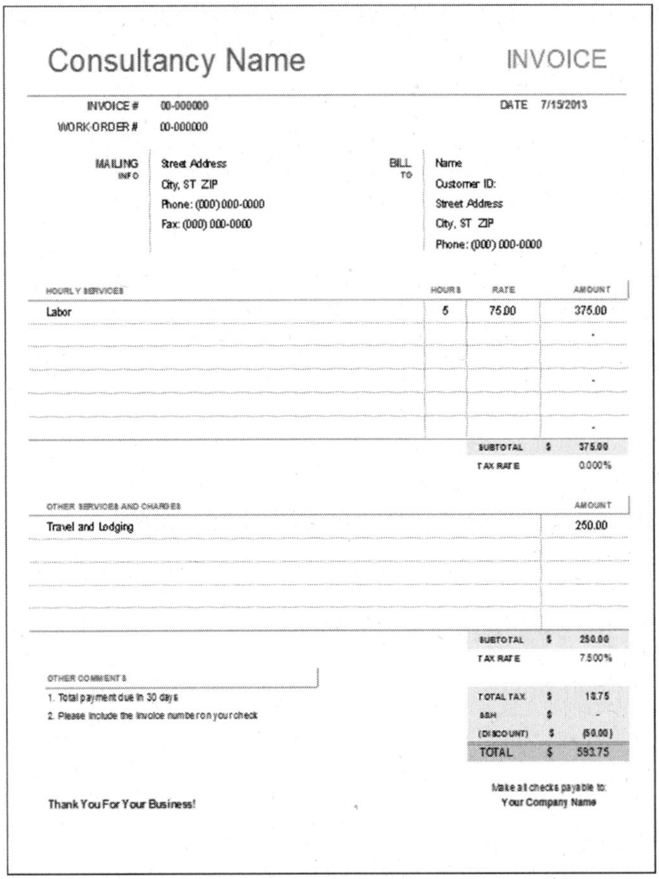

Consultancy Name INVOICE

| INVOICE # | 00-000000 | | DATE | 7/15/2013 |

WORK-ORDER # 00-000000

MAILING INFO
Street Address
City, ST ZIP
Phone: (000) 000-0000
Fax: (000) 000-0000

BILL TO
Name
Customer ID:
Street Address
City, ST ZIP
Phone: (000) 000-0000

HOURLY SERVICES	HOURS	RATE	AMOUNT
Labor	5	75.00	375.00

| | SUBTOTAL | $ | 375.00 |
| | TAX RATE | | 0.000% |

OTHER SERVICES AND CHARGES	AMOUNT
Travel and Lodging	250.00

| | SUBTOTAL | $ | 250.00 |
| | TAX RATE | | 7.500% |

OTHER COMMENTS
1. Total payment due in 30 days
2. Please include the invoice number on your check

TOTAL TAX	$	18.75
S&H	$	-
(DISCOUNT)	$	(50.00)
TOTAL	**$**	**593.75**

Thank You For Your Business!

Make all checks payable to:
Your Company Name

Figure 18-2:
A social media consulting invoice can look like this.

For example, assume you charge $20 per hour for social media management and $40 per hour for HTML web programming. If you put in five hours of social media management, then that service would equate to $20 × 5 hours — $100. If you also did 5.25 hours of programming, this service would equal $40 × 5.25 hours — $210.

Your billable rate may vary based on the task; it's important to make it clear that your hours correlate to the work performed and tasks accomplished.

✓ **Work breakdown:** List your deliverables to the most detailed level possible. Instead of listing "research," for example, explain what your research entailed. What resources did you use? Did you have to create a working spreadsheet to document your research? Do you have any documentation that details your findings? Again, the more detail, the better!

- ✔ **Payment flexibility:** Define exactly when the payment for your services needs to be submitted. You should have a clear idea of how your employer or contracting company wants to pay you: direct deposit, check, PayPal, or otherwise.

  We recommend a net 30-day payable period from the date that you deliver your invoice. Indicate that a penalty fee may be associated if the invoice isn't paid in this time period.

- ✔ **Offer a discount:** Give more hours than you've promised and include a line item under your gross total that shows how much the entity is saving as a result of your discount. Put the net amount owed in the next line.

Don't forget to claim this income as a W-2 employee or a 1099 contractor when performing your tax return. This additional work qualifies as taxable income; not claiming this money or depositing the funds in personal accounts can get you into trouble with the IRS!

Asking for what you want

Some people dance around what they want. Be clear. You're trading your time and expertise for experience and monetary compensation.

If you're not sure what to ask for, here are a few suggestions:

- ✔ Higher compensation for the overall projects or your hourly rate
- ✔ More designated hours to get the work done efficiently
- ✔ Tools, software, or educational programs that can aid your efforts
- ✔ Additional manpower to delegate tasks and assignments
- ✔ Future benefits or guarantees for additional work

During your weekly report and progress meeting, ask questions that have decision makers saying "Yes." These examples can get you started:

- ✔ Are you satisfied with my work so far?
- ✔ Am I exceeding your expectations?

Explain a clear benefit or value statement that correlates to sales, productivity, or additional results. When the management validates that this would be of interest to them, this is the perfect time to ask for whatever you need to better do your job.

The conversation may look something like this:

> **You:** *Would you like me to add another 10% sales increase to the top line, Mrs. XYZ?*
>
> **Mrs. XYZ:** *Absolutely. How can we make that happen?*
>
> **You:** *Well, I typically put in three pro bono hours but I feel confident that if I were compensated for five extra hours per week that I could conduct the additional testing necessary to take our sales to the next level. Would you be willing to add another three or five hours to my billable time?*
>
> **Mrs. XYZ:** *Five hours is no problem. Consider it done and please add this to your invoice.*

In this scenario, five more billable hours mean about 20 more billable hours per month and 250 hours per year. Better results, more experience, and more money: This whole "asking for what you want" thing sure can be fruitful! Don't forget to ask for this in a new agreement or put it into your existing signed agreement as an addendum.

Don't be afraid to demand your value. Ask for more than you believe you deserve in terms of compensation, resources, and hours allotted. Getting less than you expected is the worst that can happen. No one will ever offer a higher hourly rate or more hours to get the work done, so it's important to start high and be willing to go down.

Setting standards for the future

While building a consultancy can be a tremendous opportunity for the future, making the most of your full-time employment is certainly more of a guarantee.

You can't assume that organizations will do the "right thing" and "take care of them in the future." In the contract that both parties sign, make your wants known and clearly establish where this path is leading.

To get what you're looking for, emphasize how you can fill the company's needs and guarantee that everything is done properly by using a contract. When you do this, you're focusing on the company's benefit rather than your own and they'll be more likely to grant you exactly what you wanted in the first place.

Here are a few examples of where your work may lead in the future:

- ✔ **Guaranteed work in the future:** The entity promises to give you the first right of refusal for additional work if, and when, the time comes. If you define that your work and deliverables meet certain standards, then you might as well guarantee that you can keep the same work in the future — or even add to your responsibilities.

- ✔ **Pay or billable hour increases:** Pay increases are typical with pay-for-performance agreements (such as social media advertising) when you meet thresholds, but it's wise to ask for both higher pay and more hours when completing the same type of work in the future.

- ✔ **Additional consulting opportunities:** This is another first right of refusal area; you should be given the highest priority for future jobs and projects. It's important to ask what future work will include and to be able to dictate how your work should progress.

- ✔ **Right to showcase work:** A great way to garner more business and greater responsibility is by getting permission to show off the work and its results. Many companies are finicky about this issue, so it's important to have a clear understanding that a job well done grants this privilege.

- ✔ **Recommendations:** Even if future work isn't in the cards, it's nice to have a guarantee that you'll get a positive recommendation. This recommendation is even stronger when it comes on behalf of your employer to someone that they have a relationship with. Furthermore, featuring recommendations in your proposal template, your website, on LinkedIn (see Figure 18-3), and on other promotional materials is great social proof.

- ✔ **Referrals:** The greatest compliment is a direct referral on behalf of your employer. Ask if the company is willing to direct more business your way whenever possible, and periodically check with them to prospect more work in the future. Every happy client should turn into three more clients.

Don't ask *if* your employer knows anyone who could use your services. Ask *who* would benefit from your skills set.

They'll know of at least three different sources that would be interested. To make this strategy even more efficient, ask the company to make a phone call in your presence and set up an initial discovery meeting for you. This warm introduction will exponentially increase your close rate for additional clients and work opportunities.

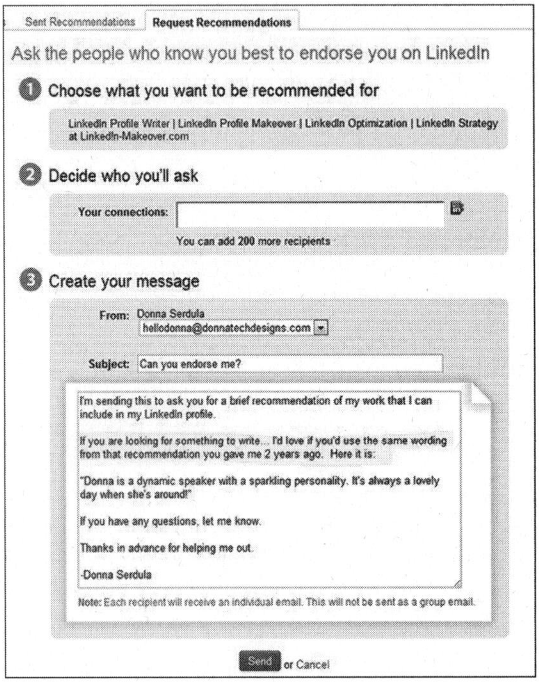

Figure 18-3:
A LinkedIn endorsement is good business.

The figure shows a LinkedIn "Request Recommendations" screen with the following visible text:

Sent Recommendations | **Request Recommendations**

Ask the people who know you best to endorse you on LinkedIn

1 Choose what you want to be recommended for

LinkedIn Profile Writer | LinkedIn Profile Makeover | LinkedIn Optimization | LinkedIn Strategy at LinkedIn-Makeover.com

2 Decide who you'll ask

Your connections: [   ]

You can add 200 more recipients

3 Create your message

From: Donna Serdula
hellodonna@donnatechdesigns.com

Subject: Can you endorse me?

I'm sending this to ask you for a brief recommendation of my work that I can include in my LinkedIn profile.

If you are looking for something to write... I'd love if you'd use the same wording from that recommendation you gave me 2 years ago. Here it is:

"Donna is a dynamic speaker with a sparkling personality. It's always a lovely day when she's around!"

If you have any questions, let me know.

Thanks in advance for helping me out.

-Donna Serdula

Note: Each recipient will receive an individual email. This will not be sent as a group email.

Send or Cancel

Social Media Reporting

A vast majority of brands only care about results.

The reporting aspect of your work is so important. Report your results to the company at least once per week.

Reporting involves providing the important numbers that the company is interested in and interpreting the data and overall results. Figure 18-4 shows one example of a social media report. Yours might include these types of numbers.

The following sections set you up to report weekly.

Including important information

Your social media position dictates what kind of information you include in your report. For example, if you're in a social media management role, include this type of information:

✔ **Sales:** Conversions are by far the most important aspect. This means web-tracking pixels generated by the social media platform, internally, or through a third party and installed on your company's website. Sales also can be measured by a scannable bar code, QR code, or a specialized promo code.

✔ **Contact information:** Companies know that "the money is in the list." In other words, having the address, phone number, or email address of current and potential customers lets the brand control when to market to the end user.

✔ **Impressions:** The total number of people who potentially saw your message account for *impressions.* This number's effectiveness is typically related to factors such as click-through rate and engagement.

✔ **Engagement:** These numbers vary by platform, but engagement's often measured by shares, Likes, and comments on your company's social media posts.

Figure 18-4:
Your social media report might include hard and soft conversions, transactions, and revenue.

Use an email marketing provider such as iContact to gather more data. We prefer Bronto email software because of its tools, support, and direct-response mechanisms.

Many social media platforms have reporting functionality. Set up a weekly 30-minute meeting to review the information and receive affirmation from the people you report to that you're on the right track.

Though many of the platforms have reporting tools, you can use a website such as socialreport.com or sproutsocial.com to create any type of social media report imaginable. Your social media report should have the following:

- ✔ **Summary:** Highlight key information. Use bullet points to highlight the overall accomplishments and the most relevant information. Be prepared for questions.

- ✔ **Graphical presentation:** This may include graphs, pie charts, infographics, and other visual aids. Make your progress more aesthetically pleasing and approachable. Figure 18-5 shows an example of a graph.

- ✔ **Progress:** This may either be in bullet form or by visual aid. Make sure management can clearly see the progress that you're making. Show the progression of your efforts from week to week (and on a yearly basis, if applicable).

You lead the meeting. Keep these specifics in mind:

- ✔ Come in at allotted time and meet for the agreed upon amount of time. Again, we suggest 30 minutes.

- ✔ Create an agenda with time allotted for reviewing the summary, visual aids, and overall progress.

- ✔ Document your notes from the meeting and upload the meeting minutes into a shared platform such as a Google Drive or Dropbox.

Creating a weekly evaluation plan

A weekly evaluation plan helps you stay on top of deliverables and ensure that you have the same expectations as the company.

Your *social media report* shows how you're progressing. Your *weekly evaluation plan* is a way to get feedback on your results. You can combine the two reports.

Lead with the social media report to highlight your contributions. Ask for a weekly evaluation after you present your findings. When the decision makers convey that they are happy with your results, you're likely to get a favorable review. That means that in the future, the decision markers are less likely to question your involvement, hours worked, or compensation. If your results were anything less than favorable, ask questions to find out where you can improve.

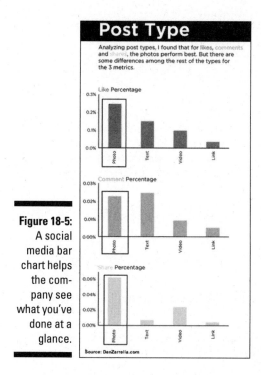

Figure 18-5:
A social media bar chart helps the company see what you've done at a glance.

Your weekly evaluation report should have the following:

- ✔ **Specific deliverables:** Deliverables are detailed in the social media report that we mention in the preceding section. Review the specific high-level deliverables and give the decision makers your progress and future projections during your weekly reporting meeting. You're asking your superiors for any feedback for improvement as it pertains to deliverables.

- ✔ **Hours worked or project progress:** Review the hours you put in throughout the week. How were your hours allocated this week? Did you meet, go over, or go under the amount of time that you personally designated for the project? If you went over your weekly hour allotment projection, what needs do you have? If you're working on a project basis, how far along is the project and when will it be completed? Do you need any help or other resources to complete the work?

- ✔ **Compensation terms:** Briefly remind them what the billing amount is based on the benchmark that you've met or the hours that you've worked multiplied by your agreed-upon hourly rate. When you remind them (bi-weekly or monthly), emphasize your hourly rate rather than the project's total cost. If you break down your work into smaller dollar amounts, then you're less likely to be scrutinized.

Some of the feedback that you get may hurt your ego or be disheartening.

✔ Stay professional.

✔ Use their advice.

✔ Maintain your position as the resident expert.

If the company questions your methods or suggests a tactic that doesn't work with your strategy, you can politely decline. However, you should clearly explain your line of thinking and educate your bosses if you're respectfully declining their opinions. After all, they're helping you pay your bills!

Ensure that your review system has a consistent grading scale (1–5 or a letter grade). Include these factors in your review:

✔ **Deliverables:** Go over your weekly analytics reporting and evaluate whether you met your weekly goals.

✔ **Workplace standards:** Review your attendance, punctuality, appearance, and overall adherence to the employer's rules and standards.

✔ **Intangible qualities:** Evaluate whether you've been proactive and have demonstrated leadership. Evaluate your attitude and demeanor.

✔ **Overall performance:** Combine all the factors and give yourself an overall rating for the week.

No superior wants to hear excuses. If you fell short on your goals, or on any part of your performance review, own up to your mistakes, apologize for the shortcoming, and create a plan to make sure you don't repeat this setback. Top-notch social media pros accept responsibility for their performance and take action rather than complain or feel bad for themselves.

Pinpointing your benefits

Solely working for money is one of the quickest ways to make your work, happiness, and overall performance deteriorate. We've both made the mistake of not giving a thought about what we were going to get out of a working arrangement. We sacrificed happiness and time that we could have been spent with friends and family. Quality of life is more important than making more money (if the way you make your money is making you miserable). Recognize that even though you might need to make short-term sacrifices, you need an equal or bigger payout or you'll burn out.

Part VI
The Part of Tens

Get the top ten interview tips at
www.dummies.com/extras/gettingasocialmediajob.

In this part . . .

✔ Find out how to set yourself apart from job competitors and fellow employees.

✔ Stay away from the top mistakes made by social media professionals.

✔ Keep current with the top ten social media resources.

✔ See more at www.dummies.com.

Chapter 19

Ten Social Media Best Practices

*L*ots of sources offer social media best practices. True social media pros can pick through the information and establish what works. We do that for you here, saving you significant time and confusion.

This chapter details the top ten critical activities for social media professionals.

Defining Your Mission, Vision, and Purpose

All excellent social media marketers constantly refine the mission, vision, and purpose of the social media accounts that they represent.

Here's how we define those three intricate components:

✔ **Vision** is your end goal — in ten years. Your social media presence is trying to accomplish your vision.

✔ **Mission** is defined by how the social media engines will help you accomplish your vision. A mission is your day-to-day guide for meeting your social media objectives. Your mission helps you accomplish your ultimate vision.

✔ **Purpose** is why your social media engines exist. Your purpose ensures that you strictly define what the social media presence looks like.

Developing a Listening Strategy

Monitoring the brand and discussion around relevant industry is more quantitative, but listening is considered an equally, if not more important, qualitative factor.

Define not only how you're going to talk, but more importantly, how you're going to listen. Your strategy should strictly define how, who, what, where, and when you'll listen to the general social media landscape. Most importantly, documenting the listening process helps you track and enhance your presence and makes you more efficient.

Formulating a Highly Functional Decision Tree

Have a plan for when the brand makes a mistake or has a crisis. This happens no matter how great your social media presence and overall management. Figure 19-1 is an example of a high-level decision-making plan.

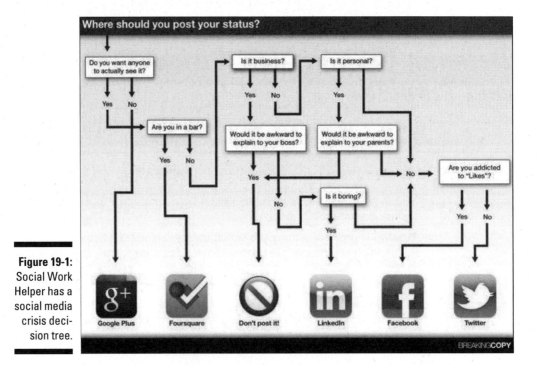

Figure 19-1: Social Work Helper has a social media crisis decision tree.

Strictly define what level of management can make specific types of decisions. Decisions can vary from

- ✔ Knowing specific product or service information
- ✔ Releasing sensitive or proprietary information
- ✔ Addressing legal issues
- ✔ Issuing refunds
- ✔ Handling consumer complaints

Establishing Proactive Rather Than Reactive Goals

Proactive goals are important. If you aren't aware of why you're participating on social media, then you're probably just following suit and "doing what you're supposed to." Always just reacting is a recipe for failure.

Proactive goals come from critical thinking, from planning, and from clearly defining an expected outcome. Weekly, monthly, and quarterly planning comes into play. *Reactive goals* are developed on the fly out of fear or a lack of preparation.

Serving Customers and Prospects

Most brands venture into social media with the hopes of building their sales and use the social web as a *push* platform where they broadcast information similar to that of traditional media. The top pros know to use social media as a *pull* platform. They weave content and context together to form relationships with consumers.

The best way to build content and context is a firm commitment to serve your customers and prospects. Answer their dire questions, provide a higher level of service than competitors, and demonstrate commitment to serving their desires.

Developing Engagement Standards

Engagement standards define the timing of your responses, the types of consumer feedback that you'll respond to, the voice in which your brand speaks, and so forth. Engagement standards are your litmus test, helping you decide how, why, when, and what to say on social media at all times.

Chapter 12 explains voice; Chapter 3 discusses automation; Chapter 16 addresses post timing.

Abiding by Your Engagement Standards

Engagement standards are just words unless you use them. Ideally, management establishes accountability. Create your own daily rituals in terms of maintaining a consistent tone, creating content, and connecting with others.

While you're searching for a job, create one remarkable content piece per week and spend the rest of your time connecting and helping others via social media.

The same engagement standards will apply when you become a successful social media professional. Almost all of your time needs to be designated to cultivating connections and communicating in order to provide help to your intended audience.

Organizing Accountability

Top social media organizations always have very clear-cut roles and responsibilities carved out. However, since social media as a whole is constantly changing, the roles evolve. This gives you the tremendous ability to define your job clearly and take on the tasks that you know will make the biggest lasting impact.

If you're not sure what your job entails, ask. You should know who is responsible for what critical activities and who you report to.

Conducting Continuous Improvement

Question your approach and strive to improve. Upper management typically has a tougher time understanding social media and its impact, so it falls on social media departments to provide quantitative evidence — higher direct sales, improved customer satisfaction, engagement ratios and overall consumer brand impressions — of improving the brand.

Chapter 7 details the tools you need to offer proof of your value.

Remaining Transparent

Social media is all about remaining open, honest and letting the world see "the real you." Transparency is the absolute best way to build trust with your community. Give your audience behind the scenes access to your business by creating behind-the-scenes media such as a pictures, videos, live streams and blog entries and then sharing them on social media. This is the best way to build trust, respect and to get others to like you.

People do business with people, not logos. It's in your best interest to completely unveil the people who represent your business. In turn, customers will show more interest in the business and be more willing to engage and share your social media posts.

Chapter 20

Avoiding Ten Common Social Media Job Mistakes

In This Chapter

▶ Listening too little

▶ Forgetting your audience

▶ Being verbose . . . or silent

▶ Promoting inconsistently

Nearly every company and person has tried to figure out how to leverage the social media phenomenon for financial gain. Many unscrupulous activities have arisen, and misinformation floats freely.

The following common tactics are terrible for business and always result in failure.

Setting Unrealistic Goals and Expectations

Unrealistic personal goals and impractical employer expectations are by far the biggest problem in social media.

Most marketers and businesses look at social media as the newest "push" medium and frequently use the channel as the freshest way to promote and sell their products and services. The problem is that social media isn't one-way communication. It emphasizes two-way conversation between the brand and the consumer.

Social media takes time. When companies rush in thinking they'll get sales by promoting their goods and services, they're in for a rude awakening.

You're at a party, so strive to be the party guest everyone wants to be around. Don't be the huckster that is always trying to sell themselves and their stuff.

Forgetting to Consistently Promote

Many companies don't promote their products in a consistent, effective manner. Oftentimes, a brand enters the social media space promoting their products nonstop. When they gain no traction, they give up. On the other end of spectrum, brands may focus all of their efforts on "making friends" with their consumers and fail to ask fans to buy something.

Promote and ask for a particular action from your fans between 5 percent and 20 percent of the time. If you post every day of the month, you should include a call to action between two and six times during that month.

Talking and Never Listening

Companies tend to talk about their brand, products, and services, but not to listen to consumer feedback. Never observing conversations around their brand, competitors, and industries is another mistake. The brand's losing valuable insight and annoying their current and potential fan base.

It's always in a brand's best interest to set up keywords related to their brand on social media monitoring software such as Hootsuite.

By doing this, brands are able to see exactly what their current and target customers say about them and have the option of collecting this information for improvement purposes and/or responding to the social media posts.

Focusing on Yourself Rather Than Community

A brand is formed within the community. What does the larger social media community say, think, and feel about your brand when you're not around? You can talk about how great your brand is and prove why you're the best, but unless the community truly believes this, you're fighting a losing battle.

Exhibiting a company's values and acting as a brand advocate on social media is especially important when you're searching for a job.

We can't stress it enough: Figure out how to best serve the social media community rather than serving your own needs and wants.

Updating as Part of a Schedule

Many social media "gurus" will have you believe that you have to make daily posts — but if your brand constantly puts out boring updates, then your targets won't be prone to responding and you're less likely to be seen.

Only update genuinely newsworthy posts. Your audience will pay attention. This is true because most social networking engines have internal algorithms that measure how engaging content is. If your content isn't Liked, commented on, or shared, then the likelihood of it being seen is much lower.

Engaging Too Little

Engaging too often is a problem. On the flip side, not posting enough makes your brand seem uninteresting. Find a healthy balance of engagement that makes your fans feel compelled to talk about your brand when you're not around.

Software such as Nimble will remind you when to touch base with your key audience on social media, and you choose whether communication is on a daily, weekly, monthly, quarterly, or yearly basis.

Communicate with customers once per quarter at a minimum. Stay aware and measure how receptive your audience is to your communication.

Branding Inconsistently Across Platforms

Brands might suffer from multiple social media personalities. Would you ever want to hang out with someone who acted completely different from one day to the next? Absolutely not. The same holds true on social media.

Beware of these common inconsistent branding:

- ✔ Value propositions, brand values, slogans, and profiles.
- ✔ Messaging that doesn't fit the audience. Remember the Four Rights: the right message on the right platform at the right time with the right people.
- ✔ Imagery that isn't consistent. Chapter 12 talks about brand imagery.
- ✔ Constantly changing voice, tone, and personality. Establishing these elements of your brand are also discussed in Chapter 12.

Failing to Establish a Lead-Generation Strategy

Often a brand focuses on communication but doesn't have a plan for turning fans into customers. Many brands fear that consumers will think the brand is trying to use their relationship for personal financial gain. Though that perception is a possibility, it's more important to establish value.

Without a strictly defined sales process in place, a brand is doomed to have conversations with consumers all day long but never get results.

Your lead-generation strategy should usually, but not always, include the following types of actions:

- ✔ **Marketing data:** Name, email, phone number, home address, and other forms of contact
- ✔ **Special offer or promotion:** Any sort of specialized pricing, bonus, or gift that a consumer will receive
- ✔ **Direct sale:** Acting on behalf of your employer to ask for the sale of a product or service

Concentrating on Too Many Social Media Sites

Avoid participating on a platform because it suddenly has lots of users, or the engagement rate is high, or because an article tells you to.

Concentrating on too many platforms leads to loss of focus. That's like a musician who tries to learn six instruments at the same time.

Focus on LinkedIn and Twitter while you're looking for a job. These two platforms are the best for professional positioning and communication.

While working in the field, your employer's customers will use different platforms, but the Big Five — encompasses Facebook, Twitter, LinkedIn, Instagram, and Google+ — are a safe bet.

Getting Too Personal

Establishing a distinct brand personality helps your employer stand apart from the competition and gives followers an idea of the people behind the logo. However, don't get too personal with your social media profiles.

For example, reacting negatively to critical feedback or sharing views on polarizing topics like politics and religion can harm your brand's reputation and turn off your followers.

Chapter 21

Ten Ways to Stand Out from the Crowd

*T*here's more noise online than there has ever been before. Former Google CEO Eric Schmidt says, "Every two days now, we create as much information as we did from the dawn of civilization up until 2003." With that much information, how can you break through?

The theory is simple but difficult to execute: Be better than everyone else. It's a good thing you're reading this book; you'll know how to be worth talking about in the social media world — especially important among your potential hiring managers.

This chapter reviews the top ten ways to separate yourself from competition and capture precious attention.

Standing Out Positively

There *is* such a thing as bad press. Negative feedback on social media is amplified because every single person has a voice.

Focus on positive ways to cause your potential hiring firms to feel compelled to talk about you. It takes no talent to be the naysayer or do something shocking or controversial.

It takes true talent to build a genuine relationship with and make your audience feel great about themselves.

When you find a company you like,

- ✔ Promote a philanthropy or charity that the company has started on social media.
- ✔ Volunteer your time to tackle a project on behalf of the hiring company.

Thinking for Yourself

A lot of social media users follow common wisdom. For example, just because one social media "guru" says it's best to tweet at 12:37 PM EST on every other Tuesday doesn't make her correct.

Use what works best, proven by your metrics, when communicating with your current and potential fans.

Taking Chances That No One Else Will

Most social media job applicants are so afraid of alienating prospective companies that they won't say anything slightly offensive. That makes for potential vanilla employees that don't stand for anything.

Taking chances and slightly offending an audience is worth your while if it's genuine and builds a stronger connection with the people that you're truly trying to connect with anyhow. It's better to be something big to a smaller niche than be inconsequential to the entire social media spectrum.

Being Willing to Fail

Take a few bigger bets.

Social media agency owner Gary Vaynerchuk gave up the helm of a profitable wine retail business to start his own web TV show about wine. This willingness to fail — to leave what he was comfortable with — landed him on virtually every late-night television show and made him a social media superstar.

If what you're doing is completely comfortable, then you're not doing it right.

Strictly Defining Your USP

A *unique selling proposition (USP)* separates you from all of your competition. Your employer should have a USP among its social media presence and as a whole within your segment.

If you don't know your USP, answer the following question: Why should your target employer hire you above anyone else? Maybe you specialize in making remarkable infographics, having the largest social media network, or achieving the lowest cost per acquisition on social media advertising platforms.

From a social media perspective, you should be able to clearly explain to employers why they should hire you. Your goal is to develop a true USP that none of your competitors can replicate.

Thanking Stakeholders Genuinely

Your fans, friends, and potential employers will inevitably be grateful for your social media efforts and will want to thank you. Your mission is to be genuine and go beyond what your competition does to express that gratitude.

We have a few ideas:

- **Thank someone for no reason.** Try thanking a prospective employer and saying how much you appreciate and respect their company (even if you didn't get the job).

- **Tweet a coffee.** Starbucks allows you to set up an account and "tweet a coffee" to anyone (send that person a $5 gift card). Check out `starbucks.com/tweet-a-coffee` for more information.

- **Show appreciation for criticism.** Your personal brand might not be for everyone, but thank them for voicing their opinion. They might not be your coworkers today, but they might be in the future. Every connection matters.

Under-Promising and Over-Delivering

Easy to say; tough to do.

Say you're running a social media advertising campaign on Facebook and you promise your employer a $45 cost per acquisition and deliver results in five days (though you feel extremely confident that you can achieve a $37 cost per acquisition in just three days). Even if you don't meet your own expectations and end up at a $42 cost per acquisition and four days, you've still under-promised and over-delivered.

Challenge yourself to go beyond expectations. This separates good from great.

Building Context with Every Connection

Positioning yourself as content expert is vital, but it's more important to build a relationship with your prospective hiring audience. It's your job to know what touches the hearts and minds of anyone you meet; people base decisions on emotions and justify with logic.

If you can create genuine conversation around topics that your hiring targets care about, then they're more likely to back you as a candidate. Create a spreadsheet or use a social customer relationship management (SCRM) database such as `nimble.com` to add notes about particular people and figure out what influences their thinking and feeling.

Demonstrating Experience, Knowledge, and Influence

One key to social media is clearly and effectively positioning yourself as an authority figure. Though engaging in conversation and talking about personal topics on social media is great, it's better to showcase prospective employers or clients your core abilities.

These cornerstone pieces show off your experience, knowledge, and influence:

- ✔ **Building a personal brand website:** Consider creating your site on a social media platform such as `tumblr.com` or `path.com`. Chapter 12 talks more about building your personal brand.

- ✔ **Publishing valuable information:** This may include *white papers* (marketing documents used to entice potential customers to learn or buy), infographics, or videos and then promoting the content with your social media accounts.

- ✔ **Making introductions:** If you know that a decision maker who you're courting is looking for a particular connection or needs a recommendation, make that person's life easier.

Choosing to Be Different

Most social media aficionados tend to fall in line. They say and do as they're told by the rest of social media. Your job, of course, is to break through and brand yourself.

Being a person who is different and worth knowing is a deliberate choice, and you have to exercise it daily.

Here are some bona fide ways of showing just how different you are:

- **Demonstrating your knowledge on video:** All other social media applicants are going to talk about their knowledge and skills. Why not use screen-capture software and demonstrate how well you know the responsibilities and qualifications for a particular job? Chapter 3 talks more about creating quality video.

- **Building a personal website:** Your site should showcase your knowledge and skills, but it also should allow people to know who you are. You can set up a beautiful, responsive site through `strikingly.com` or `tumblr.com`. Check out `brooksbriz.com` for an example of how to make a remarkable personal brand website.

- **Creating bold content:** If you identify a trend or a problem, then step up and say so! It's good to be noticed for making a statement and showcasing thought-provoking analysis.

Chapter 22

Top Ten Social Media Resources

S ites continually pop up and fight to be the top social media resource. There's not just one, but many resource sites providing valuable insight, data, news, tips, and tricks across media.

This chapter reviews the top sites for social media pros and what you stand to gain by paying attention to them.

Technorati

Technorati is technically a search engine company that serves as a publisher advertising platform. In essence, Technorati showcases the top content creators from hundreds of interests and fields.

If you're looking for the influencers within your particular field, try this site. Submit your own blog as well.

Quantcast

Quantcast specializes in accurate audience measurement and real-time advertising. The site features traffic and demographic data for literally millions of websites. Signing up gives you more advanced analytics;

membership is free. Quantcast was the first rating company to rely largely on direct measurement rather than traditional panel-based methods that powered all other media outlets.

If you're looking for more information about social media metrics and traffic knowledge, then there probably isn't a better place to find it than Quantcast.

Social Media Examiner

The main goal for `SocialMediaExaminer.com` (SME) is to help business people efficiently use all social networks. SME offers periodicals loaded with best practices, lists, and tricks to help you separate yourself from the pack. It broadcasts a weekly podcast and oversees communities for some of the biggest social media managers in the game.

Mashable

Mashable is often seen as the central hub for all social media news. Though the website's primary focus is social media news, it also delves into topics such as mobile marketing, online video, start-up business, web development, and technology. As a result of its ability to cover so many topics through the lens of social media, Mashable is often referred to as a one-stop shop.

Mashable is a great starting point for social media news. Because it covers such a width of topics, critics think its quality has gone down. Our opinion is that you should consider Mashable's information but always balance it with numerous sources.

If you're a Samsung smartphone or tablet user, use Mashable's app. It has a feature called Velocity, an algorithm that predicts when a story is about to go viral. You'll automatically get an update. With this app, you'll always be in the know!

Alltop

Alltop categorizes top headlines from popular topics all across the web; social media's the focus at `social-media.alltop.com`. Alltop curates all the content in terms of its popularity. When you're searching through Alltop, you'll often find top social media sites such as SocialMediaExaminer.com or `Techcrunch.com` but you'll also discover news sources that you didn't know existed. All the top sites are listed, along with their top-five trending stories. This is a great place to stay informed, and you can add your own blog to their directory.

Digital Trends

Digital Trends offers the best high-tech lifestyle and technology news, with reviews, guides, how-to articles, informative videos, and niche podcasts. Digital Trends tackles consumer electronics as well, including tablets, 2-in-1 convertible computers, and smartphones.

Knowing how social media works is effective, but understanding how technology impacts social's amplification and application is even better. Keep your eye on Digital Trends.

Social Media Today

Social Media Today (SMT) is a community for public relations, marketing, and advertising professionals who understand that social media is vital for their communication. SMT provides a lot of great insight and hosts lively debate around the tools, platforms, software, and personalities in social media. Even if you're not in one of these fields, the synthesis and discussion that SMT provides is great.

Reddit

Reddit is a very intimate community of users who generate news links; the audience votes to promote the story. Reddit is a very popular site and almost always breaks stories before the traditional outlets have heard about them.

It's important to frequent Reddit for the latest social media news. If you can find trends and topics in real time on Reddit and promote the content through social media, then you can get a flood of website traffic.

Twitter

Twitter is the "purest" social network in that it allows the most seamless, open communication between two parties. In fact, with a hashtag or keyword, virtually anyone can see content and then reply. Users frequently treat Twitter as an outlet to post links from thought leaders or recent news.

Visit `search.twitter.com` and type a keyword. You'll see every tweet from all over the world around that topic.

Social Times

Social Times (ST) is a news site dedicated to social media with a few unique twists. First and foremost, ST features less information than many other news sites, but its news is of the highest quality; its infographics are beautiful; and it features the top social media courses through its partner, `mediabistro.com`. Additionally, ST features the top social media jobs currently on the social media job market. The positions are constantly rotating, so act fast!

Glossary

Talk the Talk

activity: A metric that tries to establish how many customer service hours the company saved and contributed to the bottom line.

aggregated: Data collected from several measurements and compiled into a summary.

analytics: The data or statistics gleaned from systematically reviewing information to determine how customers feel about your brand. Measured analytics include number of website page views, average duration on the site, and total page views per session.

applicant relationship systems (ARS): Contact or customer relationship management tool used to gather information that can be searched at a later time.

assessments: Linked employment processes. They measure a job candidate's knowledge and skills in specific areas of competence. Assessments are used during the interview and hiring process for job candidates.

automating: A technique for controlling a process through the uses of mechanical or social tools. Social media automating refers to the automatic posting of information as predetermined by the originator.

behavioral interview questions: Interview questions that ask the candidate to draw upon past experiences and share performance examples.

best practice: Established method of doing something that consistently generates results that are superior to other actions.

billable hours: The standard charging procedures for social media consultative services rendered after considering overhead and expenses, time required for marketing and administration, and other projects competing for your time.

bird dog: Finding leads or sales or facilitating introductions for another party. This term is usually reserved for real estate, but it's applicable for building rapport and good will with influence in social media.

body language: A means of communicating wordless messages.

bottom-line efficiencies: Cutting costs associated with the business function.

bottom-line sales: Increase or decrease in net earnings or sales growth.

brand: Name, design, feature, and culture that distinguish one company from another.

brand equity: The value of having a well-known brand. It takes into account financial performance, the ability to launch related brands, and consumer sentiment. Strong brand equity leads to more predictable income and increased cash flow, and can be an asset that can be sold or leased.

call to action: Instruction to an audience to generate an immediate response. Asking viewers to Like your Facebook page is a common call to action.

chronological résumé: An overview of work history, beginning with your most recent experience and working backward.

click-through rate (CTR): A means of measuring the success of an online campaign. It's a ratio showing how often people who see your advertisement end up clicking the associated link.

collateral: Supportive material that reinforces a company's brand. Common collateral includes t-shirts, key chains, coffee mugs, and other items with the company's logo.

community management: Handling a common resource or issue within a group that's connected through a shared interest. In social media, community management is used to build loyalty and further the brand's infiltration.

consultant: A professional who provides advice in a particular area of expertise.

consumption: The number and relative percentage of people who consumed your company's content.

contact management system (CMS): Contact or customer relationship management tool used to gather information that can be searched. Also known as ARS or CRM.

contact relationship management (CRM): *See* contact management system.

content: the value or substance of the information being shared.

contractor: A person that takes on a particular role, job, or service for a defined period of time.

conversion: Shows sales and the bottom line, including overall impressions, CTR, and engagement ratios.

cost per 1,000 impressions (CPM): A metric used in marketing for benchmarking purposes. It calculates the relative cost of an advertising campaign or message in a given medium.

customer relationship management (CRM): Also known as *contact relationship management (CRM)* or *applicant tracking system (ATS)*. A system for managing an individual's or company's interactions with current and prospective customers. The system uses technology to organize, synchronize, store, and automate information (including name, contact information, and notes).

deliverables: The requirements of a project. They define accountability and agreed-upon commitments related to a project.

elevator pitch: Brief presentation of your skills and experience (or product or service) given to an authority within a company you wish to work for or with.

endorsement: An action of support to someone or something. Endorsements can be found on LinkedIn profiles. Also known as a *testimonial*.

engagement: A combination of reach, audience growth rate, and the number of users who have interacted with your brand in any way.

equity: Ownership interest in a company.

functional résumé: Format that gives an overview of skills and experience emphasizing the content of the experience rather than dates of employment.

impact mapping: Defining what you're looking for. Providing evidence that you're making a positive difference.

impressions: The measure of the number of times an advertisement is seen.

infographic or infograph: A visual image used to represent information or data. It may include charts, pictures, of diagrams, and typically uses shapes and color to share information.

key performance indicators (KPI): A measureable value that demonstrates how effectively a company is achieving important business objectives.

lead generation: Lists of potential customers or clients generated upon the likelihood of interest.

mentions: Online references to someone or something.

metrics: The criterion by which something is measured, or the results obtained.

mission statements: An organization's purpose and primary objectives. These statements are set in the present tense and explain why the organization exists as a business.

native: Type of advertising or marketing on social platforms where posts are integrated into social media streams.

networking: A supportive system of sharing information and services among individuals and groups having a common interest. In the job search, networking generates job leads and referential information.

non-government organization (NGO): An organization that's neither a part of the government nor a conventional for-profit business. Usually, NGOs are set up by ordinary citizens, but can receive funding from governments, foundations, businesses, or private citizens.

objective: Goal or judgment that isn't affected by personal feelings, but rooted in facts. Subjective refers to being influenced by opinions.

one-way communication: Communication that informs, directs, or persuades. It's direct from the sender to the receiver. Conversely, two-way communication is a back-and-forth exchange, where both parties transmit information.

open environment: Surroundings that are varied and unpredictable but used to generate creativity, collaboration, and new ideas.

open rates: An indication of how many people view or open a given email or link.

overall social reach: The total number of people who could have seen your message, campaign, or advertisement.

pay-to-play: When money is exchanged for services or the privilege to participate.

picture quote: A quotation visualized and used for motivational or marketing purposes.

platform: A web-based technology that enables the development, deployment, and management of social media services and solutions.

presence: Social media recognition for a person or business. The ability to be found on social platforms consistently.

pro bono: Work done on a voluntary basis rather that through traditional payment.

push: Push information is information received based upon personal preferences, like subscribing to a newsletter. As new information is generated, it's automatically forwarded to you. *Pull* information refers to information sent following a direct request.

qualitative: Method for measuring the quality of something rather than the quantity.

quantitative: A type of information that's based in numbers or data.

reach: A measure of audience growth rate.

résumé: An overview of an individual's professional skills and experience used to to find a job. Can be text, images with text, or video format.

search engine optimization (SEO): Increasing traffic from unpaid search results on search engines. The more frequently a site appears in the search results list, the more visitors it gets from the search engine's users.

silo: A system, process, or department that's isolated from others.

situational interview questions: Interview questions that place the candidate into hypothetical scenarios to better understand how he will handle similar situations in the future.

SMART goals: Objectives that are specific, measurable, attainable, realistic, and time related.

social media: An inclusive term referring to websites and applications that allow users to create and share content, or to participate in online networking.

social proof: A phenomenon where people assume the actions of others in an attempt to behave correctly in a particular situation. When a situation is ambiguous, people assume others have more knowledge than they do.

stipend: A form of salary. It's a periodic, fixed payment for something specific such as taking a course while you work a full-time job.

subject matter experts (SMEs): A person who is an authority in a given area.

targeting: An advertisement or branding campaign focused on a particular customer segment that the company believes will most likely be interested in the product or service provided. Also known as target marketing.

testimonial: A personalized recommendation.

thumb streaming platform: When a user monitors multiple social networks. Users thumb through a site's content at a rapid pace.

tone: The manner and delivery of speech, and is best associated with volume, inflection, and pace of the spoken word or brand message.

top-line sales: Gross sales; income received for goods or services over a period of time.

unique selling proposition (USP): A sales method used to differentiate a product or service from that offered by the competition. It's what makes one better than another.

vanity metric: Data collected about a company or its users that isn't used in decision making, but is used to build credibility. For example, millions of people visiting a website page.

vertical: Service or support provided to a specific industry, profession, or group of customers.

viral: The spreading of information rapidly on the Internet.

vision statements: Uplifting, inspiring statements that define an organization's purpose and focus on its goals and aspirations.

vlog: Short for *video blog.* It is a blog in which the postings are primarily done in video form.

website clicks: Also known as *page views,* the number of times a visitor views a page on a website.

Index

• *J* •

• *K* •

• T •

Notes

Notes

About the Authors

Brooks Briz is a seasoned speaker, consultant, and entrepreneur in the tech start-up industry. Brooks founded Brizness Marketing Consulting, LLC, and he has helped hundreds of tech start-ups build their top-line sales and attract top-notch talent through intensive marketing strategy, social media planning, text message marketing, sales consulting, and much more.

Brooks can solve your most daunting social media problems. If you don't have the right strategy, implementation, or people in place, Brooks will diagnose the situation and fix it. Not only will he alleviate the obstacles that you face in social media but he'll work with you to form the plan guaranteed to bring you top-line sales and brand equity for years to come.

Brooks also authored a book in 2014 about in-house social media management that was specifically geared toward the food and beverage industry. All of the proceeds of *#Hungry? Fuel Your Restaurant Sales with Social Media* (www.hungrybook.org) benefit No Kid Hungry. To find out more about Brooks' marketing and sales consulting, please visit www.brizness consulting.com. To discover more about Brooks personally, please visit www.brooksbriz.com.

Brooks is originally from Silver Spring, Maryland. He received his Bachelor of Science degree in Economics and Management and his MBA from the Franklin P. Perdue School of Business at Salisbury University. Brooks currently lives in Raleigh, North Carolina. When not writing or consulting, Brooks coaches high school lacrosse at Broughton High School, serves New Hope Church, and speaks about sales, marketing, and people development throughout the United States.

David Rose is the vice president of recruiting with YELLOW DOG Recruiting (www.yellowdogrecruiting.com), a national recruitment company specializing in the placement of leaders within the hospitality industry. He leads a team of professionals dedicated to identifying top candidates for leadership roles within some of the world's leading restaurant, food service, retail, grocery, hotel, and gaming companies.

Prior to YELLOW DOG, David was the manager of talent acquisition for American Express in Fort Lauderdale, Florida. He led a team driven to identify candidates opportunities within the network's largest service center, in addition to the oversight specialized recruitment throughout the United States.

Before American Express, David was the senior recruitment manager with Compass Group, the world's largest food service provider. He also held roles as client services manager with OMNIPartners, a research recruitment company, and as a management recruiter with Roth Young Personnel Services of Washington, D.C.

Throughout his career, David has worked to focus on the identification of leadership-level professionals. His specialties include relationship building, inclusive recruitment, strategic development, career coaching and counseling, succession and career planning, branding, and information sharing.

David holds a Bachelor of Science degree in telecommunication from the University of Florida in Gainesville, Florida. He lives in Fort Lauderdale, Florida, with his two children.

David can be found on Twitter (www.twitter.com/YELLOWDOG_01), Facebook (www.facebook.com/YELLOWDOGRecruiting), and LinkedIn (www.linkedin.com/in/yellowdogrecruiting).

Dedication

This goes out to anyone who has ever felt intimidated by social media and/or the job search process. May this book serve as your guide to a fruitful social media career and a long and prosperous life. When you have questions, need guidance, or just want to introduce yourself, please email me at `heybrooks @brooksbriz.com`. Thank you for reading this book and I trust that it will bring you tremendous value!

—Brooks Briz

Dedication

To Bryce, Maxwell, my parents, grandparents, Peter, Scott, Andrea, David, family, friends: Thank you for your loyalty, support, and inspiration, without which I would not be the person I am today.

To all the career-minded readers, take it one step at a time. Know that nothing happens the way you envision. Processes and people will always delay interview and hiring processes, but the adventure of discovering your perfect job makes it all worthwhile. Use this book as a source to help you refocus. You must be strategic about your career, and this book will help you build a foundation for your future. I am eager to hear how this book helps you. Reach out at david@yellowdogrecruiting.com.

Thank you for reading this book.

—David Rose

Authors' Acknowledgments

I'd like to recognize the following: God, you, David Rose, Amber Sersen, Amy Fandrei, Tonya Cupp, Pat O'Brien, Paul Dunay, Stan Phelps, my newhope Church family, the entire Wiley Publishing team, `FilterEasy.com`, `ENDcrowd.com`, and all of my friends and family.

For anyone that I didn't thank directly, please know that I have you in my heart and mind. Thank you for your support.

—*Brooks Briz*

I've had a personal goal of writing a book for a long time. I am the child of educators, and was subjected to continuous grammar correction throughout my formative years. As I grew, I became the person my friends asked to proofread papers and projects. Professionally, I have written articles, reviews, and blog posts, lectured to classes and organizations, and participated in panel discussions related to the search for career happiness.

Writing this book, in collaboration with Brooks Briz, has been a tremendous experience. I offer my sincere appreciation to Brooks for his partnership and vision.

The following people were especially important in creating this book, and I offer my gratitude: Bryce Rose, Maxwell Rose, Scott Rosenburg, Andrea Navarro, Susan Rose, Jack Rose, Peter Rose, Jack Pockriss, Maralynn Mash, Joshua Schneider, Gregg Rosenburg, Andrew Strauss, Toby Srebnik, and Daniel Rose.

Finally, the team at Wiley Publishing deserves acknowledgment, and my sincerest gratitude, for seeing the opportunity and need for this book, and for coaxing each chapter out of me while providing valuable guidance to a first-time author. Their patience and support made the challenging task of meeting deadlines much easier.

—*David Rose*

Publisher's Acknowledgments

Senior Acquisitions Editor: Amy Fandrei

Project Editor: Tonya Maddox Cupp

Technical Editor: Nancy Holland

Editorial Assistant: Claire Brock

Sr. Editorial Assistant: Cherie Case

Project Coordinator: Kumar Chellapa

Project Manager: Mary Corder

Cover Image: ©iStock.com/Anatoliy Babiy

ple & Mac

d For Dummies,
Edition
3-1-118-72306-7

one For Dummies,
Edition
3-1-118-69083-3

cs All-in-One
Dummies, 4th Edition
3-1-118-82210-4

X Mavericks
Dummies
3-1-118-69188-5

gging & Social Media

ebook For Dummies,
Edition
3-1-118-63312-0

cial Media Engagement
Dummies
3-1-118-53019-1

rdPress For Dummies,
Edition
3-1-118-79161-5

siness

ck Investing
Dummies, 4th Edition
3-1-118-37678-2

esting For Dummies,
Edition
3-0-470-90545-6

Personal Finance
For Dummies, 7th Edition
978-1-118-11785-9

QuickBooks 2014
For Dummies
978-1-118-72005-9

Small Business Marketing
Kit For Dummies,
3rd Edition
978-1-118-31183-7

Careers

Job Interviews
For Dummies, 4th Edition
978-1-118-11290-8

Job Searching with Social
Media For Dummies,
2nd Edition
978-1-118-67856-5

Personal Branding
For Dummies
978-1-118-11792-7

Resumes For Dummies,
6th Edition
978-0-470-87361-8

Starting an Etsy Business
For Dummies, 2nd Edition
978-1-118-59024-9

Diet & Nutrition

Belly Fat Diet For Dummies
978-1-118-34585-6

Mediterranean Diet
For Dummies
978-1-118-71525-3

Nutrition For Dummies,
5th Edition
978-0-470-93231-5

Digital Photography

Digital SLR Photography
All-in-One For Dummies,
2nd Edition
978-1-118-59082-9

Digital SLR Video &
Filmmaking For Dummies
978-1-118-36598-4

Photoshop Elements 12
For Dummies
978-1-118-72714-0

Gardening

Herb Gardening
For Dummies, 2nd Edition
978-0-470-61778-6

Gardening with Free-Range
Chickens For Dummies
978-1-118-54754-0

Health

Boosting Your Immunity
For Dummies
978-1-118-40200-9

Diabetes For Dummies,
4th Edition
978-1-118-29447-5

Living Paleo For Dummies
978-1-118-29405-5

Big Data

Big Data For Dummies
978-1-118-50422-2

Data Visualization
For Dummies
978-1-118-50289-1

Hadoop For Dummies
978-1-118-60755-8

Language &
Foreign Language

500 Spanish Verbs
For Dummies
978-1-118-02382-2

English Grammar
For Dummies, 2nd Edition
978-0-470-54664-2

French All-in-One
For Dummies
978-1-118-22815-9

German Essentials
For Dummies
978-1-118-18422-6

Italian For Dummies,
2nd Edition
978-1-118-00465-4

Available in print and e-book formats.

Available wherever books are sold. **For more information or to order direct visit www.dummies.com**

Math & Science

Algebra I For Dummies,
2nd Edition
978-0-470-55964-2

Anatomy and Physiology
For Dummies, 2nd Edition
978-0-470-92326-9

Astronomy For Dummies,
3rd Edition
978-1-118-37697-3

Biology For Dummies,
2nd Edition
978-0-470-59875-7

Chemistry For Dummies,
2nd Edition
978-1-118-00730-3

1001 Algebra II Practice
Problems For Dummies
978-1-118-44662-1

Microsoft Office

Excel 2013 For Dummies
978-1-118-51012-4

Office 2013 All-in-One
For Dummies
978-1-118-51636-2

PowerPoint 2013
For Dummies
978-1-118-50253-2

Word 2013 For Dummies
978-1-118-49123-2

Music

Blues Harmonica
For Dummies
978-1-118-25269-7

Guitar For Dummies,
3rd Edition
978-1-118-11554-1

iPod & iTunes
For Dummies, 10th Edition
978-1-118-50864-0

Programming

Beginning Programming
with C For Dummies
978-1-118-73763-7

Excel VBA Programming
For Dummies, 3rd Edition
978-1-118-49037-2

Java For Dummies,
6th Edition
978-1-118-40780-6

Religion & Inspiration

The Bible For Dummies
978-0-7645-5296-0

Buddhism For Dummies,
2nd Edition
978-1-118-02379-2

Catholicism For Dummies,
2nd Edition
978-1-118-07778-8

Self-Help & Relationships

Beating Sugar Addiction
For Dummies
978-1-118-54645-1

Meditation For Dummies,
3rd Edition
978-1-118-29144-3

Seniors

Laptops For Seniors
For Dummies, 3rd Edition
978-1-118-71105-7

Computers For Seniors
For Dummies, 3rd Edition
978-1-118-11553-4

iPad For Seniors
For Dummies, 6th Edition
978-1-118-72826-0

Social Security
For Dummies
978-1-118-20573-0

Smartphones & Tablets

Android Phones
For Dummies, 2nd Edition
978-1-118-72030-1

Nexus Tablets
For Dummies
978-1-118-77243-0

Samsung Galaxy S 4
For Dummies
978-1-118-64222-1

Samsung Galaxy Tabs
For Dummies
978-1-118-77294-2

Test Prep

ACT For Dummies,
5th Edition
978-1-118-01259-8

ASVAB For Dummies,
3rd Edition
978-0-470-63760-9

GRE For Dummies,
7th Edition
978-0-470-88921-3

Officer Candidate Tests
For Dummies
978-0-470-59876-4

Physician's Assistant Exam
For Dummies
978-1-118-11556-5

Series 7 Exam For Dummies
978-0-470-09932-2

Windows 8

Windows 8.1 All-in-One
For Dummies
978-1-118-82087-2

Windows 8.1 For Dummies
978-1-118-82121-3

Windows 8.1 For Dummies
Book + DVD Bundle
978-1-118-82107-7

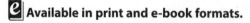 **Available in print and e-book formats.**

Available wherever books are sold. For more information or to order direct visit www.dummies.com

Take Dummies with you everywhere you go!

Whether you are excited about e-books, want more from the web, must have your mobile apps, or are swept up in social media, Dummies makes everything easier.

Leverage the Power

For Dummies is the global leader in the reference category and one of the most trusted and highly regarded brands in the world. No longer just focused on books, customers now have access to the For Dummies content they need in the format they want. Let us help you develop a solution that will fit your brand and help you connect with your customers.

Advertising & Sponsorships

Connect with an engaged audience on a powerful multimedia site, and position your message alongside expert how-to content.

Targeted ads • Video • Email marketing • Microsites • Sweepstakes sponsorship

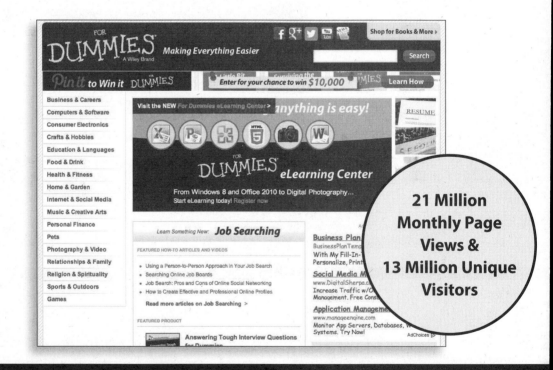

Custom Publishing

Reach a global audience in any language by creating a solution that will differentiate you from competitors, amplify your message, and encourage customers to make a buying decision.

Apps • Books • eBooks • Video • Audio • Webinars

Brand Licensing & Content

Leverage the strength of the world's most popular reference brand to reach new audiences and channels of distribution.

For more information, visit www.Dummies.com/biz

FOR
DUMMIES
A Wiley Brand

Dummies products make life easier!

- DIY
- Consumer Electronics
- Crafts

- Software
- Cookware
- Hobbies

- Videos
- Music
- Games
- and More!

For more information, go to **Dummies.com** and search the store by category.

FOR
DUMMIE.

A Wiley Bra